THE PERSISTENCE OF SLAVERY

A VOLUME IN THE SERIES

Childhoods: Interdisciplinary Perspectives
on Children and Youth

Edited by
Rachel Conrad, Alice Hearst, Laura L. Lovett,
and Karen Sánchez-Eppler

THE PERSISTENCE OF
SLAVERY

AN ECONOMIC HISTORY OF CHILD TRAFFICKING IN NIGERIA

Robin Phylisia Chapdelaine

UNIVERSITY OF MASSACHUSETTS PRESS

Amherst and Boston

ISBN 978-1-62534-524-0 (paper); 523-3 (hardcover)

Designed by Deste Roosa

Set in Carta Marina and Adobe Caslon Pro

Printed and bound by Books International, Inc.

Cover design by Deste Roosa

Cover art by Deste Roosa, adapted from "Iron Collar and Chains Used by Slave Traders, early 19th cent.," *Slavery Images: A Visual Record of the African Slave Trade and Slave Life in the Early African Diaspora,* accessed March 10, 2020, http://slaveryimages.org/s/slaveryimages/item/389 (CC BY-NC 4.0). Background image from Freepik.com.

Library of Congress Cataloging-in-Publication Data

A catalog record for this book is available from the Library of Congress.

British Library Cataloguing-in-Publication Data

A catalog record for this book is available from the British Library.

A portion of chapter 3 was published in a previous form as "Girl Pawns, Brides and Slaves: Child Trafficking in Southeastern Nigeria, 1920s" in *Children on the Move in Africa: Past and Present Experiences of Migration,* ed. Marie Rodet and Elodie Razy (Oxford: James Currey, 2016). Reprinted with permission.

For my children, Caleb and River,
and for all the trafficked children
whose stories we may never know

CONTENTS

ILLUSTRATIONS

Maps

Tables

PREFACE

In December 1929 the *New York Times* reported the murder of forty-three Nigerian women. Colonial officers shot these women as they participated in the 1929 *Ogu Umunwaanyi* (the Women's War) in Igboland located in Southeastern Nigeria.[1] In the weeks following, it became evident that additional women had lost their lives or suffered injury. In the aftermath of the uprising, the British Colonial Office conducted the Aba Commission of Inquiry, during which dozens of men and women testified about what they believed had caused the Women's War. The outcome of the inquiry suggested that women rioted because of the fallout from European colonization—the threat of taxation, decreased export profits for women's commercial goods, increased import prices for daily essentials, along with growing dissatisfaction with their male Nigerian counterparts, mainly warrant chiefs and members of local native courts, whose abuses women could no longer bear.[2]

This book was born from my initial interest in the 1929 Women's War after reading Judith Van Allen's renowned article, "Sitting on a Man," during graduate school. The article outlines the women's grievances against British officers and Nigerian men and their subsequent physical and oral demonstrations through which they expressed their frustrations.[3] Motivated by Van Allen's critique, I read through the more than one thousand pages of inquiry testimony.[4] When I found the mention of child pawning sprinkled throughout the testimony in relation to tax payments and moneylending arrangements, my interest in the women's protest shifted to examining the use of children and their labor as vehicles for economic exchange. Thus, this book looks beyond the most commonly touted complaints as the reasons for the Southeastern women's unrest by seeking out how the colonial political and economic conditions changed and undermined Nigerian women's social standing and economic solvency, resulting in their inability to provide for and maintain their children. It became clear that nefarious moneylenders, child traffickers, and slave dealers subjugated numerous children to lives wherein they engaged in coercive productive and reproductive labor. I argue that the persistence of child slavery and various forms of child trafficking can be understood only when children and their labor are evaluated within local and global socioeconomic conditions. Despite earlier abolitionist attempts to end slavery, access to children's bodies represented monetary wealth and social security. Domestically enslaved children exemplified the new face of slavery in the early twentieth century and beyond. This new form of slavery developed alongside "legitimate commerce" in Africa and has not received sufficient attention, unlike that of earlier forms of slavery, mainly chattel slavery associated with the transatlantic slave trade.

Oral interviews, British and Nigerian archival materials, newspaper holdings, and missionary and anthropological accounts have provided the bulk of the material used for this book. These items include personal correspondence, newspaper and magazine articles, formal correspondence between British officers, court records, provincial and intelligence reports, treasury reports, League of Nations documents, missionary records, and anthropological memoirs. In particular, the colonial reports entitled I. Tribal Customs and Superstitions of the Southern Province of Nigeria; II. Practice of Pawning Children as Security for Debts of Parents and *Slave Dealing and Child Stealing Investigation* (1933–35) provided substantial information about the development of League of Nations committees focused on women and children throughout the colonies and shed light on colonial authorities' perception of child-dealing operations throughout Southeastern Nigeria.[5]

While conducting research in Ibadan, Nigeria, in December 2011 and January 2012, I planned to travel to Enugu (Southeastern Nigeria) to conduct oral interviews. However, on January 1, 2012, President Goodluck Jonathan rescinded fuel subsidies afforded to Nigerians, which doubled the price of fuel and provoked a nation-wide strike. At that time, I had twenty-four hours to leave the country before the Lagos Murtala Mohammed International Airport shut down for an indeterminate amount of time. Encouraged by members on my dissertation committee and university guidelines, I made the difficult decision to evacuate the country in the midst of the unrest. My experience is not unique, as it is known that scholars who cross national borders to conduct research have to contend with social and political realities that erupt in social dissidence and sometimes violence. When faced with this type of dilemma, we have a choice to stay and continue our work or to leave so as to ensure our safety.[6] In my case, I had limited research funds and could not remain in the country indefinitely, therefore I chose to prioritize my well-being by removing myself from any threat of violence. Owing to the advanced age of some of the interviewees, it was necessary to move forward with the interviews in a timely fashion. While this is not an ideal situation for any historian, I chose to commission the oral interviews upon my return to the United States.

With the assistance of Austin Ahanotu and Anayo Enechukwu, local historians of Enugu, Nigeria, as well as research assistants, we identified nearly two dozen respected elders, many of whom are chiefs, and other community members living in Aba, Calabar, Enugu, and Owerri. They were selected on the basis of their age, place of residence (sites where the 1929 Women's War occurred), and knowledge of practices relating to child pawning. The research assistants acted as interview facilitators and interpreters and documented how Southeastern Nigerian residents understood the institution of pawnship and how the institution changed over time. The questions posed are as follows: Did they have any knowledge of child pawning? Could they describe the conditions under which a child was pawned and the terms of the agreement? Could they explain whether it was a socially accepted practice during the 1920s–30s (and in some cases, the 1940s)? Did Nigerians pawn children so as to pay colonial taxes, and if so, how did moneylenders treat pawned children? Did pawns have contact with their biological parents? Could they describe the connection between pawning and bride price payments? Finally, could they discuss contemporary uses of houseboys and house girls in the present time period (as a way to identify [dis]continuities)? The answers to these questions have created an invaluable trove of information about the use of children in social and economic exchanges; however, limitations to this book exist.

Despite the numerous available archival resources, it has been impossible to quantify the exact number of pawning cases that transformed into marriage or slavery (or vice versa) during this period. Still, we do get a glimpse of child pawnship, slavery, and marriage through anecdotal evidence and by analyzing the available case studies found in court records and other colonial archival materials.

ACKNOWLEDGMENTS

I am indebted to the dozens of people who assisted me in achieving the completion of this book. This work came to fruition with the guidance of my mentors at Rutgers University: Carolyn A. Brown, Judith A. Byfield, Temma Kaplan, and Seth Koven. My interest in child pawning in Igboland led me to meet many wonderful and insightful people, and I am deeply thankful for all of those who agreed to be interviewed and allowed their stories to be shared. I also extend my sincere gratitude to the research assistants who conducted interviews on my behalf when the political environment prevented me from doing so. I could not have managed Nigerian archive logistics without the assistance of my dear friends Abiola Oladunjoye Ayodokun and Osuolale Joseph Ayodokun in Ibadan and my colleague David Imbua located in Calabar. In addition, while researching in London, Mohammed and Fatima Sessay and Mama Veneka graciously provided pleasant company and lovely accommodations.

Many sources of financial support aided my research endeavors. I am grateful for the funding received from the Rutgers Center for Historical Analysis and History Department, the American Historical Association's Bernadotte E. Schmitt research grant, and Duquesne University's Wimmer Family Foundation. This project is the culmination of research conducted at the National Archives of Nigeria (Calabar, Enugu, Ibadan); Rhodes House Library (Oxford); the National Archives (England); the British Library (England); and the School of Oriental and African Studies (England). I appreciate each director, librarian, and staff member who helped me locate the appropriate materials.

Along my journey I have been blessed to have a number of academic acquaintances and friends who provided chapter comments and served as informal mentors. My goals would not have been achieved without the support of Saheed Aderinto, Ana Lucia Araujo,

Keisha Blain, Mariana Candido, Paula Fass, Abosede George, Allen Howard, Susan Kent, Benjamin Lawrance, Paul Lovejoy, Susan Martin, Marc Matera, Oghenetoja Okoh, Lara Putnam, Marie Rodet, Laura Ann and Benjamin Twajira, Judith Van Allen, and Mari Webel. Additionally, I would not have survived the tumultuous graduate school years, where the idea for this book took shape, without the laughter of my cohort: John Adams, Lindsay Braun, Kate Burlingham, Darcie Fontaine, Leigh-Anne Francis, Vanessa Holden, Stephanie E. Jones-Rogers, Christopher Mitchell, Sara Rzeszutek, Shanita Tartt, Rebecca Tuuri, and Elizabeth Marie Villefranche. Additional moral support from Munir Bayyari, Danielle Docka-Filipek, Richard and Meghan Frazier, Josh and Breanne Grace, Scotty Kennedy, Tosha Khoury, Brent Little, Paulette Moore, Lynn Shanko, Katrina Stevens, Audrey Stewart, Brian Vierra, Molly Warsh, and Raul Zamudio kept me going. Their generosity of time and spirit cannot be measured.

I am very appreciative of my colleagues in Duquesne's History Department. Thank you to John "Jay" Dwyer, John Mitcham, and Philipp Stelzel for reading chapter drafts and providing critically insightful comments. I also thank my research assistants, Megan Crutcher, Aubrey Parke, and Lauren Eisenhart-Purvis, for their diligent work and attention to detail.

My family has provided an enormous amount of emotional and financial support along this journey. I thank my parents, Robert and Ermalinda Moore, for their endless encouragement. I also acknowledge my younger brother Clarence Rodriguez Stewart's sacrifice when he moved from California to live with me and my young sons in New Jersey so that I could travel abroad and conduct research. I also appreciate the weekly phone calls shared with my older brother, Paul Taylor, and his wife, Ana, who made sure that I was staying the course. Finally, I thank my husband, Kyle Davison, and sons, Caleb and River, for putting up with my hectic schedule and for their never-ending love, humor, and support.

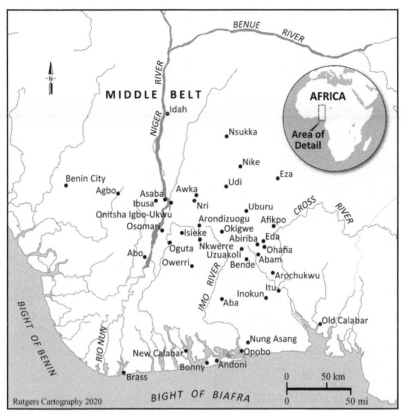

FIGURE I. Bight of Biafra Map. Created by Michael Siegel.

THE PERSISTENCE OF SLAVERY

INTRODUCTION

Nwigwe, on a certain day in November 1926, in the Province of Owerri did steal the child Ihuoma under the age of twelve from her lawful guardian and parent at Avutu and detained her knowing her to have been stolen.

—*Particulars of Offence, Provincial Court of the Province of Owerri,*
Okigwi Division, June 12, 1929

Nwigwe's trial occurred almost three years after the alleged offense.[1] He stood accused of participating in the kidnapping of twelve-year-old Ihuoma in the Province of Owerri located in Southeastern Nigeria. Ihuoma testified that a man named Mbakwe took her from her home and delivered her to Nwigwe and his friend Okoronkwo. Traveling by canoe, they went to Umuokpara, where he consulted with two other people in the privacy of their house about what to do with the girl. At the end of the meeting, Nwigwe concealed the girl under a mosquito net as they left the house. He then took her to the bush (forested area) until it got dark and waited for yet another person to meet with him to discuss the girl. Scared, Ihuoma began to cry. Nwigwe covered her mouth with his hand told her that if she made any noise a policeman would shoot and kill both of them.[2]

Eventually, through the efforts of Ihuoma's brother, she returned home. Ihuoma's story is unique, but not because she was kidnapped. She was one of the lucky children who returned to her family after being stolen. Otherwise, her story is an example of a common experience shared by many children throughout Southeastern Nigeria during the 1920s and 1930s. Ihuoma's account illustrates that child-dealing practices often involved several people, various modes of transportation, and constant efforts to evade police detection.

The Persistence of Slavery: An Economic History of Child Trafficking in Nigeria offers the framework to understand a child's economic positionality in society—*the social economy of a child*. This analysis enables us to construct a comprehensive history of the primacy of the child's social and economic role. By mapping the history of the Bight of Biafra (current-day Nigeria) from the transatlantic slave through the early twentieth century, we can identify ongoing methods of appropriating children's bodies and their labor through the institutions of slavery, pawning, and child marriage. This book illuminates the political and economic changes that resulted from British colonialism and the sociopolitical implications that led to child trafficking. The United Nations defines child trafficking as "the recruitment, transportation, transfer, harbouring or receipt of a child for the purpose of exploitation."[3] The chapters that follow reveal the methods by which guardians transferred children and describe the decision-making process of child dealers and, in some instances, how children enacted their own agency. Although their choices may have been a reaction to the political, social, and economic conditions of the time, I argue that adults and children actively sought ways not only to cope with personal economic realities but to overcome and at times profit from local economic instability as well. Unlike other histories of children and childhood in Nigeria, I apply a conceptual approach, the "social economy of a child," as an ideology that asserts that children are valued as kin, meaning family members, and as laborers and protected as dependents, yet also used as collateral in a variety of ways when parents or guardians suffered from economic insolvency. I show how a child's status changed when a guardian attempted to gain some form of profit from the child's labor and that such an analysis is essential to understanding Nigeria's economic history. At the core of this book is the argument that child trafficking, child slavery, and other forms of coerced labor persisted beyond the nineteenth-century antislavery movement because children functioned as transmitters of wealth through which Nigerians negotiated their social and economic position.

WHO IS A CHILD? HISTORIES OF CHILDREN AND CHILDHOOD

Human rights activists have been especially attentive to the use of child labor in the Global South, while some scholars have called for historical explorations of children's productive activities in the past so as to formulate policies for ending it in contemporary society. To analyze African childhoods, scholars must contend with contemporary images of African children as victims. Modern news cycles often represent African children as abandoned, exploited, used in warfare, emaciated, and diseased.[4] In 2004, Beverly Grier, a historian of Africa, pleaded with other Africanists to "take children more seriously in their research," arguing "that children have shaped and continue to shape history in Africa in significant but hitherto largely untold ways."[5] Grier's suggestion came at a time when scarce research on children's contributions to family economies existed.[6] The static notion of "African childhood" must be challenged and understood as a "social construction that varies in time and space." Scholarly theories about what constitutes "childhood" are largely based on social and political factors, which include the "patriarchy, capital, colonial and post-colonial states, and children themselves."[7] Looking to early twentieth-century reformers concerned about child welfare in the Global South offers some insight into what those political motivations might have been.

From the 1920s onward, child advocates and human rights activists made evident their interest in children's health programs, access to education, and child labor conditions resulting in the formalization of scholarship in the social sciences.[8] Evelyn Sharp's 1931 report on the International Conference on African Children, organized by the Save the Children International Union, serves as a comprehensive collection of the investigations and reform efforts focused on the well-being of children throughout imperial holdings. As part of the document, G. Mondaini's Royal Institute of Economic and Commercial Science (Rome) report underscored instances where increased child pawning, slavery, marriage, and labor abuses transpired with the influx of European colonialism and industrialization. To reinforce the pattern, Sharp detailed instances of child pawning as "illicit slavery" like that which existed in Liberia.[9] The case of Liberia is significant because of the global attention garnered regarding recruiting and labor practices, which sent laborers to the island of Fernando Pó located off the coast of Nigeria, in the Guinea region.

Spain had established the colony of Fernando Pó in 1778 and struggled to procure labor for its palm plantations during the early decades of the twentieth century. At issue were the disreputable, independent labor recruiters who swindled prospective laborers into signing labor contracts with false promises.[10] The subpar working conditions and labor abuses of the mid-1920s resulted in the 1930 Enquiry Commission to Liberia, an investigation requested by Liberians. Subsequently, the League of Nations' International Commission on Slavery determined the process of recruitment and the resulting labor conditions to be indistinguishable from "slave raiding and slave trading," essentially describing "contract workers" as "slaves." By September 29, 1930, the president of Liberia, C. D. B. King, issued a proclamation demanding an end to all forms of pawning and the release of domestic servants. In the aftermath of the investigation, the British Foreign Office promised the Liberian government that the League of Nations would address the issue in January 1931.[11] It is evident that concerns about the welfare of African children in the colonies from the 1920s to the 1930s, specifically regarding the institution of pawning and domestic slavery, received increased global attention. It is within this historical context that I examine child trafficking in its various forms in Southeastern Nigeria.

The study of children as historical subjects is necessary to fully understand the complexities of social, cultural, economic, and political histories. Yet scholars have only begun to consider "children" and "childhood" as formal categories of analysis in the past few decades. Early thinkers, however, did call upon the intellectual community to pay attention to childhood as a significant moment in a person's life. Scholars have granted credit to Jean-Jacques Rousseau (1712–78) for identifying adolescent needs and philosophizing that the life experience of a child, known as "growing up," was a process worth paying attention to.[12] It was not until the twentieth century that historians truly focused on children and childhood as legitimate categories of research. Philippe Ariès diverged from beliefs that children existed as miniature adults, positing that children and the historical concepts of childhood changed over time.[13] He argued that childhood, a social construction, formed during the modern period, creating domestic spaces fraught with tension and violence based on hierarchies and discipline. And as notions of childhood expanded, so too did histories of children and childhood.

Since the 1960s, historians have continued to map the lives of children and adolescents. Scholars increasingly situated children's histories in the context of family histories, emphasizing intimate relations in the household.[14] By the 1980s, histories of children and childhood experienced a downturn, and women and gender came to the fore.[15] Histories of children developed as an offshoot of and at times in tandem with histories of women and the family, and by the last decade of the twentieth century, children's contribution to the household became a major interest.[16]

Comprehensive histories that focused solely on children and childhood developed during 1990s as children's productive activities faced intense scholarly inquiry.[17] Childhood scholars have drawn

attention to topics spanning childrearing, girlhood, children's literature, psychology, adolescence, disabilities, orphanhood, and labor,
among others. Related to the central category for analysis in this
book, child labor, Paula Fass and Mary Ann Mason have asserted
that parents' love for their children did not exclude the need for their
labor as it was a matter of survival and "that the value of children
was still measured in the services they performed."[18] This argument,
while valid, stops short of prioritizing the children's bodies and
associated labor as the literal embodiment of transferrable wealth
and as producers of wealth. To fully understand the value of children,
we must center their productive activities within family economies.

Child labor is most visible in the poorest sectors of society. As
Colin Heywood has observed, "People today react indignantly to
reports of children still working in the 'sweatshops' in Western societies, not to mention the millions employed in the poorer countries
in the world." In part, this attention to and anxiety about child
labor invited academic interest in agricultural communities that
use very young children as farm laborers and hired hands. It is clear
that class distinctions come into play when the study of child labor
is pursued. Hugh Cunningham suggests that "the most obvious
manifestation of poverty is the division between children who are
an expense to their parents throughout childhood and beyond, and
those who, through work of some kind, contribute to their family
economies."[19] This analysis falls short of recognizing the value of
a child's corporeal being. It is the child's body and labor that can
translate dependency and expense into economic contribution and
wealth. Childhood dependency is a condition in which parents and
guardians have access to and control over children's movement and
their productive activities. It is this control that has garnered growing attention, especially when exploitative practices are identified.
The concern about child welfare is broadly based on the child's age
and ability to invoke personal agency and maintain personal safety.
Therefore, reviewing how various stakeholders define *child* is crucial.

Defining children as a protected group that should not be exploited is relatively easy. Doing so according to age, however, is a bit more complicated. The British and American laws that attempted to circumvent the use of child labor generally defined "childhood" as lasting until age fourteen to sixteen (depending on country and locality), after which adulthood began. However, the selection of a specific age seemed arbitrary to some. In 1911, Scott Nearing, secretary of the Pennsylvania Child Labor Committee, asked, "What is the purpose in setting an age limit for child labor and why was that limit set at fourteen?" He suggested that childhood should be defined according to the child's maturity and not marked by national standards.[20] Nevertheless, the terms *child* and *childhood* are largely informed by Western labor laws that developed during and after the Industrial Revolution as social reformers set out to define children as a protected demographic so as to keep them safe from labor abuse.[21]

The drawback of using the Western classification of maturity as a measure by which childhood is demarcated is that it does not take into consideration other cultural norms that distinguish children from adults. As Audra Diptee and Martin Klein have noted, numerous concepts about childhood existed throughout the African continent during the colonial era, which included notions of age as well as experiences. In Igbo society, for instance, the age-grade system "is the most important agent of socialization apart from the family." It is a collective of the same or similar aged individuals within a community who are trained to participate in duties that serve their families and the public. Under common leadership, children prepared for their role in society according to their age grade. For example, Uche Dike explains that boys spent leisure time by participating in "hunting, fishing, playing," and learning activities together.[22] Should any member of an age grade behave in an immoral manner, it was up to the collective to reprimand the guilty party. These self-monitoring groups remained intact until after marriage. It is through this pattern that boys and girls became men and women through various initiation rites. Lisa McNee explains that should a young person fail to undergo the appropriate initiation(s), "they would remain a child in the eyes of society regardless of his or her age." However, the colonial period served as a unique moment when children and youth challenged prevailing social structures.[23] The social norms and expectations that informed the behaviors of children and parents in Nigeria's precolonial era transformed with the onset of colonialism and in this way further challenged the notion of childhood.

The Persistence of Slavery fills a historical void by highlighting how British colonialism altered childhood for the most vulnerable. Even though other scholarship has focused on the history of children and slavery in a global context, as well as the productive labor and sexual abuse of children, there exists no other book that details how children, through their fluid statuses—pawns, slaves, child brides, and traffickers—were essential in wealth procurement for families, communities, and the colonial state.[24] Some scholars have explored more contemporary modalities of child slavery, which demonstrates a shift from the predominate practice of focusing on the adult male slave, but they fail to offer a comprehensive account of the widespread trafficking of children at the end of the transatlantic slave trade and beyond. The following chapters provides an in-depth breakdown of humanitarian efforts and legislative attempts to identify and end child trafficking and slavery in colonial Southeastern Nigeria.[25] In contrast with previous scholarship, I illustrate how economic conditions, including moneylending, introduction of new colonial currencies, and the fluctuation of indigenous currency values shaped the movement of children under various forms of guardianship. Other historians of child slavery and of children and childhood have not explored this symbiotic relationship as a central category of analysis.

Africanists *have* documented the increased need for domestic labor as the transatlantic slave trade came to an end, concentrating on child mobility, constraint, and opportunity, with limited attention to humanitarian and antislavery efforts.[26] In contrast, my work stresses the importance of individual actors—humanitarians—who demanded an account of the varied uses of Southeastern Nigerian children, as well as the contributions of women who participated in the 1929 Women's War, thereby creating a rich colonial record that documented known forms of child pawning, child slavery, and child marriage.

By all accounts, historical scholarship on children in Nigeria during the colonial period is limited. The texts that do exist, however, illuminate the ways in which children, families, and colonial authorities attempted to negotiate the changing social, economic, political, and cultural terrain. To date, the most comprehensive book on Nigerian children highlights the interplay between urbanization, the British social workers' salvationist project, and elite Lagosian women's modernization efforts in Western Nigeria. Abosede George shows that in their attempt to combat "unruly" children and youth, chiefly girl hawkers, British reformers and Nigerian women fought to control Nigerian children's productive activities.[27] George largely focuses on the cultural consequences of British colonialism as European gendered expectations determined acceptable behaviors for girls. My work diverges from George's in that I prioritize the primacy of economic outcomes related to children's movement and labor, arguing that the colonial environment disrupts Nigerian childhoods in ways that British cultural assimilations could never remedy.

Other more recent works that focus on Nigerian colonial childhoods examine how the label "modern children" came to define Nigerian youth. Saheed Aderinto posits that "modern African childhood" is born from Christian missionary efforts in West Africa during the early decades of the nineteenth century. He claims that "mission education laid the foundation of the modern conception of childhood" through the introduction of Western notions about religion, leisure time, labor norms, language, and personal identity. The educated class influenced the characteristics of modern African childhood well into the first decades of the twentieth century. While Aderinto acknowledges that colonial childhoods developed against the backdrop of families' social and economic position, he mainly highlights constructions of childhood in terms of access to education. Such constructions include the consumption of colonial propaganda related to childrearing, allegiance to empire, acceptable forms of child labor, mobility, multiculturalism, and social programs. Missing from this analysis is how modernization, largely understood as a process born from imperialism, produced the globalization of Nigerian commercial markets that depended on child labor. As part of this modernization process, the codification of colonial law and moneylending practices created modern childhoods wherein certain groups of children became vulnerable to trafficking and slavery.[28]

Scholars have also analyzed the history of children's involvement in social clubs, legislation concerning adolescents, and child labor.[29] Yet, much of the scholarship concentrates on Western Nigeria, thus reflecting the glaring absence of books and edited volumes attentive to children in Southeastern Nigeria during the colonial period. However, when commodity commerce replaced the international trade in slaves, the Aro (Igbo subgroup), the main agents of the slave trade, began to depend on agriculture to withstand the massive change in trading norms in order to maintain an influx of income.[30] As palm oil production increased, as did the need for credit, so too did the demand for labor and moneylending. It is within this context that we can understand how children and their labor filled those needs.

Documenting how children's bodies represented collateral in financial practices is central to understanding the interdependency of personal finance, social contracts, and external, local, and global factors. Anna Mae Duane argues that "although children are often excluded from the calculus of who counts as a slave, they have long been central to defining slavery itself," precisely because of the child's vulnerability and dependency on others.[31] Children should be historicized, in their own right, as slaves. As such, my work emphasizes the vulnerability and dependencies of children, which allowed for their subordination and enslavement. Analyzing Southeastern Nigerian oral narratives from those who remember how children became pawns, child brides, and slaves produces critical insight.

Children continued to be an integral part of the local and colonial economies after the transatlantic slave trade (1519–1867), during which slavers seized 1.6 million Africans from the Bight of Biafra. By mapping the movement of children, as embodied forms of wealth and as transferable laborers, this book distinguishes itself from others. The study of the social economy of children during the colonial period allows us to once again revisit "slavery's twentieth century problem."[32]

REVISITING SLAVERY'S TWENTIETH-CENTURY PROBLEM

What is slavery? The answer to that question depends on whom you ask. In this contemporary moment, it is likely that those focused on modern-day slavery would provide examples of sex trafficking during the Super Bowl, child slavery in Ivory Coast cocoa farms, or perhaps prison labor in the wake of the COVID-19 pandemic where New York prisoners make sixty-five cents or less per hour producing antibacterial gel.[33] These are twenty-first-century examples of various forms of forced or coerced labor, but the questions remains: How did we come to define these phenomena as instances of slavery? The 1926 Slavery Convention defines slavery as "the status or condition of a person over whom any or all of the powers attaching to the right of ownership are exercised."[34] If we assume that there is a link between historical patterns of chattel enslavement, domestic slavery in Africa, and forms of oppressive modern-day servitude, would we be correct? To answer these questions, it is necessary to explore early efforts to end the transatlantic slave trade, the European seizure of African territory, the development of the cash crop industry, and the expansion of other mercantile enterprises.

The transition from subsistence farming peasants to wage-earning and taxpaying colonial subjects did not happen spontaneously in the twentieth century. When Africans did not meet colonial labor needs, administrators instituted coercive practices that resulted in "emerging labor systems" that were "more oppressive than slavery," often involving child labor. Suzanne Miers and others have regarded the resulting tyrannical labor systems as slavery's twentieth-century problem. To further elucidate the contradiction, Jean Allain argues that even though many Western countries denounced slavery, colonizers believed that imperial holdings could not be civilized without forced labor.[35] So how, then, did forced labor differ from slavery?

The 1885 Berlin Declaration set in motion a reconfiguration of the use of African labor. The attendees of the 1884–85 Berlin Conference agreed to support the end of the slave trade by land and sea. In an attempt to gain unanimous agreement to legitimize imperial holdings, representatives promised to ensure the well-being of and improve moral standards (according to European norms) of indigenous peoples and denounce domestic slavery. Not until the signing of the Berlin Act of 1890, through which Europeans championed their colonizing mission under the guise of raising Africans from their "heathen" state and ending slavery, did European powers plot out territorial boundaries for nearly all of Africa.[36] Decades before the Berlin Conference, when profits from the transatlantic slave trade waned, the formalization of their influence on the continent increased as Europeans sought other methods to reap economic returns from Africa and its peoples. At the behest of Western demand, plantations and cash cropping multiplied, especially in West Africa's palm oil industry, and labor needs surged in the decades that followed. For example, Calabar dominated the palm oil trade in Southeastern Nigeria from 1906 to 1929. Women generally controlled the palm kernel trade, while men governed the trade in oil.[37] Clearing land, planting, harvesting, transporting, and participating in public works projects helped build and maintain agricultural trade. The British surmised that this process of developing legitimate trade would ultimately curtail the slave trade.[38]

In the face of "legitimate" agricultural and commercial development, vigorous efforts by abolitionists to end chattel slavery throughout the Americas and the Caribbean fell short as it related to domestic slavery in colonial Africa. The trade in palm oil, ground nuts, and other agricultural goods required domestic slave labor that ensued concurrent with and subsequent to the transatlantic slave trade. Robin Law coined the term "'legitimate' commerce" as a way to describe commercial activities that could not successfully thrive without forced labor and argues that "in-part, this growth in slavery within West Africa reflected the increased use of slave labour in the production and transport of exports for 'legitimate' trade."[39] As a play on words, the development of "legitimate" commerce, as opposed to the transatlantic slave trade, created an environment that necessitated and profited from coerced labor. Even more so, the advent of colonialism in Africa produced heightened labor mobilization and control, trends that persisted throughout the colonial era.[40] Abolitionists sought to end slavery in the late eighteenth century and more readily focused their efforts on immobilizing the transatlantic slave trade in the early nineteenth century.[41] With potential access to new forms of wealth, both Africans and colonial officials set out to amass the labor needed for commercial enterprise.[42] Therefore, the ways in which colonial administrators deployed African labor merits consideration as a way to understand why some indigenous customs regarding child slavery went largely unchecked.

Many nineteenth-century abolitionists and humanitarians celebrated the collapse of the transatlantic slave trade as a noteworthy success even though domestic slavery rose exponentially in its aftermath. This "reinvention and reconfiguration" of slavery deserves scholarly consideration, especially as it relates to children. Prior to colonization, slavery on the continent of Africa served many purposes. Individuals became enslaved as a result of wars, misdeeds, and being born into slave lineages. There existed "open and closed slave systems," and those born in a closed slave system were generally precluded from discarding their social status. Open slave systems provided opportunities for slaves to achieve "status mobility," and it was not uncommon for slaves to be integrated into family structures.[43] Otherwise, some societies expelled "criminals and abnormal children" by selling them to people outside their community or used them for ritual sacrifices and for "settling conflicts." The heightened reliance on child labor occurred with twentieth-century European incursion on the African continent. Benjamin Lawrance submits that this period should be considered "the beginning of the age of child enslavement."[44] If historians of slavery reimagine this period as a time when African child labor was central to colonial economic structures, the reverberation of the abolitionist movement falls short of absolute triumph.

Expanding beyond the 1926 Slavery Commission definition and its 1953 amendment, scholars have defined and redefined historical and contemporary applications of slavery. Slavery, as an institution, denied the slave of any legal rights, making him or her a form of commercial property, a "capital investment." For instance, Martin Klein summarizes a slave as an "outsider, someone who is 'seen as property,'" adding that "the dependence of a slave originated in an act of violence and its continuance required action." Paul Lovejoy explains that slaves did not control their own labor, sexuality, or reproductive abilities, which ensured that the owner had access to any financial or human capital that resulted from owning the slave.[45] No matter the formal definition, labor practices akin to slavery proliferated throughout the African continent.

Contract labor, more accurately described as forced labor, became the common method of securing labor for public works projects. Even in the face of international scrutiny, colonial administrators understood that ending all forms of forced labor would diminish colonial earnings and "threaten both the production of exports and the generation of revenues." Moreover, prohibiting men and women of high social status from maintaining their slaveholdings would "have alienated local collaborative elites and disrupted the economic base of their power."[46] In addition to slavery and contract labor, pawning was another method by which individuals leveraged labor and secured access to loans.

Southeastern Nigerians utilized the institution of pawnship as the main way to guarantee loans during the economic stress caused by colonial policies. And through this method, hundreds, if not thousands, of Southeastern Nigerian children were thrust into domestic slavery.

Pawnship, a form of legal dependency in which a pawn was held as security, became a widespread labor condition in various parts of Africa in the twentieth century. The pawn's labor paid the interest on a debt until the debtor reimbursed the moneylender. Paul Lovejoy and Toyin Falola explain: "Kinship, marital bonds, or some other clearly recognized social status was supposed to safeguard individuals from excessive abuse, prevent the transfer of pawns to third parties, or obstruct other acts that the debtors might consider inappropriate or illegal."[47] In addition to pawning a child or young dependent for a loan, chiefs and elders in the community offered youth, in their place, to perform conscripted labor for the colonial administration.[48] In precolonial pawning cases, parents and guardians expected to redeem their children once the loan had been repaid. Distinct from pawning, panyarring was a form of foreclosure on a loan.[49] If a debt remained unpaid, debt collectors could "seize" the debtor or his or her dependent until they received the payment.[50] In the case of girls when parents failed to repay the debt, their daughter likely became the moneylender's bride or that of one of his or her dependents. Nefarious moneylenders also sold pawned girls to work as prostitutes.[51] Even though betrothing young girls to a man was a normative practice, reselling them to strangers was not.

A variety of sources help inform the growing economic histories focused on debt and the mobilization of juvenile labor in Africa. European merchants, seamen, and anthropologists documented pawnship practices. Martin Chanock describes the institution as a normal moneylending system practiced during colonialism. The social contract created by a moneylending agreement would "cement 'relationships of obligation and dependency.'" Current scholarship dedicated to the institution illuminates how the practice of pawning enabled Africans to engage in commercial activities, pay debts, formalize marriages, bury family members, and survive famines. More specifically, the research presented by Lovejoy, Falola, Judith Byfield, David Richardson, and Felix Ekechi historicizes pawning, taking into account global economic factors. These works help us understand how Africans mitigated their economic circumstances in the face of colonialism.[52] However, attention to the exchange of children and their labor is incomplete, resulting in limited perceptions of the methods by which Africans dealt with colonial economic distress. My analysis adds another layer to existing histories by prioritizing children's lives and productive activities as they existed as pawns and in other economic capacities and serves as an example of an economic anthropology that centers children.[53]

Insolvent populations pawned children for temporary loans for a variety of reasons.[54] As the Igbo-speaking people attempted to deal with the faltering economy, many borrowed to meet fiscal responsibilities. Such individuals sought patrons, known as *ogaranya* ("persons with some property"), for the purpose of obtaining loans. Fundamentally, the pawn existed as both a dependent of another individual and part of an economic transaction. The nature of that dependency—as a subordinate to another family member or as a pawn to a nonrelated *ogaranya*—generally determined whether pawns, especially children, would ever be redeemed. While pawning existed before colonization, the institution became more prevalent as Nigeria's internal economy became increasingly integrated with the international economy. At such time, pawning had become a "legal category of social and economic dependency" often certified before witnesses.[55] After Nigeria became a British protectorate in 1901, the British allowed Nigerians to pawn themselves and some dependents when circumstances necessitated. Archival materials provide confirmation that this practice continued well into the 1930s albeit transformed. Evidence shows that a once legal and public practice (when an adult pawned himself) evolved into a social and economic institution, which resulted in the creation of what some consider one of the darkest elements of Nigeria's shadow economy during British occupation.

BRITISH TRADE AND OCCUPATION OF NIGERIA

During the nineteenth century, the transition from supplying slaves during the transatlantic slave trade to the development of the prominent palm oil industry created a need for credit systems in Nigeria, which allowed Britain to establish control over trade operations and oversight of credit agreements. Credit agreements allowed sellers and buyers to operate along Nigeria's coast. In 1856 the British established a Court of Equity in Calabar to monitor and rule on disputes between the local traders and British firms.[56] The 1860s were an especially turbulent time for established oil traders and suppliers because of the constant struggles over access to oil-supplying regions in the interior and oil prices. During this period the demand for credit increased as African brokers and small-scale traders sought to access it. The requirement that traders submit large capital deposits resulted in growing demands for credit by small-scale traders who did not have the prerequisite funds. In this context, moneylending transactions increased as did disputes over loans, and resulting debt cases demanded colonial intervention.[57]

By 1870, the British established Courts of Equity in Opobo, Brass, Okrika, in the Niger Delta and in the west from Bonny to the Benin River. The courts' goal to maintain "a certain amount of law and order among the wild 'gentleman' of the commercial community of the coast" suggests that moneylenders acted recklessly when handing out loans.[58] The Courts of Equity continued to settle disputes over trade and debts between European merchants and African traders as a way to maintain peace and the flow of goods.[59] The economic crisis of the 1880s, during which palm oil prices plummeted, caused loan defaults and resulted in bankruptcy for some of the largest European trading firms. For example, the National African Company (later the Royal Niger Company) that established a monopoly in the palm oil trade on the Niger River went bankrupt when oil prices fell, leaving them with numerous outstanding debts.[60]

In another instance, the court intervened in German merchant transactions that allowed African traders access to large amounts of credit, resulting in frequent disputes when debts went unpaid.[61] Over time, managing the mounting debt cases became untenable. The credit disputes that existed between Europeans and Africans spurred British attention, and by 1900 Britain had imposed the

Recovery of Credit Proclamation, which prevented British intervention in recovering debts for other European traders. The prevalence
of moneylending caused so many inquiries that "it was considered
that 'trust' was given out to such an extent, and so recklessly, that
legitimate trade was being seriously damaged by it."[62] The British
argued that the breakdown of moneylending agreements directly
destabilized trading markets and sought more control over the trade.

Colonial Nigeria evolved in several stages as the British gained
more control over the trade in palm oil during the mid-nineteenth
century. The British formalized its occupation of Nigeria with the
Anglo-French Convention of 1898, and in 1900 the area was divided
into the Colony of Lagos and the Protectorates of Southern and
Northern Nigeria. As high commissioner of Southern Nigeria
(1903–6) and the governor of the Colony of Lagos (1904–6), Sir
Walter Egerton (1858–1947) was appointed to oversee the merger
of the northern and southern administrations in 1904.[63] The amalgamation resulted in the development of three focal provinces in
the south with capitals in the Eastern Province at Calabar, the
Central Province at Warri and the Western Province of Lagos.
Each province had an assigned commissioner.[64] In order to gain
control of the region, the British led a military assault, the Aro
Campaign of 1902, on the slave-owning elite of northern Igboland.
From 1904 to 1909, the army slaughtered hundreds, and the British
forced thousands who survived to work on infrastructure projects,
such as "road construction, stream clearance, and the building of
government guest houses."[65] In 1906 the southern territories were
united into Lagos Colony and Protectorate of Southern Nigeria. In
an attempt to streamline administrative practices across Nigeria, the
British enacted a plan to unify the colony by establishing indirect
rule, a system in which they aimed to appoint local chiefs to oversee
assigned localities in the southwestern, eastern, and central parts
of the country under British governance. In 1905, Lord Frederick

John Dealtry Lugard, who later served as governor in Northern and Southern Nigeria (1912 to 1913) and governor-general (1914 to 1919), issued a memorandum that mapped out his goals, which included the development of a railway system, a plan to regulate trade in natural and agricultural resources, and, perhaps the most often written about, the development of a judicial system based on a uniform policy.[66] By 1906, Southern Nigeria's governing structure was comprised of four district commissioners, three district officers, and nine divisional commissioners, all of whom worked under the high commissioner (figure 2).

In 1914 the Colony of Lagos and the two protectorates of Southern and Northern Nigeria became the Colony and Protectorate of Nigeria. By World War I, the political boundaries and administrative

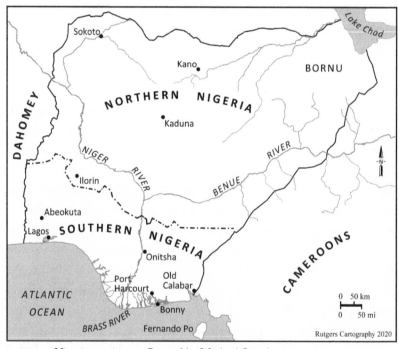

FIGURE 2. Nigeria, 1906–1914. Created by Michael Siegel.

structures had been established. The formal creation of the Colony of Nigeria transformed the Bight of Biafra's economy and radically changed the indigenous forms of governance, which ultimately affected the lives of children.[67] The administration moved quickly to develop an infrastructure that would create an export-oriented economy, which it hoped would lead to self-sufficiency. When the British first introduced systems of compulsory labor for public works projects, they extracted labor from coastal canoe houses (defined in chapter 1). They also commissioned village leaders, some of whom they designated as warrant chiefs, to supply personal slaves, pawns, and other dependent persons for work. As a result, chiefs forced children and men to comply with colonial work orders, producing unfree labor systems, a policy that attracted the protests of antislavery humanitarian groups in England and sparked a debate within the Colonial Office about the wisdom of using corvée labor.[68]

By 1914, Lugard finalized plans to implement Nigeria's new governance structure.[69] At the time of Lugard's appointment as governor-general, the Southern Nigeria Protectorate encompassed a patchwork of colonially structured polities and scattered native courts in the southeast. To his "orderly" military mind, this was chaos. Lugard initiated governance changes that sought to create a common, rationally organized local governing system. Lugard refined the system of local government, known as "indirect rule," that allowed the appointment of local men as warrant chiefs who carried out the colonial administration's orders in Southeastern Nigeria. This form of rule mirrored what Britain had applied in the Islamic north and allowed Nigerian men to function as judges over native courts. However, imposing indirect rule on Igboland proved problematic because, unlike the north, the region consisted of small, autonomous units without chiefs. The previous indigenous system was largely based on councils of men and sometimes women related by kinship, lineage, and seniority in spiritual and professional capacities. Therefore, the newly appointed chiefs drew the ire of their subordinates. The warrant chief system and colonial court structure did not replicate native governing practices and would be cause for social upheaval.[70] The application of Lugard's policies had notable economic consequences and labor implications for Southeastern Nigerians.

CHAPTER OUTLINE

The Persistence of Slavery is organized into five chapters, followed by a conclusion. Chapter 1 surveys the development of British colonial rule in Nigeria and documents how the advent of colonialism transformed local governing bodies, domestic slavery, and economic conditions. In the era of conquest, I focus on the transformation of the local economy into a colonial economy, the move from the transatlantic slave trade to the trade in palm oil products and other agricultural goods and its effect on domestic slavery. Conflicting colonial policies about coerced labor, primarily in the canoe house systems (trading centers), attracted international attention that resulted in antislavery critiques about the use of child laborers, especially pawns, in the trading institutions.

Chapter 2 looks closely at the post-1914 Lugardian reforms of indirect rule. New rules governing coercive labor and moneylending agreements left some Igboland residents seeking economic relief. Additionally, the implementation of the warrant chief system and removal of the district officers who provided oversight of the native court system left residents vulnerable to warrant chief abuses. I explore how local inhabitants with limited access to colonial authorities became reliant on warrant chiefs, court clerks, and other court members to mediate disputes. By analyzing court documentation of debt cases and evaluating how the influx of British currencies affected Nigerian personal and commercial activities, this chapter illustrates the particularly difficult economic realities that some families, especially women and children, endured.

Chapter 3 considers the development of concern for the well-being of African children that grew with increased organizational attempts to end child pawning, marriage, and domestic slavery. Women's groups, antislavery lobbies, and humanitarian organizations, based primarily in the League of Nations, shifted their attention to the trafficking of women and children in an effort to end domestic slavery in Africa.[71] This chapter also examines the reformist agenda at a time when British policies focused on generating revenue from Nigeria as the success of the colonial economy necessitated various forms of coerced labor.[72] While social reformers in Europe, the United States, and Canada worked to improve the well-being of children in their respective countries, they also began to define acceptable conditions of African childhood. And it is within this context that my analysis pays critical attention to girls as child brides, slaves, and pawns as concerns about human trafficking increased.

Chapter 4 offers a new perspective on the 1929 Women's War by reconsidering the women's motives for participation. In addition to the well-known reasons cited for the uprising—taxes, decreased export prices, and increased import costs—women lost their children through the institution of pawnship when they needed loans to pay colonial taxes. I examine the increased tensions between women and political authorities, mainly the warrant chiefs. The chapter also shows the similarities and differences between the 1925 women's dancing movement and the 1929 revolt. We see a continuation of concerns about financial instability, the decrease of women's political influence, and a desire that women's economic endeavors be secure from male infringement. This chapter shows that, among other reasons presented by scholars for nearly fifty years, the overall economic stress of the late 1920s propelled women to protest the loss of their children through pawning.

Chapter 5 focuses on the aftermath of the 1929 Women's War and the ways in which colonial officials responded to international pressure to investigate child trafficking and examines British ambivalence about ending the traffic in pawns. By pressuring colonial officials to investigate child dealing, the League of Nations ensured the development of colonial records that identified specific stakeholders in child trafficking practices. In particular, this chapter provides an overview of women and children as victims and as traffickers. Identifying women and children as trafficking agents upends the assumption that women and children should have been defined as mere dependents in need of protection.

The Persistence of Slavery is a significant contribution to histories of Africa, children and childhood, women, slavery, and labor. Human rights groups and policymakers are seeking ways to understand the legacies of human trafficking so as to develop policies that would limit and, if possible, end child trafficking. Understanding the long history of human trafficking in Nigeria will assist that effort. The limitations of this book are represented in the types of the available archival material. Court and colonial records are likely to have misrepresented some Nigerian accounts and lack a significant number of firsthand testimonies from children. I rectify this absence through the use of oral testimonies by including oral histories from current-day residents of Aba, Calabar, Enugu, and Owerri that offer rich details and describe the cultural practices that allowed a child to move from one form of guardianship to another.

Politics, Social Relations, and Trade in the Bight of Biafra

The women and children are employed in collecting palm-oil; the men, in trading to Brass and Eboe, [and] kidnapping their neighbors.

—*MacGregor Laird, Scottish trader, 1832*

T he last century of the transatlantic slave trade saw the normalization of child trafficking as slaving, pawning, kidnapping, and the sale of children escalated. More than any other region, the Bight of Biafra drew significant numbers of children into the slave trade as its inhabitants developed many individual and group methods of seizing children and employing their labor. With no central government to regulate their actions, long-distance traders from throughout Igboland and beyond, local middlemen, women, and children developed human trafficking strategies without drawing much European attention, evading significant opposition from local authorities.[1]

This chapter surveys the development of British colonial rule in Nigeria and how the advent of colonialism altered local governing bodies, domestic slavery, and economic conditions. The transformation of the local economy into a colonial economy, specifically the transition from the transatlantic slave trade to commercial trade in palm oil products and other agricultural goods, unveils the way in which domestic slavery developed. Conflicting colonial policies about coerced labor, mainly in the canoe house systems (trading centers), attracted international attention, resulting in antislavery critiques about the use of child labor, especially pawns.

Analyzing the history of various forms of child slavery in eighteenth- and nineteenth-century Atlantic commercial trading systems provides an understanding of Nigerian childhoods during the colonial era and offers an anthropological reckoning of how African traders and families negotiated access to children and their labor in maritime environments. The transition from the transatlantic slave trade to "legitimate commerce" (as described in the introduction) and the implementation of colonial taxation schemes profoundly transformed the deployment of child labor in Southeastern Nigeria. The capital market served the local economic interests of wealthy men and women, leaving the poorest individuals to pawn land or kin.[2] As noted in the quotation from Scottish trader MacGregor Laird above, there existed an interconnection between the growing palm oil industry, child labor, and kidnapping.[3]

Historians have focused on pawnship and the consequences of commercial production as it relates to gender, but other modes of analysis are imperative.[4] Chima J. Korieh notes that scholars have focused on how entire societies transformed, as a consequence of commercial developments in the Biafran hinterland, but do not evaluate individual responses to the change. His critique acknowledges that women's labor increased when commercial activities expanded—a major theme in African colonial scholarship—"but such a narrow assessment ignores the coincident increases in . . . children's labor inputs as well."[5] The focus of this chapter fills this historical void by mapping out how children's labor is reimagined and deployed during the eighteenth and nineteenth centuries.

EARLY CASE STUDIES

The use of children as pawns, whether as collateral for commercial goods, for monetary loans, or in slaving ventures, has not yet been fully explored by historians of Southeastern Nigeria. There has been little written about economic transactions on which the labor of children was based. Even when there are available sources, there are limitations, such as a lack of firsthand accounts or faulty memories.[6] In the paragraphs that follow, the personal histories of Olaudah Equiano (also known as Gustavas Vassa, ca. 1745–97) and Peter (no last name given) help us understand how children became part of West African economic transactions.[7] The pattern of relationships and networks that sustained child dealing gives historians insight into the complex and wide-ranging system that enabled the abduction and captivity of freeborn children.

These accounts offer a window through which to see how child traffickers transferred children from one guardian to another and how pawning practices resulted in the enslavement of children. In Equiano's case, his parents left him and his sister at home alone on the day that kidnappers snatched them. The kidnappers strategically waited until the parents had gone to the farm before enacting their plan. Accompanied by their trafficker, Equiano and his sister traveled all day and took shelter in a small home, stationed along a trade route, where they ate and then slept through the night. In the following days, the child dealer sold Equiano's sister first and then Equiano, after which various slave dealers continued to buy and sell Equiano over the several days' journey. At some point Equiano ended up with a chief, who worked as a blacksmith, and while in his care, Equiano labored as an apprentice, working with bellows, as well as a cook's assistant for about a month. Subsequently, Equiano was sold after the death of the chief's only child. It is likely that the chief sold Equiano to secure the funds to pay a debt brought on by his daughter's funeral. Equiano's personal account depicts a trade network comprised of numerous actors. Some facilitated the actual abduction; others took responsibility for securing a rest house in which they could hide along the route; still others acted as intermediaries when buying and selling the children.[8]

In another example, Laird recounted the story of an adolescent named Peter, which he documented during his trade ventures in the early nineteenth century. Peter's father, a well-respected trader who operated along the Niger Delta and the Cameroonian coast and in Fernando Pó, purchased a canoe from a canoe trader. He paid half the cost of the vessel and left his son, Peter, as a pawn to guarantee that he would return and pay the debt. Before Peter's father returned, Peter's guardian, the canoe trader, offered him as collateral to a slave trader to whom he promised slaves, and in exchange, the canoe trader received goods and payment in advance. When Peter's guardian returned with slaves in tow, Peter assisted him in carrying provisions onto the slave ship to prepare for its departure. But before Peter could leave the ship, the slave trader apprehended him, causing the canoe trader great angst.[9] Remanded on the ship, young Peter watched as the canoe trader yelled at the slave trader, demanding that Peter be allowed to disembark the vessel, but it was too late. The slave trader who had Peter in his possession sailed off. Peter could not escape, and his guardian could not retrieve him. In that moment, Peter's status as a pawn switched to that of a slave.[10] The slave trader violated the conventions of trade and pawning by kidnapping Peter, whose status as a pawn should have been protected. However, that was not the end of Peter's story.

A British warship seized the slave trader's ship on Sierra Leone's coast, a colony established for liberated slaves, after which one Colonel Nicolls adopted him and enrolled him in school, while the majority of other freed slaves performed hard labor.[11] After five years he was able to return to his village and reunite with his mother. By then, he called himself Prince William of Bimbia (Cameroon), which signifies that he had made a name for himself, most likely as a commercial trader. Peter's story is a reflection of the precarious status of child pawns during the slave trade era.[12]

Equiano's and Peter's stories provide examples of the interdependence of children, security arrangements, and the transatlantic economy, offering historians important clues to understand the vulnerability and economic embeddedness of children. The social economy of the child dictated the circumstances under which a child became a slave or pawn. A fundamental contradiction of pawnship is that the pawn is someone who is both a dependent within a kinship network and part of an economic transaction. Pawnship, as a credit system, relied on the protections that kinship relations provided.[13] Kinship also provided a moral code that facilitated community cohesion and linked village inhabitants through social contracts, based on dependencies and protection. Social relationships maintained by trust and mutual responsibilities held these groups together. However, by the eighteenth and nineteenth centuries, many of these conventions and mores collapsed under the pressure of the transatlantic slave trade and the development of legitimate commercial activities. Pawning underwrote and connected indigenous moneylending agreements to the slave trade, while at the same time making pawns more vulnerable to slavery.[14]

THE BIAFRAN HINTERLAND AND THE ARO

The Biafran hinterland's physical geography and ecology shaped the political, social, religious, and economic systems that affected the vulnerability of children. The area consisted of three main environmental regions: the northern grasslands, the fertile palm belt, and the salt marshes on the coast. Each had its own geography resulting in specific forms of economic specialization. In the north (approximately 140 miles from the coast), the environment encompasses savanna-like grasslands and has lower rainfall than the areas to the south. John Oriji argues that Abam warriors (Aro slaving partners) operated in the north as it was a key source area for slaves during the seventeenth and eighteenth centuries, as well as into the first half of the twentieth century. Igbo-speaking peoples and their neighbors lived in densely populated villages, some approximating one thousand people per square mile, with many perched on infertile, eroded escarpments where they could barely eke out a living by farming. Although this offered some protection from slavers, the land was not sufficient to support all inhabitants. Some village members from different clans felt compelled to sell a child to secure the means to feed those remaining. Near them, in the more fertile valley, prosperous farmers called Nkanu allied with the Aro slave traders. The land in the north yielded yams, cassava, corn, and beans. To the southeast, near Enyong Creek, inhabitants successfully grew oil palms, bananas, and cassava. In the south, inhabitants also farmed a variety of vegetables, oil palms, corn, and bananas. They were willing buyers of their less fortunate neighbors' children, whom they used to tend their fields or sold to slave traders headed for the coast.[15]

The Igbo, Aro (Igbo subgroup), Ibibio, Ijaw (Ijo), and Efik lived in the area that extended from the Niger Delta to Cameroon (from the Niger River in the west to the Cross River in the east) and dwelled in communities that were often democratic, overseen by senior men and women whose membership in secret societies committed them to appeasing deities. Very few acted as aristocratic rulers. Rather, each village group self-governed their communities through the creation of specialized entities. It was an area that is fragmented into many small villages, with no history of a precolonial empire or powerful indigenous state as was the case with the Oyo Empire of the Yoruba in Western Nigeria.[16] Internal trade systems, which date back to the Neolithic era, linked these distinct cultural groups. This "primordial trade" lasted for centuries and saw the exchange of foodstuffs, handiwork goods, and other items. The internal trade in goods continued as the transatlantic slave trade surged. Adiele E. Afigbo argues that initially "elite members of the community" throughout the region dominated the internal and foreign slave trade, not solely the Aro. The Aro, Awka, Nkwerre, Abiriba, and Umunoha competed for authority before the transatlantic slave trade until the Aro captured the oracle, Ibini Ukpabi (meaning "drum of the Creator God," see chapter 2), from their Benue-Congo rivals. It was not until the seizure of the all-important oracle that the Aro began to dominate the internal and external trade in men, women, and children.[17]

The Aro established their capital and spiritual home in Aro-chukwu, near the Cross River where they housed the Ibini Ukpabi mystic shrine.[18] As a ruling society that was both feared and respected, other Igbo groups looked to the Aro for advice and to settle disputes. As it pertained to Aro trade activities and their travel throughout the region, many in Igboland considered the Aro "God men" and afforded them protection as they developed a complex trade system in the Biafran hinterland. To support their trade ventures, the Aro controlled key markets, dispensing fellow Aro and other business associates to form villages intermittently along trade routes.[19] Marrying women in each of the satellite villages was especially useful because it, too, expanded and maintained Aro influence in the region.

During the eighteenth and nineteenth centuries, the Aro acted as the premier group of agents who organized and executed slave transactions, which led to the sale of thousands of Africans at the coast.[20] They secured slaves from the interior whom they filtered through the network of public markets, private compounds, and satellite villages. As chief perpetrators in child dealing, the Aro became synonymous with "constant warfare and kidnapping," and by 1900 they had established a trade diaspora of more than 150 settlements across 80,000 square miles of the Bight of Biafra.[21]

Because the Aro targeted women and children, communities developed practices whereby they would hide. One Igbo resident stated, "I noticed that every large tree in a prominent position had a recently-erected wooden platform in the topmost forks, which were to serve in case of an Ada attack; a point of vantage for shooting, and also a refuge for property, women and children." Although individuals throughout the region worked together to avoid capture, many could not escape the demand for slaves. Danger of enslavement increased with the development of plantations in the New World, resulting in Aro refinement and expansion of their trading networks.[22] The geographic nature of the region proved ideal for Aro slaving activities.

The Niger, Cross River, Benue River, and Bight of Biafra coast served as natural boundaries for the Aro trading diaspora. This is significant because the relationships and trade routes developed for the capture, transport, and sale of men, women, and children during the transatlantic slave trade provided the infrastructure for the subsequent trade in children during the colonial era. The Arochukwu satellite villages that spread throughout Igboland held their own markets, mainly dealing in horses, cattle, beads, and slaves, sometimes operating separately from other local markets.[23] The Arochukwu trade reached as far north as Idah, as far east as Isiokpo, and as far south as Itu and southeast at Calabar.[24] The trade extended as far as Awka and northeastward to Nike as well. Another route spanned from Arochukwu northward through Afikpo and Uburu to Ezza (Eza) and Izzi country and south to Bende and Uzuakoli. The Aro also coordinated their business at the "*Agbagwu* trade fair which played a prominent part in the marketing and trading life of the Ibo people" and attracted traders from throughout the hinterland.[25]

The areas that would eventually become colonial provinces known as Calabar, Ogoja, Onitsha, Owerri, and Rivers housed the major market towns where both the sale of slaves for transatlantic trade and the subsequent sale of domestic slaves, especially in children, took place. Specific market towns and source areas for child dealers included Awka, Onitsha, and Udi in Onitsha Province; Aba, Owerri, Bende, Okigwi (Okigwe), Orlu, and Uzuakoli in Owerri Province; Uburu, Calabar and Cross River in Calabar Province; Degema in

Rivers Province; and Afikpo, Ikom, and Obubra in Ogoja Province (see figure 1). Many of these regions also provided slaves to the Delta city-states, supplying the canoe houses with thousands of slaves who manned trading canoes and, in the case of Calabar, worked on palm plantations.[26] When dependent on the transport of goods along rivers and other waterways, the Aro relied on the Efik, the Opobo, and Bonny people for assistance and passage.[27]

The many rivers and streams that penetrate the interior became important byways that facilitated the area's engagement with the transatlantic slave trade and subsequent palm oil trade. Although it was difficult and treacherous for traders to move over land in many parts, the waterways allowed for easier access to the coastal societies where European traders were based. Important rivers, all of which flow north to south, including the Imo, the Anambra, the Orashi (Urashi), and the Cross, connected the inland region to slave traders.[28] The most important river, the massive Niger, divides the west from the east and functions as one of the key entry points into Igboland and Nigeria as a whole. The rivers allowed travel into the interior and access to the region's integrated trade. It is through these waterways that the Biafran population became as much a part of the global Atlantic trading system as did the New World. This new era of trade also led to shifts in authority and power.

Previous forms of accountability based on kinship and social relations broke down. Former democratic forms of political involvement eroded as wealthy men overruled older men in village councils. Men no longer achieved political power or social influence through seniority. Ugo Nwokeji describes the period of the transatlantic slave trade and the decades that followed as ones that departed from old value systems, allowing for new levels of violence.[29] A new system of validation, known as "title-taking," emerged and institutionalized the power of merchants. The new wealth gave rise to the development of governing councils made up of those who bought titles, rather than elders whose former authority was based on gerontocracy.[30] The house system is one example through which we see men ascend socially who could not otherwise do so.

THE CANOE HOUSE SYSTEM

In response to the demand for slaves during the sixteenth, seventeenth, and eighteenth centuries, kinship-based village systems developed corporate trading and political institutions called the "house" or "canoe house" along the Niger Delta, which stretches approximately 270 miles along the Atlantic coast and 120 miles north to south and is located between Lagos in the west and the Calabar in the east (see figure 1). The Niger River flows through connected waterways into the Gulf of Guinea and connected inland slavers to slave ships along the coast. The houses operated as trading enterprises and governing bodies that generally included a male head, his family, and dependents. The integrated political systems of the Niger Delta city-states (mainly Ibibio, Ijo [Ijaw] and Efik) varied.[31] Some functioned as monarchies and others as republics, but each was fiercely independent.

Every waterway entry point and trade post housed its own ruler who controlled all aspects of trade.[32] As interest in palm products grew, the houses facilitated the palm product trade with Europeans. The house ruler negotiated with European traders and worked with satellite villages in the interior to service the demand. Kenneth Morgan notes that in the case of Bonny and Old Calabar, "credit was tightly controlled and granted by British merchants to the heads of Canoe organizations that fetched slaves from the interior." In addition to slaves who manned trade canoes, there existed other subordinates who engaged in warfare with competing houses. Other dependents included indigent free people, pawns, children born to residents of the house, and elders unable to care for themselves.[33]

Old Calabar and Bonny are examples of fishing villages that developed into autonomous mercantile communities made up of family-based merchant houses. In the first decades of the eighteenth century, the Efik in Old Calabar had become a small yet important group that sold slaves. As their trade families grew, they began to branch out to places such as Creek Town, Old Town, and Duke Town, located on the Cross River estuary. The Efik dominated trade relations with Europeans, especially slave transactions, and their tendency to learn English and purchase European guns gave them an overwhelming advantage over the hinterland region and leverage when dealing with the middlemen who delivered the slaves.[34] By the mid-eighteenth century, the Efik came to incorporate slaves who worked on canoes as rowers and traders. Even though they appeared to be outsiders, slaves often shared common interests with their masters and fought on their behalf. In time, some slaves became rich through their personal trading ventures, gained respect, and even held slaves of their own. As the house populations increased, slaves cleared land and built huts for freemen, wives, apprentices, and other slaves. These wards, called *ufok,* grew dramatically during the nineteenth century.[35] Generally, an *obong*, or paramount leader, served as the ruler of a large house and represented his lineage in commercial transactions with Europeans.[36]

The house system depended on the existence of credit, which enabled the head to secure slaves and oil for trade. Between the 1830s and the 1850s, Old Calabar exported the most oil of all the Niger Delta ports. Soon afterward, Calabar and Bonny exported the large majority of oil reserves. The increase in oil exports directly correlates with the increased demand for slaves and pawns, given the need for labor.[37] Paul Lovejoy and David Richardson argue that the city-state of Bonny came to dominate the trade in slaves in the early decades of the eighteenth century precisely because of its ability to access credit, which was reinforced by the secret association Ekpe.[38]

During the 1830s, Laird and R. A. K. Oldfield noted that Brass traders bought palm oil for four to five pounds a ton and transported it from the interior of Igboland to Brass Town for Bonny house traders. They traded the oil for "muskets, powder, red beads, white baft [also known as "bafta," a woven textile], bandanas, romals, coarse stuff hats, pipes, tobacco in leaf and looking glasses." Unlike Calabar, Bonny and the other city-states had almost no arable land and relied almost entirely on trade for foodstuffs.[39]

Bonny operated as the political and economic epicenter of the Bight of Biafra during most of the nineteenth century, and its history offers unique insight into how the house system opened up avenues for slaves to attain great wealth.[40] One example is Jaja, an Igbo slave, who became a powerful trader in the house system. Jaja was born in 1821 in Amaigbo, located in current-day Imo state, and sold to a house head at Bonny when he was approximately twelve years old. The house head deemed Jaja stubborn and insubordinate and gave him away to a prominent trader in the Anna Pepple House in Bonny, where he excelled as a slave, and by 1861 Jaja ranked as one of the house's most productive traders. When the house ruler denied him from taking political office, Jaja left and founded Opobo, his own trading state, with the intention of competing with Bonny, and he eventually became known as the king of Opobo.[41] Jaja is an exceptional example of an enslaved child who eventually forged his own success as a trader in a trading house.

The last century of the slave trade and the expansion of trade in palm oil, gum, and kola nuts, among other items, during the first half of the nineteenth century prompted the growth of internal slave labor and eventually led to the Delta's oil wars in the 1870s and 1880s.[42] In the following decade, prominent Efik traders controlled much of the trade activity along the Cross River.[43] British explorer and colonial administrator Harry H. Johnston wrote that as he traveled the Cross River in 1888, the fight over control of the trade spurred even the young children of Old Calabar to arm themselves with machetes and knives as they stood guard in the river awaiting anyone who dared travel without permission. Historians have outlined the economic importance of the house trading operations, but current scholarship does not provide an in-depth analysis of how British intervention allowed for the prolonged use of domestic slaves through the implementation of the House Rule Ordinance and subsequent moneylending regulations.[44]

THE NATIVE HOUSE RULE ORDINANCE OF 1901

The British abolished "slavery" as a legal category in 1901 in Nigeria.[45] However, there was one exception: dependent populations residing in canoe houses. By the early twentieth century, the canoe house trading firms continued to accommodate freeborn persons, slaves, pawns, apprentices, and the elderly indigent. The approval of the Native House Rule Ordinance of 1901 serves as one of the most severe examples of Britain's refusal to fully combat slavery. The ordinance reinforced the power of the men who controlled the largest collections of slaves in the colony: the headmasters of the canoe houses. The ordinance became the target of British antislavery activists who had pressured colonial governments to end slavery since the mid-nineteenth century. By 1909 the Anti-Slavery Society and Aborigines' Protection Society joined forces as the London Auxiliary of the Anti-Slavery and Aborigines' Protection Society (AS & APS). Within one year, the London AS & APS invited similarly minded supporters in Lagos to create a subcommittee in Nigeria. This organization committed itself to addressing the mounting grievances aired by Africans throughout Britain's colonial empire and sought out support for their antislavery stance, with an emphasis on challenging the Native House Rule Ordinance of 1901.[46]

The law prohibited the newly freed slaves from leaving the houses, ensuring the maintenance of trade revenue. Members of the AS & APS had to contend with long-standing policies relating to the use of forced labor in Nigeria. Severe punishments for slaves who fled discouraged others from doing so.[47] The Native House Rule Ordinance reads as follows:

"House" means a group of persons subject to Native law and custom by the control, authority, and rule of the Chief, known as Head of the House. Every member of the House shall from and after the commencement of the Ordinance be subject to Native law and custom. Every member of the House who refuses or neglects to submit himself to the control, authority, and rule of the Head of his House in accordance with Native law and custom shall be liable on conviction to a fine not exceeding fifty pounds, or imprisonment with or without hard labour for any term not exceeding one year, or both. Where a member of the House is charged upon the oath of the Head of a House or the representative with an offence under the last preceding section, the Commissioner before whom the charge is made may issue a warrant directing the person wanted therein to arrest and bring before him such member of the House to be dealt with for the offence with which he is charged. Any person wandering abroad and having no means of subsistence may be arrested By any Officer of any Court within the district in which such person is found without a warrant and brought before the Commissioner of such district and questioned about his means of subsistence and in which House he belongs. Any person who resists or obstructs the lawful apprehension of himself or any offender under the Ordinance, or escape from any custody in which he is lawfully detained shall be liable to a fine not exceeding fifty pounds and imprisonment with or without hard labour.[48]

The British drafted the ordinance provisions to defer to native law and custom because it ensured the existence of a long-standing labor population. The government dissuaded anyone who would have otherwise fled by penalizing escapees. The ordinance did not mention persons who pawned themselves or their dependents to the houses, even though it was known that "relations, pawns and slaves" lived in the houses. Antislavery proponents recognized this omission and worked to secure the rights of pawns in addition to the slaves who remained in the houses. The Native House Rule Ordinance of 1901 served the trading interests of the house heads and the British trading firms by allowing them to maintain a cheap source of labor until the beginning of the First World War.

Established in 1910, the local affiliate of AS & APS in Lagos made the repeal of the Native House Rule Ordinance of 1901 its first point of business. One AS & APS member explained: "The Society is not intended to oppose the Government but to help it and to prevent British rule from being justly regarded by subject Native Races as oppressive and British honor and prestige being trailed in the mud by heartless and conscienceless Moneygrabbers. Connections with the cosmopolitan Society would broaden our sympathies and widen our interest in our fellow humanity in Africa and elsewhere."[49] John H. Harris, secretary for the Lagos AS & APS, referred to the house heads as "moneygrabbers" because the head controlled and benefited from pawn and slave labor. It is obvious that AS & APS members believed it was their duty to act as the colonial government's moral guide. The members' efforts generated enough support to change the language of the ordinance. In 1912, the amended ordinance gave slaves the right to buy their freedom. Support grew to ban slavery in the houses altogether, and the ordinance was repealed in 1915.[50] However, during the almost fifteen years that it was in effect, the ordinance generated an ongoing debate regarding the use of servile labor in house systems that illuminated internal British tensions. As the Lagos AS & APS called attention to the lesser known and perhaps least understood form of labor procurement, that is, pawning, colonial officials from other regions weighed in on the issue.[51]

Anti-Slavery and Aborigines' Protection Society members and other reformers began to focus on the children who resided in the houses. One such reformer was Richard Edward Dennett (1857–1921).[52] In 1902, the Colonial Office hired Dennett as a forest service officer, allowing him to travel throughout Nigeria, and during his tenure there, he wrote about the local customs of the Igbo, Ibibio, Yoruba, and Hausa. He focused on the ways by which a person might lose independence to a house head. In September 1911, he penned an article entitled "Development of Native Governments in Southern Nigeria" in which he highlighted the distinct difference between the European understanding of slavery via slave trafficking and the native custom of pawning, arguing that pawnship was a condition that few in Britain fully understood.[53]

Dennett believed that Nigerian elders mainly pawned the young as security for debts and that children formed most of the pawn population. He criticized his fellow British officers for completely overlooking the various prevailing institutions that fostered child labor akin to slavery.[54] To draw attention to this complex issue, Dennett continued to publish opinion pieces in the *Nigerian Times* as a way to highlight the legal and moral conflict that existed between the abolition of the slave trade, the denunciation of domestic slavery, and the codification of the Native House Rule Ordinance of 1901. He openly criticized the government's implementation of the ordinance on the grounds that it allowed and encouraged house heads to rule as coercive despots, holding people, who should have been legally free, as slaves. Having a deep understanding of the way that pawnship operated in the Congo, Dennett wrote about "children

in pawn" as distinct from child slaves, explaining the intricate relationship between the debtor, lender, and pawn as well as the process
of redemption.[55] However, obtaining freedom under the ordinance
remained illegal. Slaves' inability to leave the houses or even to buy
their own freedom continued to be a long-term concern. Despite
Dennett's widely publicized objection to the house systems, colonial
authorities defended the ordinance, arguing that the supply of cheap
labor had to be preserved.[56]

The growth of the palm product trade further expanded Nigeria's
economy in the last half of the nineteenth century. Likewise, the
widespread and increased use of the steamship brought with it
both advantages and disadvantages for local oil traders. Steamships
increased the capacity for long-standing traders of the houses to
multiply along the Delta states while limiting the influx of smaller-
scale traders with fewer resources. When new traders participated
in the palm oil business, they ran low-cost operations and earned
small profit margins, allowing for some success in the oil trade during
the second half of the nineteenth century. Martin Lynn asserts that
these newcomers increased competition at a time when the market
began to contract, which allowed for the continued incorporation
of child labor as both slaves and pawns.[57]

A few years after the publication of Dennett's articles, acting governor F. S. James reflected on the continued exploitative employment
of children. According to James, "It is rather curious to see that the
joint opinion of the D.Cs [district commissioners] tend[s] to show
that slave-dealing that is now in existence is mostly in connection
with children (principally girls). The main object for the continued
demand for slaves by the Bonny, Opobo, Degama [*sic*], I may say
all the big coastal towns inhabited by middlemen, is to obtain the
necessary labour for their trading canoes—the people required are
boys not girls."[58] The focus on female slave dealing was usually
concerned with what colonial officials believed to be child marriage,

whereas attention to boys in the house system usually referred to the slave population. When boys and girls entered the houses as pawns or slaves, boys often worked as porters, apprentices, and canoe paddlers—one of the most demanding types of labor—while girls farmed, performed domestic work, and traded. When parents sought to redeem their pawned children from a house, their efforts usually proved unsuccessful. For example, a divisional court in Aba sought to prosecute Chief Ben Stowe of Bonny for holding a girl against her and her parents' will for three years. The district commissioner transferred the case to Opobo, the chief's hometown, resulting in an acquittal. The court did, however, sentence "his unfortunate accomplice to eighteen months in jail."[59]

The social and legal statuses of persons living in the houses remained a point of contention for colonial authorities. Referring to house members, District Commissioner F. E. G. Johnson observed that "the rights of members never have been, and now possibly never will be, satisfactorily defined."[60] Consequently, colonial authorities hesitated to prosecute house heads when they had large numbers of children in their possession because of the number of excuses given for having them. To make it even more difficult for child pawns to get released, house heads claimed that when they received young dependents, they "cared for, supported, trained and assisted" them "in many ways," and that by freeing all house dependents, they would be left alone in their old age with no means of support. Referring to the common ideology that defines family and kinship responsibilities, a house head believed that any dependent he supported while the dependent was young owed him continued service in his old age.[61] Indebted to the house heads, who provided labor and revenue resources, the British remained hesitant to address the antislavery lobbyists' concerns.

In April 1914, Head Chief Dore Numa, native political agent of Warri, described the different types of members that resided in the house systems throughout Southern Nigeria in his letter to the governor's office. In the case of pawns, Numa noted that people lent out their relatives for money "in the same way as the whiteman [*sic*] places articles of value in security for money borrowed." Numa further explained that all of the pawn's labor or profit acquired from that labor paid the interest on the initial loan. Once redeemed, the house head forced the pawn to leave with a shaved head and naked except for a loincloth, for which relatives paid six shillings, after which the pawn could (re)claim freeborn status. According to Numa, pawns generally preferred to follow the custom of repayment rather than be freed outright. Any other path to freedom would stigmatize them, which would prevent them from returning to their home village. Other chiefs claimed that freeing all dependents from the house systems would increase crime rates.[62] Preoccupied with social control in the new colony, the specter of hundreds of freed former slaves concerned Lugard and other British authorities.

In addition to Chief Numa, another chief who was also a house slave argued in favor of the Native House Rule Ordinance.[63] In 1914, he responded to rumors that the ordinance might be repealed and referred to the biblical story of Joseph as proof that God ordained slavery. When Joseph was a slave, wrote this chief, he was able to enhance his personal wealth and became a rich man. According to this perspective, house slaves need not be freed because they, too, could become rich without manumission. He also suggested that slaves had no land to which they could return, which was necessary to farm and subsist, and that freedom might actually be a detriment to a slave's ability to survive. He claimed that many of the house slaves had large holdings of silver, gold, livestock, and even other slaves. Using himself as an example, the chief argued that because he was both a slave and a wealthy man he would be forced to give his slaves to his master upon emancipation.[64]

Trying to convince his counterparts, the chief continued, "Oh, slaves in Nigeria are alright[.] [T]hey should remain as the[y] are, live [*sic*] us to remain as we are."[65] Self-interest is clear in this example. The house assigned slave rankings, and heads allowed certain slaves who had become successful traders to hold a percentage of their trade profits. This slave had accrued some wealth while trading on behalf of his master, which appears to be a modification of the system by incorporating incentives to retain the support of willing slaves. In any case, the master ultimately owned all that the slave acquired because the master owned him. It is possible that his master treated him well and did not relegate him to the colonial labor teams sent to build railways when the British demanded that chiefs provide a certain quota of laborers.[66] It is more likely that this particular house slave did not want to lose all of his worldly possessions upon leaving. Another scenario is that since he had grown up in the house system from age six, he had no familial village to which he could return.[67]

Points of contention on dependency status in the house system highlighted the concerns of both slaveholders and slaves, but it was not an issue that pitted the British against Nigerians. For example, Christopher Komulu Johnson, a Westernized African and the editor of the *Nigerian Chronicle*, published a response to Numa's letter:

We do not in any way agree with his views or arguments. We do not believe that a custom, however good it may be to the native when he was isolated and not exposed to the crashing wheels of modern civilization, when land-hunger and the spirit of exploitation had not driven foreigners into our shores, ought to be allowed to continue when they are being taken advantage of and used by aliens against the true interest of the nation. We in conjunction with other local contemporaries and notably the Anti-Slavery and Aborigines Protection Society of London and its Organising Secretaries the Rev. J. H. and Mrs. Harris have for years called public attention to the objectionable and inhuman change that has come upon the House Rules System since it has been backed up by Southern Nigeria Ordinance.[68]

Johnson's response clearly represented a competing opinion about the house systems in 1914, highlighting the views held by AS & APS, the Colonial Office, sympathizers like Dennett, native leaders, and other dependent populations.

Preventing house heads from slave dealing proved difficult in the years from 1901 to 1914. According to the ordinance, if house heads acquired a slave before 1901, he could legally retain the slave. This loophole enabled some house heads to obtain slaves after 1901 and claim that they had received the slave before that date. Some British authorities believed that, according to the ordinance, all slaves were made house "members," reversing their own and their children's former enslaved status. If a child's parents did not reside in the house, heads commonly claimed that a sick child was given to them to be healed. Heads also maintained that parents often died while the child remained in house, and he therefore had a responsibility to care for the parentless child. Upon questioning, house heads often agreed to free a child but claimed that they first needed to recoup the expenses paid for rearing the child.[69] Since neither the colonial state nor extended family were willing to pay the childrearing expenses, children often remained in the house's captivity. Undoubtedly, house heads made it nearly impossible for children to gain their freedom. Likewise, Richard Roberts's analysis of laissez-passer, meaning "official permission to move from one district to another" in the wake of emancipation, illustrates the assertive efforts made by slave owners to maintain slaves when the French colonial regime deemed slavery illegal in 1905.[70]

The actions taken to stall the release of slaves in Nigeria are not unlike practices in colonial French Sudan, where slave masters litigated slave debts in courts. Additionally, in 1912, District Commissioner Reginald Hargrove commented that prosecuting slave dealers remained difficult because in order to prosecute house heads and others for slave dealing, someone had to testify against the accused. Children, he claimed, were too young to testify effectively. Hargrove believed that any witness who came forward was probably complicit in obtaining the slave, leaving successful convictions out of reach.[71]

By August 1914, the work of the British AS & APS had declined due to the onset of World War I. Temporarily decreasing their efforts, they believed that the war would be short-lived and that they would soon return to their human rights efforts in Africa.[72] This was not the reality, however. The years following 1914 saw an increased use of forced labor on the African continent, and it was not until the 1920s that Western humanitarians again refocused significant attention on child trafficking and other forms of child dealing in the colonial provinces of Nigeria.

CONCLUSION

The Bight of Biafra's social relations, political institutions, and trade practices transformed as the transatlantic slave began to wane and Britain increased its efforts to colonize the region. With the onset of British colonialism came the upending of indigenous forms of government and social relations, where young men with access to new forms of wealth rose to power at the expense of the ruling society of elders. The twentieth century was a period of radical change and violent slaving incursions that caused fear and insecurity throughout Igboland as mercenaries and kidnappers traveled freely around the Biafran hinterland. Unable to defend themselves for fear of Aro retribution, many parents lost children to commercial kidnappers, and those in need of loans suffered when moneylenders violated the principles of child pawning and moneylending. New forms of social stratification throughout the region developed as new elites emerged and challenged existing governing traditions and mores.[73]

Children occupied a variety of subordinate social positions during this era. Historical accounts show how slave traders accepted child pawns as credit when they advanced guns, alcohol, and other goods to local "big" men and how middlemen traders supplied slaves to villages and canoe houses in need of labor.[74] Pawnship became increasingly visible between the 1820s and 1840s when the trade in palm products gradually replaced the transatlantic slave trade. The growth of commercial transactions in Nigeria during the late nineteenth and early twentieth centuries incentivized the sale of children into slavery to work on palm plantations and the exchange of child pawns or pledges as collateral for funds. Canoe houses held junior and senior slaves, where both children and adults worked as traders and in other capacities.[75]

In the years that followed, Nigeria's economy experienced a shock when the colonial government began to demonetize "native" currencies (i.e., cowries, manillas) and replace them with British silver. In so doing, London unintentionally created a dual currency in which money changers dictated exchange rates. This negatively affected family economies.[76] Poor men continued to borrow from native credit-lending bodies made up of kinsmen. Generally, individuals who had made payments to the lending societies would then have the opportunity to borrow when in need, but many lacked this resource. The crisis forced families into debt, as they pledged either land or dependents, including their children, to obtain a loan.[77]

CHAPTER 2
Colonial Policies and Coercive Labor: Trade, Slaves, and Debts

I send you Nwobani and Ekelebisi in this Division [Okigwi] to whom ex-Court member Ovuebe of Obowo is said to have pledged two children, Ahuibo and Nwaenyinya to pay a judgement debt.

—District officer, Okigwi, February 28, 1929

During the 1910s and 1920s, the warrant chiefs who served as native court judges frequently engaged in and endorsed slave dealing, often presiding over the courts and constituencies with absolute and coercive power. In 1922, the district officer of Ahoada described the warrant holders as "irresponsible boys" and "ex-criminals, ex-slaves or rogues."[1] The warrant chiefs and court clerks issued exorbitant court fines and demanded bribes, which left Nigerians with limited options by which to acquire funds to pay debts. As noted in the statement above, the defendant paid a court fine so excessive it required pawning his two children.[2] British officials remained hesitant to check the power of warrant chiefs, court clerks, and other slave-owning rulers because they did not want to decrease the labor supply needed for colonial infrastructure projects and agricultural efforts. Forced and bonded child labor also remained a thorny issue throughout the colonial period: legislation concerning pawns and forced labor, the restructuring of the native court system, the introduction of British currencies, and British perceptions about pawning ran counter to most attempts to end child dealing.

This chapter addresses these post-1914 Lugardian reforms by analyzing the removal of British oversight that had provided checks and balances in the native court system, the policies that left residents vulnerable to court clerk and warrant chief abuses, and the oppressive moneylending agreements that led to child pawning. Through the use of court documentation of debt cases, treasury records, and child-dealing accounts, this chapter illustrates the particularly difficult economic realities that families, especially women and children, endured at the hands of the warrant chiefs and other court representatives. Exploring these issues is necessary in order to understand why League of Nations committee members demanded an investigation into child dealing during the 1920s (chapter 3) and the eruption of the 1929 Women's War (chapter 4).

In the first decades of the twentieth century, imperial powers struggled to define and regulate coercive forms of labor. The British touted antislavery ideals and principles of civilization, but unable to retain the labor force needed to produce crucial colonial exports, they straddled the fence between publicly espousing emancipation for all in the colony while privately suggesting that some forms of coerced labor were not only acceptable but also harmless. The 1920s presented an immediate challenge to district officers and residents in the provinces as they wanted to appear to respond to humanitarian concerns while soft-pedaling any legislation that might truly enforce the use of free labor. In part, colonial authorities may not have been able to distinguish pawned persons from slaves because they often performed similar duties. A child could imperceptibly pass from one to the other, unbeknownst to the British. Even so, there was a real and meaningful distinction between the two statuses. Masters owned slaves, whereas creditors controlled the pawn's labor, owning only the pawning contract. Pawns enjoyed limited rights and privileges, mainly the right of redemption, and they could seek legal intervention if they were mistreated or if a dispute arose about the loan. Slaves did not have the same recourse.[3]

The mobilization of unfree labor and moneylending arrangements became points of contention between antislavery lobbyists and colonial authorities at a time when the colonial office sought labor and revenue from the local populations. The legal status of slavery was abolished in the Niger Coast Protectorate in 1901; however, as observed in chapter 1, colonial officials allowed certain native rulers to legally keep children as slaves, domestic servants, apprentices, or pawns.[4] As these internal inconsistencies prevailed, some British subjects in the colony and Europeans outside it began to share increasing apprehension about the use of child labor in Nigeria. The prevailing contradiction in colonial policies between the desperate need for labor and Britain's claim to oppose all forms of slavery exacerbated the vulnerability of children.

In Southern Nigeria, indirect rule consisted of four main elements: the installation of warrant chiefs; the creation of native courts; the transition from manillas to the British silver and paper notes; and the eventual implementation of direct taxation in 1926, all of which directly influenced the transfer of children. Colonial officials granted warrants (official papers) to local men whom they designated as chiefs, which empowered them to rule over indigenous matters in court. The Igbo, Ibibio, Ijo, and Efike, however, did not live in politically centralized areas and, in most instances, did not have chiefs.[5] Rather, the political process was diffuse and complex. Councils of men and sometimes women led by village elders and secret societies played a role in maintaining democratic oversight in their respective communities. Assuming that these communities had chiefs, the British initially sought out "traditional" rulers but often chose men who either lacked any form of seniority or status, were former slaves, or were members of the Aro community.[6] Analyzing the development of the colonial court system exposes how the appointment of illegitimate rulers created the circumstances within which Nigerians accrued debilitating debt and lost their wives and children through pawning.

THE COLONIAL COURT SYSTEM

The transformation of Nigerian forms of governance influenced the vulnerability of men and their dependents because the new court system oversaw matters pertaining to family and business affairs. The credit disputes that initially captured British attention shifted from Afro-European agreements to those coordinated between Nigerians and resulted in the development of policies that monitored money-lending.[7] Initially, British administrators in Lagos created the Petty Debt Court in 1863 where the court mediated loan disputes up to £50, but by 1864 the amount was decreased to £20.[8] By 1900, Britain released the 1900 Native Court Proclamation, which determined the structure of two types of native courts—the native councils and the minor courts—"endowed with specific executive and legislative powers" to preside over disputes in Southeastern Nigeria. District commissioners maintained oversight of the native councils that operated in each district headquarters and ensured that all members who received formal dispensation from the high commissioner adhered to native court rules.[9] The native councils ruled on cases involving damages of up to £200. A Nigerian "native authority or a local chief" presided over minor courts located throughout the districts, which operated at a lower level than the native councils and dealt with disputes, including debt cases of up to £25 and inheritances cases of up to £50.[10]

When the British sought to strengthen colonial courts through new legislation, the 1901 Native Court Proclamation made illegal the operation of the council of elders and secret societies to openly intervene in disputes. Seniority, gender, social status, and personal skills generally determined who would be allowed into the council of elders and secret societies. The council of elders consisted of the most senior age-grade in a community.[11] Charged with religious and financial responsibilities, these groups were an integral part of the local governing systems. Male secret societies, such as the *eze, obi,* and Ekpe (Egbo) became quite powerful because they were comprised of men who had become wealthy by trading in a wide variety of goods, including slaves.[12] In particular, the Ekpe among the Efik in the Cross River region monitored pawning cases and assumed responsibility for enforcing repayment of debts.[13] The British knew these societies existed, but their inner workings remained secret. The new regulation forced these associations, including savings clubs, to act in ways that avoided British detection. Unable to operate openly, they eventually lost power to the new colonial court system. One unintended consequence included the rise of disreputable moneylenders, many of whom the High Commissioner appointed as court clerks and chiefs.

During Lord Frederick Lugard's rule as governor-general (1914–19), the Colonial Office decreased British supervision of the native courts, which set in motion rivalries among court members. Lugard had long felt that the warrant chiefs and clerks in the local courts required more power rather than less, but his actions caused chaos in the native courts and increased opportunities for corruption, while preventing any single official from rising to an inordinately high position. In addition, global economic factors in the aftermath of the First World War (1914–18) also weakened the colonial court system. Germany had been one of Nigeria's largest purchasers of palm products, and the war resulted in the loss of the German palm oil market.[14] One consequence was that as Nigeria's economy began to weaken, London could no longer afford to employ British district officers to serve in each of the native courts, which decreased colonial oversight.[15] A newly introduced court ordinance aimed to address these issues.

The 1914 Provincial Court Ordinance formalized boundaries of the Eastern Provinces, comprised of Calabar, Ogoja, Onitsha, and Owerri, and restructured the colonial court system. Each province was split into divisions, which in turn were broken into subdivisions. As for the colonial court system, Lugard abolished the multiple local native courts, which previously retained up to six members and a district officer each. He allowed one native court for each district and appointed one warrant chief to be in charge of the court. The new native courts, subject to "traditional" law, primarily ruled on cases dealing with personal offenses and petty crimes.[16] When Lugard removed the district officers from the courts, he introduced paramount chiefs (the highest ruler) to serve as presidents of the native courts. Paramount chiefs, warrant chiefs, and court clerks operated without British intervention.[17] Lugard also established higher-level courts—the provincial and supreme courts—above the native courts.

Creating a new court structure resulted in an uneven application of judicial rule. Commissioners oversaw the provincial courts, which generally heard cases regarding violations of British law and land disputes.[18] The provincial court now served as a buffer between the native courts and the supreme court. Only large towns, such as Calabar, Port Harcourt, Degema (southwest of Port Harcourt), and Bonny housed supreme courts. This separation limited Nigerians' ability to appeal to a higher authority, leaving many who lacked the funds to travel great distances at the mercy of local warrant chiefs, clerks, and other court members. As a way to increase their personal wealth, clerks and chiefs often encouraged the losing parties to appeal, which required an additional payment. In such cases, clerks and warrant chiefs would offer loans to plaintiffs as exorbitant rates.[19]

The development of the post-1914 court system created divisions based on greed and envy between court clerks and warrant chiefs. The British granted warrant chiefs the power to rule over legal cases and charged clerks with transcribing summonses, managing the court messengers who delivered them, accepting court fees, and documenting fines. The colonial administration appointed court clerks who could read and write English, and literacy, in many ways, trumped the authority of the presiding warrant chief. A. E. Afigbo argues that warrant chiefs, who were often illiterate, had to defer to literate clerks.[20] In fact, most litigants feared the clerks more than the chiefs because of the clerks' power to document the outcome of a case and their propensity to extort money from litigants. Even though cases heard under native courts should have been determined according to customary law, often warrant chiefs and litigants were subject to the clerks' explanation of a ruling according to the "white man's," that is, British, law. The warrant chief should have been the senior court member, but his inability to read and write caused a power shift wherein many court clerks often acted with more authority than did the warrant chiefs. *Brits controlled most of court*

In addition to the clerks' propensity to subvert customary law, warrant chiefs and clerks accepted bribes, such as chickens, goats, money, women, and children, in exchange for the desired outcome. However, clerks received the lion's share of those bribes. Warrant Chief Obiukwu explained, "Ma ukpara erigh ibe ya o nagh ebu," meaning "to grow fat, an insect must feed on other insects."[21] Chief Obiukwu shamelessly admitted that to enhance his personal wealth he had to prey on his constituents. In sum, the reorganization of the native court system, with decreased British oversight, allowed the warrant chiefs, clerks, and court members to abuse and extort their constituents, intensifying the vulnerability of men, women, and children. Claiming customary rights to demand labor from local residents, warrant chiefs exacted personal services as well; they had the power to select men to serve at the pleasure of colonial officers. Elder Chief Ugwu Nwangwu Ugwu recounted that men were forced to be "carriers of goods, porters, some of them die[d] on the way carrying goods and properties of the white people."[22]

Court member abuses resulted in other wide-ranging consequences. In 1920 the Owerri district officer complained: "Although theoretically the power of the chiefs is derived from Native Custom, the chiefs themselves have done nothing to maintain the native organization[s] (if any), and in many cases, in order to maintain their various corrupt and illegal methods in an attempt [to] secure [their] position—that is in wealth—for themselves, they have deliberately disregarded the recognized elders of the town and the clubs."[23] Entire towns exhibited dissatisfaction with the warrant chiefs, many expressing that the chiefs lacked legitimate authority. In 1921, the senior resident of Owerri wrote: "What has struck me most during my short time in the Province, since I was last in it, is the lack of respect the youths had for the Chiefs."[24] The young and old often refused to respect the status of the warrant chiefs, but they had no choice but to abide by their rules for fear of retribution. One Aba resident explained that "these [court] representatives were kinsmen but were very shrewd, heartless and inconsiderate in discharging their duties." Even when local residents decided to have warrant chiefs hear their cases, it was not unusual for the hearing to end in a physical fight between litigants.[25]

Acknowledging the inherent problems in the native courts, G. N. Heathcote, the assistant district officer of Bende, complained that cases would be solved more efficiently if "some whiteman" could supervise them. Heathcote acknowledged that the previous system in which district officers oversaw each of the native courts provided protections that had been lost under the post-1914 court system.[26] The district officers' previous oversight had prevented warrant chiefs and clerks from demanding women and girls in exchange for loans that would be used to pay court fines and fees.

Colonial officials recognized that some court members abused their power to increase personal wealth. To decrease corruption, in 1914 Lugard raised the clerks' salaries. For example, in 1928 a Calabar clerk earned £240, while the warrant chief received £132 annually. Instead of eradicating fraud, the pay increases provoked warrant

Bribes run rampant

chiefs to seek new ways to further increase their own wealth. In so doing, the warrant chiefs exploited litigants by demanding even higher bribes and extra payments. The new ordinance inadvertently increased the number of debt litigants and forced impoverished persons to mortgage their women and children to settle court fines and other debts. Some court members even married the women or girls, while others sold them to willing buyers.[27] The colonial archive offers glimpses of these transactions in slave-dealing records from which certain assumptions can be drawn. For example, in 1929, native court member Eze Onyodo of Ichida of the Awka District sold a woman, Akwu Alazie, and her daughter to two men in Degema.[28] It is reasonable to presume that Onyodo received the woman and child in lieu of a court fee or fine knowing he could find a buyer for them in the well-known slave trading region of Degema, located south of Port Harcourt and east of Brass. From the 1910s to the 1920s, British attention to debt cases and moneylending practices spurred new legislation related to moneylending.

MONEYLENDING LEGISLATION

Pawnbrokers' practices came into question as a result of ongoing moneylending disputes brought before the native courts. British administrators took notice that pawning agreements lacked formal documentation or bookkeeping records as debt cases moved from local native courts to the district courts.[29] The attorney general introduced the Pawnbrokers Bill to the Legislative Council for the purpose of regulating the agreements in Southern Nigeria.[30] Consequently, on June 2, 1912, the British enacted the Pawnbrokers Bill, which mirrored the United Kingdom's Pawnbrokers Act of 1877 (originally 1872). The legislation regulated loans between 40 shillings and £20 when borrowers exchanged a pawn or pledge. The bill carefully defined a "pawnbroker" as any person whose business practice took goods or animals in pawn. It also described a "pledge" as an item pawned to the pawnbroker, and a "pawner" as the individual who provided "an article for pawn to a pawnbroker." The inclusion of the word "shop" in the bill suggests that the colonial administrators recognized pawnbrokers' businesses as legitimate only when they operated out of a permanent structure.[31] These assumptions, though in many ways accurately representing the workings of pawnbrokers' operations, did not formally recognize the various ways they conducted business. As a result, the Colonial Office rendered child pawning invisible in the Pawnbrokers Bill.

The new directive required that moneylenders display signs in their place of business, issue pawn tickets with which borrowers could redeem the pledged item(s) or chattel, and make the pledged item(s) available for one year and seven days after they were pawned. As the most significant change concerning the accruable interest on the loan, the bill limited the potential interest or profit that could be charged.[32] For the purpose of oversight, the bill also required the moneylender to purchase an annual license and pay an excise duty in order to conduct business, affording a local officer the right to investigate the moneylender's business affairs and subpoena the broker's records when a dispute arose regarding the terms of a loan.[33]

The government argued that introducing the new bill guaranteed the end of "oppressive and excessive rates of interest" levied upon borrowers.[34] The rules and consequences set forth could be applied only to those individuals who openly acknowledged their work as moneylenders. When concerns regarding persons who casually lent money to a friend (with or without a pledge) arose, officials assured the public that the rules related to only those individuals who were professional pawnbrokers who lent no more than £20. All other moneylenders were left unregulated.[35]

The Pawnbrokers Bill did not legally bind moneylenders who took no material pledges, nor did it explicitly deal with moneylenders who took child or adult pawns, even though ample evidence exists in the colonial archives that some officials actively denounced the practice of child pawning, thus making its omission significant.[36] The loan amount for human pawns usually fell within the regulated range of 40 shillings to £20. Therefore it seems reasonable that some reference to human pawning would appear in the 1912 bill if for no other reason than to discourage the practice.[37]

The absence of regulations that dealt with human pawns led to oppressive moneylending practices, resulting in inequitable moneylending agreements. By 1913, increased efforts to mitigate the interest that could be exacted from a debtor were evident in the amended Pawnbrokers Ordinance: "The Pawnbrokers Ordinance by an Order of the Executive dated 9th January has been made to apply to the Sanitary Districts of Lagos and Calabar. License for a period not exceeding twelve months has been fixed at £12. The profit allowed is one half penny for every two shillings or part of Two Shillings on a pledge for every calendar month or part of a calendar month if the loan exceeds Two Pounds. One farthing shall be paid for every two Shillings on a pledge for a fraction of a calendar month not exceeding fourteen days provided the loan is less than Two Pounds."[38] In an attempt to extend standards for pawning, the government regulated the amount of time a pledge remained with the creditor and dictated the precise amount of interest charged. It is likely, however, that when a debtor offered a child in pawn, he or she could not enforce the rules listed in the Pawnbroker's Ordinance, leaving the person subject to the moneylender's demand for heavy interest payments that exceeded the ordinance limits. The ineffectiveness of the native courts and the inadequacy of the Pawnbrokers Bill left the prevalence of child dealing unabated, allowing for the continuation of child pawning and for numerous children to be sold into slavery.

In 1911, H. Bedwell, the commissioner of the Eastern Province, complained that prosecuting slave dealers remained difficult. In a report that Bedwell assembled, colonial representative Mr. Cyril

Punch provided an overview of slave dealing in Calabar from 1907 to 1911 that outlined how challenging it was to prosecute slave dealers who dealt in children. Referring to the House Rule Ordinance of 1901, which protected slaveholders from prosecution if they acquired a slave before 1901, Bedwell wrote, "The difficulty in bringing home charges of slave-dealing becomes entitled to the benefit of every doubt urged by his Council of every Native Custom brought in defence under the House Rule Ordinance." Almost every case dealt with children. If the accused claimed that he had acquired the child before 1901, he cited the House Rule Ordinance, thus making it nearly impossible to prosecute slave dealers in 1911–12. Justice Weber of Degema noted that in many instances the district commissioner chose not to prosecute slave-dealing cases because it "waste[d] too much of time and [was] trouble." District commissioners began to choose a course of least resistance in prosecuting child-dealing cases. Therefore a person in possession of a child younger than fifteen years old would not be prosecuted if he could prove he had the permission of the parent to care for the child.[39] Sometimes the accused claimed that he acquired a girl child by paying a bride-price payment to her parents.[40] A comprehensive list of methods used to authenticate acceptable guardianship is unclear, but the pattern of limiting the resources invested in prosecuting slave dealers is evident.

The number of slave-dealing cases in all of the Southern Provinces decreased from 110 in 1913 to 75 in 1914. However, by 1915 the number had risen to 136.[41] It is likely that some of children initially taken as pawns were later sold as slaves. This is likely due to the hardship caused by disruption of the palm trade during the war, after which it remained difficult to locate kidnapped children whom child dealers had sold into slavery. The *Owerri Province Annual Report* documented that only eleven children had been liberated from 1908 to 1921 (see table 1).

TABLE 1. **Register of freed slaves in Owerri**

NAME	AGE UPON CAPTURE	SEX	ORIGIN	DATE OF LIBERATION
Lottie	17	F	Aba	March 17, 1908
Ehi Ibe	8	M	Aba	May 16, 1916
Akune	11	F	Ibibio	November 10, 1917
Iwe	12	F	Okigwi	September 18, 1917
Unufuru	10	F	Owerri	September 18, 1917
Daughter of Uche	10	F	Arochukwu	July 5, 1917
Oyibajialu	8	F	Ahoada	June 21, 1918
Obi	15	M	Bende	1919
Mbokwo	4	F	Aba	April 21, 1921
Ukaji	8	M	Okigwi	September 8, 1921
Offor	12	M	Bende	August 18, 1921
Nwane	5	F	Okigwi	September 5, 1921

Source: Register of Freed Slaves, in *Owerri Province Annual Report for 1921*.

This account of freed slaves illustrates the lackluster efforts by warrant chiefs and colonial officials to investigate and intervene in child-dealing practices.[42]

Colonial authorities declared slave dealing illegal in the Southern Provinces, but it technically remained legal until 1916 as a result of the Slavery Ordinance, a product of ongoing discussions about the nature of slavery and pawning in the canoe houses.[43] In 1915 Lugard explained that self-pawning remained an acceptable practice, but if "a man should liquidate his debt by the labour of another person—whether a child or an adult—is of the nature of Slavery."[44] After much resistance from colonial officers in the Southern Provinces, Lugard publicly argued that he did not care how "inconvenient" it was for people to stop the practice of child pawning and ordered that the Slavery Ordinance be redrafted to declare that all children born in the Southern Province be free.[45] However, "the relationship between rhetoric and action" highlights the protracted nature of discourse and implementation. Gareth Austin explains that colonial officials believed "abolition would disrupt the colonial economies and create, simultaneously, rootless proletariats and angry and enfeebled indigenous political elites." Furthermore, one of Lugard's solutions, as Christine Whyte raises in her work on Sierra Leone, preferred the "policy of 'communal labor'" that "would, simultaneously, provide labor for the colonial government, train the ex-slaves into workers, and re-order African family dynamics."[46] Even with Lugard's condemnation of child pawning and the implementation of new labor policies, the use of children as objects of exchange continued.

The eventual repeal of the House Rule Ordinance in 1915 should have decreased the trade in children, but Southeastern Nigeria's economic downturn made ending child dealing difficult because of the region's use of child labor and the increase in debt cases in which debtors pawned children to obtain loans.[47] Therefore, it is important to analyze debt litigation and the introduction of British sterling (also called "pound sterling" or "silver") and paper notes into the Nigerian market so as to understand how the change in legal tender led to the destabilization of family resources.

BRITISH CURRENCIES AND DEBT CASES

Currency reform also exacerbated domestic conditions in Nigeria and added to the complex economic changes to which Southeastern Nigerians had to adjust during the 1920s. In addition to policies that monitored moneylending and debt disputes, the British introduced sterling and paper notes because they believed the complex Nigerian monetary system to be autonomous and "primitive," leaving key monetary transactions outside the control and "eye" of the colonial state.[48] The manilla, shaped like a horseshoe, dominated the area from Calabar to Owerri and remained in use until 1948, coexisting with copper rods, brass, cowries, and, from 1901 onward, the pound sterling. The introduction of nonnative currencies presented yet another economic challenge to many families in Igboland.

TABLE 2. 1899–1911 British silver coin sent to Nigeria by the Royal Mint

YEARS	SOUTHERN NIGERIA	NORTHERN NIGERIA
1899	£ 164,000	£ 61,100
1900	114,650	127,000
1901	10,800	80,000
1902	71,000	143,000
1903	9,000	190,000
1904	41,000	189,000
1905	9,000	111,800
1906	66,000	65,600
1907	329,000	111,400
1908	2,000	109,900
1909	155,000	124,400
1910	578,600	115,050
1911 (11 months)	105,000	10,650
Total	**1,655,050**	**1,438,900**

Source: Colonial Currency, 3:8.

Table 2 above illustrates the influx of British silver coins from 1899 to 1911, with a steep increase in 1910.[49] Southeastern Nigeria's commercial activity influenced the value of the manilla and sterling, and their respective values were linked to the growth and fall of the export palm oil trade. In fact, the value of the manilla increased as more British currency entered the market, which caused the exchange rate for British currency to fall. Thus, fewer manillas fetched more British currency. Appreciation of the manilla occurred because of its growing scarcity, especially after the tender was made illegal after 1911. However, the increase in value only benefited money changers and traders. To conduct daily business at the local markets, Nigerians whose earnings were paid in British sterling had to exchange their wages for manillas. This eventually caused a financial crisis for some families because they lost money with every exchange when local traders demanded manillas, which led to the multiplication of debt cases.[50]

Debt cases increased significantly from 1915 to the early 1920s. The supreme, provincial, and native courts in the Southern Provinces heard 111 debt cases in 1915 that resulted in imprisonment for non-payment of debt. The postwar trade depression and drop in incomes are cited as the most likely causes of civil cases, as well as debt case appeals heard in the provincial court.[51] To exacerbate matters, the 1921 depression resulted in a dramatic fall in palm product export earnings from £10,395,426 in 1920 to £4,487,602 in 1921. The rural population in Southern Nigeria depended heavily on incomes related to the palm product industry, and the downturn intensified impoverishment among some Igbo-speaking communities and led to even more credit defaults.[52] The economic decline was especially visible in the cases litigated in native courts in Owerri Province that dealt with debts and other contracts, which soared to nearly fifteen thousand the same year. In 1922, 482 debt cases went on appeal to the provincial and supreme courts, and in 1923 the cases more than doubled to 1,079.[53]

TABLE 3. 1921 native court cases

	OWERRI	ABA	OKIGWI	BENDE, DEGEMA	AHOADA DISTRICT	BONNY	Total
Native Revenue Ordinance	0	0	0	0	0	0	0
Matrimonial	16	96	15	14	16	5	**162**
Land	84	147	416	36	26	3	**712**
Administration of estates	1	1	4	0	0	2	**8**
Debts and other contracts	2,602	4,113	3,202	2,823	2,032	170	**14,942**
Trespass, assault, and other	219	592	685	114	458	18	**2,086**
Liberation from slavery	0	0	0	0	0	0	**0**
Other cases	5,058	6,277	6,759	5,471	4,429	250	**28,244**
Total civil cases	**7,980**	**11,226**	**11,081**	**8,458**	**6,961**	**448**	**46,154**

Source: Report on Native Court Cases in Owerri Province, in *Owerri Province Annual Report for 1921.*

As shown in table 3 above, debt and other contract cases over-whelmingly outnumbered any other specifically categorized civil cases in 1921.[54] It is evident that the weakening of Nigeria's economy created a crisis that seriously impacted debt and credit defaults. The peak in debt case litigation occurred the same year the colonial administration began actively seeking answers about child pawning. The majority of debtors against whom moneylenders filed lawsuits resided in the southeast towns of Afikpo, Calabar, Degema, Eket, Ikot-Ekpene, Obubra, and Opobo. During the recovery, from 1924 onward, the debt cases before both the native and provincial courts declined.[55] Regardless, for the first half of the decade many Nigerians sought out ways to cope with the prevailing economic conditions.

In addition to the rise in debt cases between 1915 and 1923, four other factors highlighted the southern region's economic distress. First, the majority of individuals in Owerri found guilty of an offense chose to serve time in jail in lieu of paying a fine. The 1921 annual report notes that "under ordinary conditions, persons given the option of a fine instead of imprisonment usually pay the fines, but money being scarce, they have declined to pay fines and have gone to prison instead." Second, the amount plaintiffs sought in damages in 1921 decreased from 1920 onward. Plaintiffs knew that they could not demand what people could not pay. Third, some money changers who had previously held onto silver began releasing coins back into the market because they needed additional income.[56] Finally, numerous Nigerians who traded in legitimate goods were forced out of business owing to the loss of earnings, unveiling the trend that Nigerians increasingly lacked sources of income and access to cash.[57] These factors all worsened as the decade progressed and led to the increase of moneylending and child pawning.

NATIVE COURTS, MONEYLENDING, AND CHILD PAWNING

By the late 1910s and the 1920s it had become evident that the nature of pawning transformed when native court employees extorted fines from litigants and when Nigerian moneylenders began to sell pledged children into slavery immediately after acquiring them as pawns. Examining this change is significant because the accounts that follow reveal that moneylending agreements, court member abuses, and the breakdown of pawning practices resulted from colonial economic demands on Southeastern Nigerians. As argued by Gwyn Campbell and Alessandro Stanziani, pawning was intended to prevent enslavement, not cause it.[58] Debtees expected the moneylender to keep the child in his or her care for an indefinite but moderate period of time. Drawing attention to the transformation of pawning practices underscores how families willingly or unwillingly integrated children into debt settlements in native courts.

Warrant chiefs and native court clerks influenced pawning practices because of the power they wielded over local residents. As government employees, they also functioned as moneylenders and child dealers and coerced bribes from litigants. When unable to pay, litigants either borrowed money or suffered some other injustice. Yet, obtaining convictions against court members proved difficult, as shown in a dispute in Ichida of Awgulu District (Awka Division) in Onitsha Province.[59] In 1919, Warrant Chief Ezeonyodu convicted and sentenced a local resident, named Okanu, to eighteen months of hard labor for stealing a goat. During the course of Okanu's imprisonment, Chief Ezeonyodu deployed his own brother, Obidike, and his personal messenger, Udeke, to capture Okanu's pregnant wife, Akuaghaji (also known as Akuoyibo), and their four daughters. Amid the kidnapping investigation, Jeremiah Iwenofu, Okanu's cousin, testified that Chief Ezeonyodu did indeed take the woman and children, whom he believed the chief had either killed or sold because they could not be located.[60]

Upon release from prison, Okanu fell ill for nine months, and his condition left him bedridden, but once he recovered he petitioned the provincial court in 1922 in an effort to charge Chief Ezeonyodu with stealing his wife and children. The chief, in turn, ordered the arrest of the forty-four individuals who affirmatively testified that he had kidnapped Okanu's family. He also arrested and ordered the murder of Okanu's brother, Sammy Uzor-Eghelu, whose only crime was assisting his brother.[61] In an attempt to help Okanu find his wife and children, Sammy had written a letter to the colony's chief secretary, Sir Frank Baddeley, about the kidnapping, complaining that "bribery, which is the desideratum of the day and which is in a full swing amongst the coloured employees in the Government service in the Onitsha Province especially with the Native Court clerks, Interpreters, and Chiefs whom we failed to obtain a redress in the matter complained of."[62] In another letter to Baddeley, Sammy characterized Chief Ezeonyodu as a "tiger in human form and with whom slave dealing is a trade." The chief categorized the money he received as a bride-price payment, denying he sold at least one of the girls after witnesses accused the him of selling Okanu's daughters. The court sentenced Okanu to three months of hard labor after he unsuccessfully attempted to kill the chief with a machete for kidnapping his family.[63] Okanu heard a rumor that Chief Ezeonyodu had given his wife and children to Warrant Chief Ojiakor of Adazi. When Okanu petitioned the court to address the matter, the court messenger charged him five shillings, one yam, and one cock—an exorbitant cost for court services. It is not clear if Okanu ever reunited with his family, but it is evident that Okanu had little to no recourse when the chief abused his power and stole Okanu's family members.[64]

In 1922 the colonial government launched an investigation into child pawnship, producing evidence that child dealing was prevalent in Onitsha and Owerri in the Eastern Provinces largely due to the regions' need for agricultural laborers.[65] The Aro, who created a widespread network of satellite villages, maintained their vast pawning networks. It is likely that many of the warrant chiefs and court clerks who received women or children in lieu of a court fee later sold them to the Aro, as did many other middlemen. During the 1920s, the Aro operated in Bende and Afikpo Districts. Afikpo is unique because while there were virtually no reported cases of child pawning at the time, the number of slave-dealing cases involving children were numerous. Bende was a key regional market town known for slave dealing during the era of the slave trade, and it continued to operate in the 1920s and 1930s, albeit secretly.[66] The senior resident of Onitsha reported that the trade in children was common among some groups.[67] The coastal towns of Bonny and Opobo received trafficked children in large numbers for the purpose of utilizing their labor. Other destinations included the Efik palm plantations at Akpabuyo and Azumini, which were only fifteen miles south of the major market town Aba. The Aro and other middlemen also sold children in Onitsha, the site of West Africa's largest market located on the eastern bank of the Lower Niger.[68]

Parents whose children were victims of kidnapping or botched child pawning arrangements had few opportunities to recoup their lost children. In 1920, Aro ownership of the Long Aro Juju oracle (Ibini Ukpabi) enabled the traffickers to maintain ownership of their child-dealing networks.[69] Colonial authorities were convinced that fear of the oracle "prevented anyone from reporting their actions, or appealing to the Government for help." Southeastern Nigerians rarely challenged Aro dominance for fear of retribution. Their Nigerian neighbors saw them as the "agents of the supreme manifestation of the High God, *Chukwu*."[70] In addition, some debtors could not use native courts to mediate pawnship disputes because, ironically, complicit members wanted to avoid any connection with child pawning that suggested they approved of the practice.[71]

A study of the Owerri Province, the preeminent district in the lucrative Palm Belt, provides insight into child dealing operations. In 1923, the assistant district officer of Bonny wrote that Okigwi (also known as Okigwe), Orlu, Bende, Aba, and Degema in Owerri Province stood out as key towns where child pawning occurred.[72] All housed large markets where moneylenders and child dealers operated to meet the demand for labor on the palm farms.

Reportedly, there were at least four ways in which child dealing operated in Owerri: pawning, marriage, the outright seizure of children, and the sale of children.[73] The most common reasons for pawning included burial expenses, settling a deceased father's debts, the cost to set up a farm, title making, financing public feasts, paying court fees, paying fines for committing adultery, and hiring a medicine man (*dibia*).[74] Pawning a female child often led to the marriage of the child to the moneylender or to one of his or her family members. In this case, the moneylender canceled the loan as it would then be used as the bride-price payment. In other instances, strangers as well as relatives participated in the outright seizure and sale of children to obtain money; children taken under these circumstances rarely returned home. Though colonial officials successfully prosecuted more individuals for the outright sale of children than for pawning, the vulnerability of children was gendered: child dealers of female children often claimed that they had paid the bride-price according to custom, making it virtually impossible to prosecute them.

In 1921, Owerri officials recorded the release of only four slave children. It is likely that the numbers of freed slaves reported for the Owerri Province are underrepresented because by virtue of being pawns, the children were not identified as slaves. Of the four reported, one was a male child younger than fourteen years old, and the remaining three were girls under fifteen, two of whom were returned to their parents.[75]

To illustrate Nigeria's impoverished conditions during the 1920s, a Nguru elder of the Owerri Province described child pawning during the first two decades of colonial rule: "People who were very poor could pawn themselves to a rich man for money or pawn one of their children . . . as soon as you can pay back the money you borrowed, you are free." Chief Ohaegbulam Ebubedike, an informant from Ngwa, described pawning transactions in Aba during the 1920s: "There was no specific amount for the loan; everything was hinged on negotiation, which varies according to the need of the parents. My father once told me that he lent £40 to a family that presented their able-bodied male child for pawning as collateral. The child was left to work in my father's palace as one of his bodyguards. The interest to be precise was paid in labor. Depending on the amount borrowed, it takes parents years to repay such loans and invariably leaves the child in service."[76] His account reminds us that the length of time a child pawn remained with the moneylender always depended on the parents' ability to repay the loan. The account also shows that the nature of the agreement had to be agreeable to both parties and that it had to be built on trust. Inevitably, differences in the agreements not only existed between sets of parties but also throughout the towns in the southeast.

Variations in pawning practices depended on what or who people could pawn and what moneylenders needed or wanted. In Enugu, one elder described the phenomenon: "In the olden days people of Nigeria—they used everything for economic improvement. One can use his own child, either to get income or other things. They didn't take it as any taboo. All they knew is that God has given them fifteen to twenty children, and he has a right to loan some . . . in order to sustain life."[77] Residents of Enugu saw children as a resource through which they could survive economic hardship. Similarly, the Ogoni people, who live along the Niger Delta coast, usually pawned a farm or a daughter, and men sometimes pawned themselves when in need of a loan. The Andoni, relations to the Ijaw, pledged sons and daughters, and Kwa-speaking peoples pawned daughters or property.[78] The Orsu Igbos in the Okigwi Division practiced a form of debt collection that bordered on panyarring.[79] The practice occurred when "a person owed a debt and was unable to pay it [so] his relations were expected to do so for him; if not, any goat, sheep or child seen in the debtor's compound could be seized and held as pledge. If no arrangement was then made after this seizing had taken place the child or animal might be sold. There was no imprisonment for debt. Money was always lent at a very high rate of interest [and] if not repaid the above method of seizing was resorted to. [A] Pledge was accepted in children or goods, but if possible the relations would assist by paying up the debt and taking over the debtor's belongings."[80] The seizure of a child or property occurred only if the moneylender did not receive a pledge for the original debt, making the dependents of a debtor highly vulnerable to collection practices. To avoid the seizure of a family member or animal, families concentrated efforts to pay the debt.

As warrant chiefs asserted more authority in debt cases, Lieutenant Governor Sir Hugh C. Clifford requested that residents and district officers investigate the nature and prevalence of child pawning in the southeast in 1923. In response, district commissioner of Bende, Frank Hives, expressed his belief that child pawning did exist and that warrant chiefs and traders were the most likely to accept child pawns for loans. Upon receipt of reports noting a decline in pawning, Hives remained skeptical. He claimed that any possible declines in pawning may have been due to children's growing awareness that pawning might be prosecuted as slave dealing, which could be reported to authorities. In reporting, they could put their parents or other guardians at risk of punishment, although some children did seek out police assistance after they had been sold as slaves. In addition, debtors may have been more likely to seek repayment of debts in native courts rather than receive a pawned child because they would risk going to prison if authorities found them in possession of a pawned child. Finally, Hives suggested that increased prices for goods sold in Calabar might have reduced local traders' need to pawn children.[81]

Reasons for pawning children continued to vary depending on the circumstances throughout the 1920s. Pawning a child to someone with financial means presented the child with the potential opportunity to receive an education. Parents had to pay school fees if they wanted their children to attend school, leaving many poorer children without access to an education. Elder Abraham Okolo supported Frank Hive's belief when he recalled that parents often pawned their children to warrant chiefs who promised to educate them, though not many chiefs followed through.[82]

The use of children to mitigate expenses had become normalized in the face of new legislation that monitored moneylending and slaving practices. Letters between district officers documented the failure to uphold specific standards in pawning arrangements. For example, during a trial in 1923, an Awka chief issued a £20 fine to a man who in return pawned his seven-year-old daughter to the chief, which enabled him to temporarily pay the judgment fine. He expected the chief to keep the child until she was old enough to marry, at which time the father would use the bride-price to pay off the debt, however, the chief decided to sell the girl immediately. In another pawning transaction in 1927, an Obowo man pledged his children, Ahuibe and Ewaenyinya, to pay a court fine but was later prosecuted for doing so when police located one of the two children.[83] Regularly documented, these practices occurred throughout the southeast into the late 1920s. In February 1929, Oveuebe of Obowo, a former court member of Okigwi, was prosecuted for pawning two children in order to pay a fine ordered by the Umuahia Native Court.[84] In another case, the British administration prosecuted a man for pawning a child, for the purpose of paying a fine, and sentenced him to one year in jail.[85] In all these situations, British perceptions, whether real or imagined, must be examined to understand their ambivalent approach to child dealing.

BRITISH PERCEPTIONS OF PAWNING

From the early twentieth century until the late 1920s, British officials adopted conflicting patterns of action in response to pawning. Sir Walter Egerton and Lord Lugard had both attempted to regulate child pawning, but Egerton officially argued that a strong attack on pawning would be "premature," and Lugard did not want to distract from the war effort.[86] In December 1924, Governor Hugh Clifford (1919–25) posited that short-term pawning was not abusive and that it was an "essential feature of the fiscal, economic and social system," and that abolishing pawning altogether would "plunge innumerable families into financial embarrassment."[87]

In 1925 W. A. G. Ormsby-Gore, assistant to the secretary of state, urged Governor Clifford to take forceful action against child pawning. He gave two reasons for his request. First, Lugard was now a member of the newly formed League of Nations Commission on Slavery, which focused on female pawning, and Clifford argued that Lugard needed to fight the practice in his own country and its colonies. Second, the League's efforts focused on persuading the president of Liberia, a country whose domestic slavery policies received international attention, to condemn child pawning. Thus, it could be argued that the international movement to end pawning made it essential that the British lead by example.[88]

In response to the 1923 inquiry about pawning, colonial authorities offered varying opinions about the quality of life pawns experienced. Hives stated, "There was, nor would there be now, any hardship in being a pawn as his master would look after him very well, being responsible for him, he would not only be well fed and clothed, but would be allowed, if he desired to do so, [to] visit his parents whenever he wished, and very often his parents lived in the same or adjoining towns. No stigma of being a slave was or is attached to a pawn." But this conflicted greatly with the testimony of an elder who recalls how the Igbos in Aba preferred pawned children who came from faraway towns rather than those from nearby. The wealthy men who accepted children as pawns believed that "the pawned child may not render quality services" if they lived too close to their parents. In some cases, parents in Aba pawned their children to moneylenders from as far away as Lagos.[89] And in Enugu, many pawns did not even know where they had come from.

Hives's motivation in offering a positive view of child pawning may have been the result of his lack of authority to end the practice and his desire to save the government from embarrassment.[90] Whatever the case, it is worth considering that pawns had diverse experiences.

Another informant, Chief Ohaegbulam Ebubedike of Aba, remembered that pawns were treated "mercilessly and with contempt." His own father compelled child pawns to work on his farm and did not send them to school. More often than not, he explained, his father took in even quite young children because parents begged him for money: "In most cases, my father was reluctant in ceding their demands due to the fact that he spends huge amounts of money through the same kind of transaction. He used to say that some of the pawned children were not strong enough to give commensurate return to the money lent out to their parents, which invariably amounts to a waste of resources on his part." Even though Chief Ebubedike's father did not want to accept some of the children, he had a social responsibility to maintain those in his extended kinship system. Moreover, the chief's emphasis on the child's inability to produce some form of profit by virtue of his or her own labor underscores my assertion that *the social economy of children* must be understood as central to social and financial transactions when access to potential child labor is in question.[91] The treatment of pawned children, whether or not they performed productive labor, depended on the temperament of the receiving family.

Recalling his own feelings about the pawned children, Chief Ebubedike admits, "Honestly, we considered the pawned children as lesser human[s]; their circumstances obviously made them so no doubt. They were treated with contempt and served us as slaves. Though it is my family involved, the truth must be told. Our father made them serve us like prince[s] and princesses; there was no friendly relationship between us and them whatsoever. Some of them today are very prominent individuals and sometimes when

I meet them, I feel very shocked and ashamed reflecting on the past."[92] Ebubedike's admittance of shame is a result of his family treating pawns inhumanely, but his story also implies that some Nigerian communities found the maltreatment of pawns acceptable. According to a similar account, pawns in Aba "were treated with contempt just like any slave regime. They had no respect, honor nor integrity before their masters" and only saw their parents during holidays. One woman recalls that pawns performed the family's most "heinous tasks," often worked while hungry, and only saw their parents when they were redeemed.[93] But, the most significant aspect of this account is that as children became objects of trade, their value as beloved family members decreased in the home that received them. Despite the fact that some guardians treated pawns poorly, colonial authorities remained hesitant to intervene.

CONCLUSION

The consolidation of Nigeria as a colony exacerbated pawning practices during the first few decades of the twentieth century. Contributing factors included Nigeria's economic decline, the selection of corrupt, nontraditional rulers as warrant chiefs, a decrease in the authority of elders and secret societies that previously ruled on debt cases, and the Aros' continued participation in child trafficking. Toyin Falola and Paul E. Lovejoy assert that while pawnship was connected to poverty, poverty did not predetermine indebtedness.[94] However, by the early twentieth century, some Southeastern Nigerians used pawnship to gain access to currency or other goods for the purpose of paying colonial taxes and other expenses, which ultimately led to indebtedness. It remains difficult to quantify how often Southeastern Nigerians pawned children for loans, but personal accounts and colonial records offer some perspective on the trade in children in those cases dealing with slavery, pawning, various other forms of servile labor, and marriage customs.

On March 22, 1923, Major Harry Claude Moorehouse, an officer in the British army, expressed that he did not want to see the institution of pawnship abolished by force and insisted that pawns suffered no loss of status and were not considered slaves. It is true that pawning and slavery existed as two distinct institutions theoretically, but the examples given herein make obvious this was not always the case in practice.[95] Contrary to precolonial customs in which pawns did not generally end up as slaves, warrant chiefs and court clerks operated as moneylenders who often sold pawns into slavery. After the removal of the district officer from the native court, the warrant chiefs and court clerks were able to overcharge and extort litigants, trick them into filing appeals, and then lend them money at high interest rates to finance said appeals.

By the 1920s, corruption in the court system created distrust and chaos, and the fear of imprisonment for a debt often persuaded guardians to pawn children. In addition, long-distance traders, middlemen, and the Aro controlled the networks that circulated child pawns and sold them as slaves throughout the entire colony. Their centuries of engagement in the transatlantic slave trade allowed them to use old slave routes and market centers to secretly distribute pawned children distant from their natal homes, making it nearly impossible for parents to retrieve them.

Charged with Lugard's request in 1916 to end child pawning, and under increased pressure from international humanitarian groups, colonial authorities were forced to pay closer attention to the practice. While some British representatives attempted to end the pawning, others were inclined to let it die out on its own. The colonial state's failure to end child pawning during the early 1920s can be attributed to the colonial priority to secure sufficient labor for the palm industry, ambivalence and feigned ignorance about the true nature of pawning, and a general willingness to accept it. Whatever the reason, the inability to prohibit pawning enabled court members and other child dealers to sell pawned women and children into domestic slavery. Ironically, Lugard, who had championed efforts to end child pawning, implemented policies under indirect rule that inadvertently ensured that numerous children would habitually end up as pawns and slaves. By the end of the 1920s, global attention to the use of child labor continued to grow alongside the concern of parents whose children had been pawned and subsequently enslaved. As a result, the colonial government would be confronted with an uprising among international humanitarians who insisted that child pawning and human trafficking, in any form, cease to exist.

CHAPTER 3

International Debate on the Welfare of Children, 1920s

The commission has undertaken to get the facts about the traffic in women and children as it exists to-day over the world.

—*William F. Snow,*

Chief of the Advisory Committee on the Traffic in Women and Children, 1926

C oncern about the trafficking of girls and women for the purpose of prostitution intensified during the 1920s. As expressed by William Snow, chairman of the Special Body of Experts focused on trafficking, his committee sought to identify instances of trafficking globally.[1] As for Nigeria, these investigations into the trafficking of women and girls extended to all forms of child dealing in Southeastern Nigeria during the 1920s.[2] This chapter explores how prostitution became a topic of global concern and how that concern resulted in additional investigations into all forms of child dealing in the colony. By carefully analyzing archival case studies and oral histories, I argue that inquiries into child trafficking and girl marriage produced a complex picture of legitimate marriage as well as instances of child dealing. The overlapping characteristics made it nearly impossible for British officials to determine the difference in many cases. To complicate matters, the demand to produce a marriage certificate to prove the legitimacy of a marriage had conflicting results. The following account is offered as an example of when two parties claiming to have engaged in a common marriage practice resulted in authorities charging the father with child dealing.

In 1927 British authorities accosted an Ijaw man named Bob Onana who held a twelve-year-old Igbo girl, Uche Abeaku, in his canoe at Isu. When questioned about the girl, Onana professed that Uche's father, Maduekwe, offered her in marriage for a £20 bride-price. To confirm the legitimacy of the marriage, authorities sought out Maduekwe, who declared that he married off his daughter to "gain money," adding that Onana owed him the remaining balance of the bride-price. Even though both men claimed that they had come to a legitimate agreement, colonial authorities concluded that the marriage could not be verified because the men did not produce a marriage certificate.[3] In this case, it is possible, even if unlikely, that Uche at twelve years old had agreed to the marriage or was persuaded by her father, and thus in the eyes of the British, she could have granted her consent. However, if her father arranged her marriage before she reached the age of twelve, she could not have given her consent, which would have marked the marriage as invalid. In any case, police determined that Maduekwe sold his daughter and prosecuted him accordingly.[4]

It is difficult to fully know what happened in Uche's case because the transaction between Maduekwe and Onana could be indicative of a number of socioeconomic agreements. If we assume that Maduekwe and Onana engaged in a child-dealing scheme, it is likely that Maduekwe needed a loan and offered his daughter as a pawn, and when he failed to repay that loan, Onana took Uche as his wife. As such, Maduekwe would have awaited the final bride-price payment. Another possibility is that Maduekwe sold his daughter outright and decided to use this moment of British intervention as a way to extract more money from Onana. However, if Maduekwe and Onana arranged a marriage contract, it would not have been unusual for Onana to pay the bride-price in stages, even after the marriage was contracted.[5] The perplexing similarities of these statuses show why colonial authorities had difficulty discerning legitimate marriages from illegitimate child-dealing agreements.

GLOBAL CONCERNS ABOUT CHILD LABOR, MARRIAGE, AND TRAFFICKING

The movement to investigate child welfare in Nigeria did not occur in a vacuum. The investigations that allowed Uche, her father, and Onana to live on in the archive were born out of late nineteenth-century concerns about prostitution in Europe; child slavery and child labor conditions globally; child delinquencies; as well as ongoing cultural negotiations about what constituted a child.[6] For instance, in 1880 British reformers defined "childhood" as the period extending from birth through fourteen years of age.[7] The laws designed to protect children beginning in the 1830s set a pattern for Britain's widespread reform movement. Activists lobbied for stricter guidelines as a way to decrease what they believed to be abuses of children.[8]

In July 1885, William Stead, a popular English journalist, wrote a series of salacious articles about child prostitution, slavery, and trafficking in which he painted the horrors of child rape and forced prostitution, portraying London as an open slave market for girls. As public dismay and outrage grew, the age of consent was raised from thirteen to sixteen years as a result of the Criminal Law Amendment Act of 1885. Stead's writings and the subsequent concerns about the "white slave" traffic, denoting the movement of European women across national borders, led to larger concerns about girls, women, and sexual behavior in a global context.[9] In addition to matters of sex and sexuality, Western governments also focused on establishing child labor reforms during the early nineteenth century when the abuse of children during the Industrial Revolution attracted criticism.

In the years preceding World War I (July 28, 1914, to November 11, 1918), Western countries began to address the issue of child labor in earnest. One by one, Europeans countries made efforts to limit the hours children worked and denounced child labor in factories and workshops, but enacting legislation undermined global labor needs.[10] In the United States, Congress passed the Keating Owen Child Labor Act of 1916, "banning the interstate sale of any products produced with child labor that did not meet fundamental federal standards: no employment of any child under age 14 and eight-hour workdays for children 14–16."[11] Textile owners and others vigorously fought against the implementation of the Act. In the Supreme Court case of *Hammer v. Dagenhart*, the effort to "stop interstate trafficking of prostitution, kidnapping, fraudulent lotteries, and bootlegging" came to a halt in a five-to-four vote against the act.[12] By October 1918, the Children's Bureau of the United States Department of Labor in Washington, D.C., investigated the number of labor certificates issued to children. The issuance of certificates soared 164 percent from 727 in 1916–17 to 1,917 in 1918 to children ages fourteen to sixteen, and permitting even more flexibility, the Juvenile Court allowed children living at the poverty level to work as young as twelve years of age. While there had been some uptick in the previous years owing to the manufacturing of war goods, Julia C. Lathrop, chief of the bureau, conveyed that over 50 percent of children in Washington worked in stores and business offices.[13] On the contrary, in England, juvenile employment shifted from agriculture, clerkships, and post office work to industry and transportation services. Youth laborers under the age of eighteen years increased to 1,354,000 in 1918 from 94,000 in 1914. Through these examples we can see that children buttressed national efforts in the West, supporting the sentiment that "the child cannot exist without the nation and the nation cannot exist without the child."[14]

In the years following, child labor increasingly troubled the International Labor Organization (ILO). Though armed only with advisory powers, the organization worked tirelessly to end what some believed to be inhumane labor practices and campaigned against those industries employing children younger than fourteen years of age. For workers over fourteen, the ILO encouraged governments and employers to increase wages and limit the number of hours young employees worked.[15] As international efforts to limit the hours worked by children increased, the focus on women and girls deemed vulnerable to human trafficking expanded.

The League of Nations adopted the 1921 International Convention for the Suppression of Traffic in Women and Children, which resulted in the formation of the Advisory Committee on the Traffic in Women and Children.[16] In January 1922 the Council of the League of Nations Advisory Committee on the Traffic in Women and Children was placed under the League's Social Section, which dealt with international social issues. In an antiprostitution effort, the committee sought out instances where women and children had been trafficked for the purpose of sexual exploitation, and though it lacked enforcement power, committee representatives advised on social policy and implementation so as to curb the traffic in women and children. Its goals included raising the legal age of marriage in various countries, shutting down houses of prostitution, securing residences for homeless children, and providing services for disabled children.[17]

In 1924, the League of Nations approved the Geneva Declaration of the Rights of the Child and formed the Child Welfare Committee to develop programs to improve children's lives. Eglantyne Jebb, an English schoolteacher, social reformer, and founder of the Save the Children organization, drafted the declaration. The declaration detailed that children should be provided with the resources to enjoy happy, prosperous lives; they should be cared for; they should receive relief services when needed; they should be trained to work, while at the same time sheltered from exploitation; it initially targeted European countries, although Jebb wanted to extend the protection of children to African and Asian countries.[18] The League supported the mission and strongly urged governments to protect all children.[19]

The League of Nations' Committees and growing international concern about children's working conditions led the British government to investigate instances of child marriage, child pawning, forced labor realities and other abuses in Nigeria. League members wanted to ascertain child welfare conditions as well as how the institutions of slavery, pawnship, and child marriage affected children's lives.[20] Throughout the 1920s, British authorities acknowledged that the status of child pawns, slaves, and brides could not easily be discernible from one another but did attempt to monitor transactions whereby adults exchanged children for money or goods; they also investigated marriage agreements. As Emily Burrill emphasizes in her work on colonial Mali, administrators "attempted to render certain African practices tied to marriage as legible or understandable in the colonial framework" as a way to separate slave systems from the institution of marriage.[21] In particular, the pawning of girls and child marriage posed the greatest challenge because of the inability to distinguish between the two, as illustrated in the case of Uche. How could the Colonial Office end practices that were nearly indistinguishable?

In 1925, the League appointed the Temporary Slavery Commission to identify ways to end the traffic in domestic slaves. The commission conducted a survey dedicated to child marriage, child pawning, and child slaves, and prepared a report on conditions throughout the colonies. The report resulted in the Slavery Convention of 1926, which required that members work to end all forms of slavery, defined as "the status or condition of a person over whom any or all of the powers attaching to the right of ownership are exercised."[22]

Social activists became increasingly involved with the League of Nations in its efforts to end slavery and improve global working conditions for women and children.[23] In particular, a number of British women joined the committee. Eleanor Rathbone, feminist social reformer, independent member of the British Parliament, and an active member of women's international organizations served as an adviser to the Child Welfare Committee in 1926. In the same year, Julia Lathrop, former chief of the Children's Bureau, advocated that "the child has a right to grow normally and harmoniously into the full development of his mental and moral and physical powers." The programs that followed would be part of larger social welfare efforts to address workplace conditions and child trafficking, as well as programs to deal with delinquent children, among others. In 1928 Margaret Ada Beney, a research staff member of the National Industrial Conference Board of the United States, led an investigation into the labor conditions of women and children.[24] Later, in 1929, Rathbone; Duchess Katharine Marjory, a British noblewoman who served as the Scottish Unionist Party member of Parliament; and humanitarian Josiah Wedgwood formed the Committee for the Protection of Coloured Women in the Crown Colonies. With eight additional members, this committee focused on clitoridectomy and bride-price practices throughout the colonies. These individuals, and like-minded supporters, persuaded League members to take a more activist position in improving the livelihoods of women and children throughout the world. However, the investigations that followed did not fully consider cultural lifeways when evaluating marriage customs.

When the Marriage Ordinance of 1884 became part of legislative colonial policy in Nigeria, it was not initially at the behest of missionaries or part of the colonial effort to transform "indigenous customary law" immediately. Rather, the introduction of the ordinance based on English marriage law was meant to fill a void in the growing number of issues that the Colonial Office had not yet addressed. In time, the ordinance had profound consequences for men and women married under the law. Men could not take more than one wife, family members and community elders no longer oversaw divorce cases, and laws pertaining to personal property came under English law.[25] And even though British authorities preferred that Nigerians married according to the 1884 ordinance and its many subsequent iterations, it was the mid-twentieth century before they concentrated efforts on marriage reform. Missionaries, however, did have a greater impact on indigenous marriage patterns, as they welcomed increasing numbers of Christian converts and denounced polygamy during the early twentieth century.

Most secondary literature that maps the transformation of marriage practices in Southern Nigeria focuses on the western region of the country, mainly because Christianity took a foothold among the Yoruba decades before it became a common practice in the southeast. The issue of Western companionate versus traditional marriage was a point of considerable tension between missionaries and westernized Christian elites in Nigeria during the colonial era. The complexity of marriage systems led missionaries and British authorities to argue that marriage should be a relationship between a man and a woman—a companionate marriage—who had special rights as a couple and mutual obligations to one another. British administrators and missionaries had to contend with multiple types of marriages in Igboland, including the forms covered in this chapter, such as slave bride, child bride through pawning, as well as other arrangements.[26] As a result, colonial authorities intervened in marriage arrangements insofar as they affected pawns, slaves, and other young women and children in Igboland. Administrators expected Nigerians to sign certificates of betrothal at the moment a marriage was agreed upon and a certificate of marriage at the time of marriage, giving written consent. This also required both sets of parents to sign the certificates to ensure that the marriage was legitimate.[27]

It is essential to use the examination of marriage as a tool for analysis when considering Nigeria's history of social, political, and economic reconfigurations in light of trade relationships and the onset of British colonialism. In most West African communities, marriage encompassed and indicated the joining of kinship groups as a way to expand families and extend descendant lineages.[28] However, as with most indigenous customs, marriage changed over time. As Kristin Mann has shown in her research on Christian educated elite in Lagos from 1880 to 1915, Yoruba Christian marriages and the associated practices changed as the socioeconomic and political circumstances altered indigenous customs, which began to take on new meanings. The Yoruba responded proactively to their access to new modes of education and employment opportunities, and the introduction of Christianity. Similarly, Lisa A. Lindsay provides an overview of how economic changes during the early twentieth century in Southwestern Nigeria reshaped young men's notions of independence, their ability to marry, and their engagement in wage labor on colonial projects. With an emphasis on gender, her analysis of marriage shows that the introduction of wage labor resulted in women having to demand recognition for their own economic activities and responsibilities in the household, such as paying taxes and school fees for their children. Similarly, Igbo-speaking people and their neighbors understood marriage to be a social contract that embodied privileges and responsibilities, one that provided access to productive and reproductive labor, as well as necessitating the woman's departure from her village.[29]

Even though the League of Nations focused on the trafficking of girls and women, committee members and investigative officers did not always appreciate that it was customary for women to leave their clan upon marriage.[30] Most societies in Southeastern Nigeria practiced exogamy, a pattern whereby daughters left their natal home and lived among their husband's clan, encouraging parents of young girls to begin planning for their daughters' departures early on. For example, one Enugu elder explained that "the belief of our people is that a girl belongs to somewhere else, that is to say, she will be married outside of the place, compound, [where] she [was] born. But for boys, people want somebody who will take over for them, when they die . . . who will remain in the compound. In those old days the men would have several farmlands, and they knew . . . [a single] woman could not cope with . . . [all the] farmwork. That explains one of the reasons why people marry several wives so that they could be cutting the grass and doing all sort[s] of things that are meant for women."[31]

The process of offering a girl or young woman in marriage or as a pawn—processes that separated her from her natal village—might suggest that parents lacked an emotional connection with their child, but it is imperative to recognize that the child's intrinsic value was deeply embedded in both the domestic sphere, as it related to identity and marriage, as well as the economic potential she engendered once married or offered as a pawn. While some Southeastern Nigerians rid themselves of a troublesome or disabled child, or a child considered an outcast for other reasons, many parents maintained an affective bond with those from whom they parted.[32] It is also important to appreciate that a mother's identity was directly linked to her ability to produce children and that separation from any child produced emotional and social consequences.[33] As such, analyzing marraige customs during the 1920s helps reinforce this point.

MARRIAGE AGREEMENTS

In the case of child marriage, the betrothal could extend from a child's early years to the date of the actual marriage, during which the agreement encompassed a financial component. As was the case with Igbo patrilineal societies, the father controlled access to children, their labor, and marriage agreements. The betrothed and the two respective families, mainly the senior men and women, participated in the initiation of the marriage contract. Young men depended on their fathers and other elders to negotiate the bride-price for a future wife, likewise the bride depended on her father and senior men in her lineage to negotiate on her behalf. For the purpose of creating a formal contract, the prospective groom's family agreed on the bride-price, in some form of wealth or service, with the parents of the young woman, which resulted in the finalization of the agreement.[34]

Negotiations for girl children versus women differed little. For instance, during the early twentieth century in Onitsha and Owerri, the father of the future groom presented palm wine or gin and kola nuts as preliminary gifts but never discussed the potential marriage during the initial meetings. The father continued to bring gifts to the prospective bride's home, and after some time, he revealed his son's intentions. After extended negotiations, the future husband's family offered a formal contract or bride-price to the bride-to-be's family.[35] These transactions took on various forms. For example, a groom from Owerri would begin the courtship process by bringing palm wine to the future bride's home. An Owerri woman explained: "When a man finds a girl he likes and proposes to her, and the girl agrees, he proceeds to the parents. The man goes for the first visit with a keg of palm wine tagged *mmanya ajuju* ['inquiry drink'] where he makes his intentions known to the parents. On saying the purpose for the visit, the girl child would be called upon and asked if she knew the man. If she says yes, she will be told what the man's mission [was]. She is then asked if they should drink palm wine, and if she says yes, it [means] that she has consented to the proposal." The next stage of the proposal entailed the following: "The man will be asked again to come on a market day . . . with another keg of palm wine, *mmanya ezi-uka* ['reality drink']. [This is when] the groom will . . . be given the list of traditional items required for the marriage. And once these items (bride-price inclusive) are provided, he is said to have completed the marriage rites. They would be blessed by both families and asked to live peacefully amid singing and dancing by family and friends."[36] The process, including extended negotiations with the girl's senior family members, always required the future bride's consent, which underscores arrangements where financial distress may not be a factor and the girl has decision-making power about whom she marries. In this instance, it is helpful to take into consideration Jean Allman's suggestion that the we must consider the institution of marriage as a process, rather than a static institution.[37] Negotiations had to be entered into with mutual respect, allowing for each party's approval for the final decision to marry.

Other accounts from Aba, Owerri, and Calabar illustrate the prolonged and complex courtship and betrothal processes required in the southeast in the years leading up to the 1920s. However, as a result of rising access to wage labor and the influx of the British pound, Nigerians established other patterns. In Aba, one senior woman recalled that prior to the 1920s the father of the bride continued negotiations over time, and in return the groom presented "items like a keg of palm-wine, snuff, tubers of yam, hens, and cocks," and she further noted that by the 1920s and 1930s, men also paid a sum of around £20. Another informant from Calabar claimed that prospective grooms frequently worked for the family for an agreed-on period without wages before they allowed him to marry their daughter. Paying some form of bride-price was mandatory in most areas in the southeast, but the amount varied depending on personal preference and location.[38]

Conversely, an Ibibio informant from Calabar claimed that "people attach little to bride-price. Once they find themselves in love, they get married with or without tradition. They may have up to four children before thinking of going for traditional rights." It seems that the Ibibio exercised flexibility in courtship practices and bride-price agreements. If an Ibibio parent needed a loan, however, they would pawn a girl child with the understanding that the girl would be taken as a bride if they failed to repay the debt.[39] In other words, some Ibibio accepted the pawned child as a bride when the parents lacked money to repay the loan, just as other Igbo, Ijo, and Efik parents did during this time, even though they may not have generally required the payment of a bride-price for a legitimate marriage arrangement. Nevertheless, for parents who did accept a bride-price, the payment signified a symbolic loss and the loss of the girl's future labor capacity. Even when pawned, a girl when old enough could marry the man of her choice, provided that the debt was repaid before the marriage.[40]

The British had a limited understanding of how wives and husbands-to-be and their respective parents came to a marriage agreement. They also did not fully comprehend how families planned for their daughters' inevitable departure from their natal homes, especially in these temporary arrangements, which were dependent on whether or not a debtor repaid his loan. Owerri resident Anthony Nwadinko explained that during the 1920s, "in most cases, the bride [had to] consent to marry the groom before the bride's family accept[ed] the bride price." Even if a groom acquired a wife through pawning, "brides [were] never [thought] to be for sale. The payments attached to the bride [were] just to fulfill certain traditional obligations as no amount could buy a child."[41] What is important is that those in charge of negotiating a marriage or moneylender agreement followed specific cultural rituals not governed by colonial statutes. In many cases, the transfer of children remained virtually invisible to Europeans, leaving British authorities with limited power to alter marriage and pawning customs.

WHAT COLONIAL INQUIRIES AND ORAL HISTORIES REVEAL

At the behest of the women in the League of Nations and owing to growing concerns about pawning and child marriage, Governor-General Hugh Clifford ordered all district officers to respond to questionnaires detailing native laws and customs in the southeast.[42] Consequently, the Colonial Office spearheaded investigations into marriage arrangements they deemed illegitimate. It is evident that as a result of the strained economy child marriage agreements became part of a shadow economy of social exchanges, which brought the institutions of child pawning and slavery even closer to the institution of marriage. Therefore, it was not without cause that investigators primarily focused on child pawning. The government sought information about pawnship, especially with regard to sex, age, consent, and financial arrangements between the parents or guardians; in addition, officials wanted to know what, if anything, differentiated pawns from slaves.[43] In 1923 colonial administrators sent out questionnaires to the district officers in each of the southern divisions asking for the following information:

(a) Extent to which pawning of children as security for debt still exists in your Division/District-either openly or secretly.

(b) The position and terms which apply to a pawn.

(c) The attitude adopted by the Native Courts where cases come to light.

(d) Whether one or both parents held the right to pawn according to old custom or whether consent of both parents was necessary.

(e) Whether pawning of adults was common and whether the practice still exists.

(f) The status of a pawn i.e. how long held, how treated, whether if a female-she could be given in marriage and the dowry used to liquidate the debt or could she be taken as a wife by the pawnee.

(g) Whether the pawn invariably had to live in the house of the person to whom pawned and how it affected his or her social and political status.

(h) Should a pawn run away what was the penalty or result?

(i) Whether services rendered by a pawn extinguished any interest on the original debt, and that the principal only was paid back.

(j) Whether the customs differed with regard to Male or Female pawns.

(k) Whether a man or woman could pawn him or herself and the result from social and political aspects.

In conducting this questionnaire, residents instructed district officers to "enlist the assistance of Native Rulers" to end the practice and to make sure that those who failed to comply suffered punishment.[44] This would not be easily achieved.

The examples that follow expose why families pawned children, mainly girls, and the conditions that prevented the child from returning home. In some cases, chiefs and native courts neither dictated nor had any control over the initial stages of moneylending agreements, especially when chiefs did not function as the moneylenders. For example, Calabarian Nze Azubuike Azuka's maternal grandparents had ten children and pawned his mother to a moneylender in Calabar in order to provide for the remaining children. Azuka's grandparents believed that his mother's beauty "could attract a higher loan and thus was given out." Sacrificing one child for the sake of others is a common theme reported in oral accounts and archival materials. Even so, the girl's parents endured great sadness but justified pawning their daughter because she could attract the largest sum as a pawn.[45] The strategy to ensure economic survival necessitating the release of at least one daughter through pawning did not negate the emotive connection the parents had with the child. In fact, the emotional component is what made moneylending arrangements lucrative. In this case, the daughter remained with the moneylender for many years and eventually returned. But such was not the case in every pawning arrangement.

Another informant, a chief who lived in Awo Mbieri, Owerri, acquired one of his seven wives by accepting a female pawn. The chief's son by another wife, Ahanotu Marcellenus, recalls that the woman's father "owed my father [a debt] and subsequently decided to give out their daughter's hand in marriage to my father. And the debt served as the dowry that my father would normally have had to pay."[46] In this case, the families arranging the transfer of the daughter's pawn status to that of a wife did not engage in the betrothal customs generally practiced. Patterns such as these influenced British authorities to assume that money meant more to the parents than the child. But when parents did not have land to pawn, the acting district officer of Degema, F. Ferguson, astutely observed: "The scarcity of land in these parts of Owerri probably has some bearing on the prevalence of "domestic pawning" and children form almost the only reliable asset: land is communal and scarce."[47] The child's intrinsic value is what made him or her a fundamental element of economic activities embedded in social agreements, emphasizing *the social economy of the child*.

Colonial representatives could not easily imagine a community where females existed as both economic assets and valued family members. The senior resident in Onitsha seemed to believe that people in Southeastern Nigeria were heartless about the need to trade their children so as to pay their taxes and other debts in the 1920s. Resident H. T. B. Dew offered this observation, which must be taken with caution given his lack of information about Igbo society: "Among a very primitive people like these, among whom females are largely regarded as of such monetary value, where wives are merely bought and sold, where sexual intercourse both among the married and unmarried is to a large extent promiscuous from an early age, where ethical standards in the family affairs of family life do no[t] exist, it can hardly be a matter of surprise that the practice of pawning still remains. They would have no special customs about pawning—the pawn being merely regarded as a chattel of varying value."[48] His comments reveal erroneous assumptions based on racial hierarchies and stereotypes about African sexuality. It is untrue that special customs related to pawning practices in the southeastern provinces did not exist, as each region exercised its own distinct rituals.

Some pawning rituals accentuated the parents' desire to reclaim their children one day. In Nike, Enugu rituals varied when pawning children where, in some instances, the parties invoked the spiritually important *ala*, "earth goddess" (earth mother). *Ala* was important because she represents fertility for women and success in trade for men.[49] As a ritual that represented the father's desire to one day redeem his child, he and the moneylender stood barefoot outside as the moneylender swore that he would keep the child safe. The debtor believed that "no man will change what he said. He is afraid of the land. If you agree upon something and you disobey it, the land will kill you," signifying the important cosmic connection Nigerians had with land of their ancestors.[50] Adhering to the terms of the agreement protected the moneylender from harm.

Other Enugu residents also prioritized secrecy when engaged in pawning transactions. One resident described pawning as a "business system" and said that parties should not "advertise everything." Those in need and moneylenders shared a mutual understanding that the affair should be kept private. For example, it was typical for a father to pretend that he was going to the market or to visit a friend when he transported a child to be pawned. He and the child would visit the moneylender several days in a row, until one day when the father would return home without her. On his return, he told his family that the child chose to remain with his friend, but he would not reveal the location of the child.[51] This telling example speaks to the likely emotional consideration afforded to the child—to ensure that he or she had the opportunity to become familiar with his or her new guardian. Furthermore, the language suggesting that the child had a choice may have been invoked to quell any ambivalence about whether the child was a pawn as opposed to a slave, even if the child truly lacked a voice in the arrangement.

Anthony Nwadinko, a community elder born in Owerri in 1914, recalls the complications of pawning a child of either sex. Sometimes fathers pawned their children in secrecy so as to hide their location from their wives' families. Not revealing the location of the child prevented other family members from retrieving her. If the mother's father, uncle, or brother found out where the child was located, they would "go to the man and make him produce the child or the man would be banished. Some people have been forced to go and retrieve the child because of pressure."[52] The risk of reprimand and retrieval demonstrates the power of kinship relations and the value of the child. Most important decisions that affected the family should have been discussed and approved of by the senior family members, and pawning without consultation made the father subject to reprimand for his actions.

Other complications arose when pawning a girl child. Throughout the southeast, Nigerians crafted a number of ways to offer a girl child in marriage when engaging in a moneylending agreement. Making clear that the child had not been sold was especially important because some considered it distasteful to pawn a girl who would eventually marry the moneylender. Mrs. Anthonia Nkechinyere Ibeawuchi of Ikeduru, Owerri, told the story of one of her friends who married the son of a moneylender. Even though the practice of giving a girl as a bride in return for a payment from a creditor was frowned on, "parents had no choice [but] to engage in [the practice of pawning] since their deteriorated economic situation could not let them solve their problem." HRH Igwe Dr. Titus Okolo from Amorji, Enugu, explains that when parents offered a female child in return for payment, they would say, "You have helped me, use this female child. Marry her for the good job you've done for us."[53] The quote emphasizes that the man receiving the child had done more than merely pay a bride-price—he had helped the family out in their time of need, and the family thanked him by offering the child as a bride. One could argue that this was an instance of selling a girl child, but often such cases could not be proven because the Colonial Office did not legislate against bride-price payments.

Whereas some regions in Igboland engaged in arrangements that could be described as child-selling, residents in other areas denied the practice in their own villages. Abraham Okolo, an elder from Amorji-Nike, Enugu, stressed that the people of Nike, a former slave-trading community in Northern Igboland, never sold their own children into slavery. Selling children was considered "an abomination," but pawning was acceptable.[54] However, the elder made the distinction that during the 1920s and 1930s, people often trafficked children from regions outside Nike. Child dealers sold kidnapped children to the rich men of Nike, who never asked about their origins. Rather, both parties pretended as if the trafficker offered his own children, and in these cases, the slave owners likely used children for agricultural labor on farms.[55] It is worth noting the irony that while the Igbo in Nike considered selling children an abomination, buying them was not. Nonetheless, other regions of Igboland did see blood relatives engage in the selling of their own kin.

Family members, other than the parents, also engaged in child trafficking. Uncles, brothers, and others stole younger dependents and sold them to child dealers. In 1920, a woman from the Aro town of Bende complained that a kidnapped child had recently appeared in Aba, a major market center, where the child testified that a family member had taken and given her to Abraham Hart, a trader at Bonny. Upon questioning, Hart produced a signed marriage certificate in an effort to avoid prosecution, but the district officer of Aba believed this was an instance of either child selling or pawning. In any case, the transaction was completed without the mother's consent, and she believed that Hart should be reprimanded. Even so, Hart could not be easily prosecuted because someone in the girl's family had either to the marriage transaction or at least engaged in a scheme in which both parties claimed that the child had entered into a legitimate marriage contract.[56] The district officer of Owerri claimed that "relatives of children stolen are often employed by agents to entice the children from their homes," thus making the transaction an illegal business exchange rather than a kidnapping.[57] Of all the aforementioned examples, this might be the most absurd illustration of how the Colonial Office viewed the socioeconomic position of a child at the center of economic transactions arranged by family members.

Reports about female child dealing proliferated in the 1920s as taxes increased and prices for palm kernels and palm oil dropped. In 1921 and 1923, the district officer of Okigwe reported, "It is worthy of note that there are signs of Slave Dealing being on the wane. But there is an enormous amount of trade—in truth Slave Dealing—carried on in young girls, but convictions are practically impossible on account of Dowry being legal. These girls are bought—so called married and Dowry paid up country and then taken to the coast and passed on at an enormous profit in so called Dowry. The main form this takes in Owerri—apart from stealing children in the Onicha country—is the traffic in young children or even young women under the guise of marriage. The New Calabars are fond of that trick. They promise large dowries and pay little or nothing. On getting the woman to Degema they are sold and married off."[58] Dowry and bride-price payments continued to attract attention, especially in instances where Nigerians arranged marriage by hiring the services of a middleman or -woman who arranged a marriage partner for a girl, because this method, in practice, resembled slave dealing.

As affirmed by Enugu Chief Ugwuefi Reuben, the 1920s and 1930s colonial economy—plunging export prices, increased import products, and the implementation of direct taxation—occasioned the reconfiguration of child dealing.[59] The district officer for Obubra Division reported that "In the olden days it was the custom to pawn brothers or sisters of the debtor, not his children," but that children were more likely to be "seized" when loans went into default.[60] But by the 1920s, as previously indicated, parents began to pawn children to pay court fines after the creation of the colonial court system.

Evidence of child pawning to pay court fines existed at various levels in specific towns. In 1923, an Awka chief issued a £20 fine to a man, who in return pawned his seven-year-old daughter.[61] The debtor expected the chief to keep the child until she was old enough to marry because by virtue of the chief accepting the bride-price in lieu of the debt, the debtor would be forgiven and the father would have knowledge of her whereabouts. Rather than work according to the cultural norms that had previously assumed the child would remain with the chief until the appropriate time for marriage, the chief sold the girl outright to a third party. The child's status went from pawn to potential bride to that of a slave. In addition to debt contracting, pawning and marriage rituals, and deals gone awry, child traffickers stole children outright as well.[62]

Colonial authorities could not identify all instances of child dealing, especially because of the nature of secret associations that governed some credit agreements. They had a difficult time intervening in many moneylending arrangements because these associations held authority over social contracts. A Primitive Methodist minister, the Reverend Thomas John McKenzie, recounted his dealings in Efik Ekpe society between 1919 and 1921: "We have previously stated that in olden days the Egbo [Ekpe] and other secret societies had great power, and this was exercised at times in relation to debt. The creditor would consult Egbo and the society would fix a day [for] payment, failing fulfillment a fine of one goat and four bottles of gin would be imposed. Raids on the family of the debtor used to take place and anything was taken—cow, goats, sheep, women-folk whether they actually belonged to the man or not. A man might give one of the family to be a slave either in payment or until such time a debt was paid." Ekpe secret societies that served as a source for mutual funds and enforced debt repayment during the transatlantic slave trade continued to coerce debtors to repay moneylenders well into the 1920s.[63]

COLONIAL RESPONSE TO CHILD DEALING

It is not surprising that even while attempting to stamp out domestic slavery, the Colonial Office bent over backward to protect the institution of pawnship. Members of the administration knew why family members engaged in pawning practices. The interwar period was one of economic strife that engendered changes in the political makeup of gerontocracies, native ruling systems, and marriage systems. With regard to the League of Nations, Susan Pedersen underscores that the "effort to subject imperial rule to international control had profound effects, although they were not those that its architects and advocates expected." This is certainly the case in Southeastern Nigeria, especially for those administrators who wanted to intervene.[64] Dealing in children, sometimes one's own children, was the only way to improve one's financial fate.

The ability to seamlessly transform a moneylending contract into one of marriage became a point of contention and frustration for British officials. Owerri's district officer reported that child traffickers dealt primarily in young girls, but it was impossible to convict many of them owing to the nature of the exchange: the loan given to the debtor converted to a bride-price payment.[65] Moreover, even though some administrators understood that some girls became brides as a result of unpaid debts, they misunderstood the socioeconomic nature of the transaction: "The case of pawning female children is somewhat different, as if the debtor does not redeem his daughter within a reasonable time, she would be liable to be married by her master to the man of his choice, but only with the consent of one of the child's parents or guardians, and the marriage dowry received would be taken, or part of it, in settlement of the debt, the parents of the girl very seldom objected to the marriage, as they know that sooner or later his debt would have to be paid, and it was immaterial to him whom his daughter married, as long as he received what he considered a fair dowry fee. It must be remembered that women and female children have no say in these matters, and are only considered a man's chattels, which he can do pretty well what he likes with."[66] The resident officer, Frank Hives, misrepresented the realities of pawning practices and marriage customs. As previously noted, some girls in the 1920s were sold outright and married without their parents' consent when their parents pawned them but could not repay warrant chiefs and moneylenders. Nevertheless, in some instances a pawned girl could decide whom she married, provided that her future husband paid a bride-price that covered the debt. Parents and guardians did not simply envision these arrangements as an exchange in chattel. The British did not understand the cultural and social implications of marrying a slave.[67]

Generally, Igbo fathers had some influence over whom their daughters married and rejected marriages to certain kinds of slaves, mainly the Osu. Anthropologist Margaret M. Green noted that an Osu was dedicated to a specific shrine and lived in a segregated area as an "untouchable" because of his ritual power, devoting his time to performing rituals for the family. Even today, marriage between a person born in a non-*Osu* lineage and someone from an *Osu* lineage is often considered taboo, as it was in Owerri during the 1920s and 1930s, a fact the British failed to recognize.[68]

As early as 1914, British laws attempted to codify native marriage customs in Nigeria, effectively enabling child dealers to traffic children and avoid prosecution if they showed legal documents. Officials found that child dealers used false marriage certificates as certificates of insurance that allowed them to travel with young girls and claim that their parents had given permission for the girls to marry.[69]

Martin Chanock argues that customary law was far more dynamic than the British recognized because it involved a negotiation between stakeholders and those who had influence over a girl's life. Therefore, once the British codified the marriage law they "froze" the law in time and inhibited the possibility of personal negotiations.[70] Acknowledging that the British had little or no means to engage with local people about customary practices, some colonial officials opted to not intervene in cases where pawning directly overlapped with marriage arrangements. In fact, Mr. Butler, the district officer of Warri, advised: "It is difficult to say how the betrothal question should be dealt with and I feel inclined to recommend that no further steps be taken to make it illegal."[71]

In 1923, W. A. Ross, senior resident in Oyo Province in western Nigeria, compared the female pawn favorably to the domestic servant in England "who is placed by her mother in service where there is no one to see that the mistress does not overwork the girl and that she is properly and sufficiently fed and decently housed. This domestic is probably in a little more helpless position than the female pawn." The resident also compared pawns to pauper children in Great Britain and assured his superiors that the pawn, unlike the pauper child, is never very far from his or her family. He claimed that parents and relatives visited the child and that moneylenders permitted children to return home for holiday festivals.[72] Given the rise of Britain's middle class, where parents entrusted their daughters as domestic servants to upper-class households, it is not surprising that he used this analogy.[73] Just as officials compared slaves to serfs during the transatlantic slave trade, colonial officials often painted rosy pictures of pawning.[74]

Social standing mattered in Igbo societies, and contrary to the opinion above, Nwadinko explained that "in most cases, pawned children are treated with contempt and are looked upon as instruments to be used and discarded at will . . . [P]arental affections emanating from a family do . . . not extend to pawned children."[75] Surely the treatment of a pawn depended on the temperament of the guardian, but the various accounts herein illustrate the adverse treatment child pawns endured, making their servile status abundantly clear.

CONCLUSION

The political and economic transformation of colonialism precipitated a series of events that increased child dealing through pawnship, child marriage, and slavery. In the investigations following the League of Nations' inquiries, British authorities and other humanitarian groups discovered that the trafficking of women and children was integral to Nigeria's colonial economy. The customary practices of pawning, marriage, and slave dealing were intertwined and continued to arouse the interest of colonial authorities, missionaries, and international organizations, which were especially interested in the ways in which indigenous people incorporated children into each of these practices. However, as the League of Nations pressed colonial officials to investigate and prohibit child pawning practices that permitted young girls and women to be married against their will, they met marked resistance. Officials acknowledged that child dealers used complex networks and transport routes, making the traffic in children and women difficult to identify and end in Southeastern Nigeria.[76]

At the conclusion of their investigations, colonial administrators found that parents and guardians had various motivations for pawning children, which generated some confusion about the nature and conditions of the practice. Nevertheless, the investigation did find that, among other reasons, parents often pawned children to open opportunities for their remaining children, which shows that the value of children and their labor was connected to the most basic of economic arrangements.[77] Specifically, these case studies indicate that the socioeconomic value of a child and his or her labor defines and is defined by the surrounding economic, cultural, and political environment.

Colonial officials, missionaries, and members of the League of Nations each had different motivations for trying to change marriage customs in the southeast. The League's members were concerned with what seemed to be the child's lack of agency in choosing when and whom to marry. In particular, they wanted to ensure that every girl and woman who was married had given her consent.[78] The issue of consent would become a main focus throughout colonial Africa as women increasingly contested marriages and sought out divorce, claiming that they had never given consent, even if it had been given.[79] Missionaries wanted to transform marriage practices because they hoped to increase Christian conversion and reduce the sacri-political power that elder men held over younger men. They denounced polygyny and upheld what they believed to be the sanctity of monogamous, companionate relationships. Even so, there was no easy way of transforming indigenous marriage practices as they related to the pawning of girls.

As hard as League members and humanitarian groups worked, little was done by the Colonial Office to end child dealing during the 1920s, especially as it related to child marriages. The limited understanding of Nigerian customs and the introduction of onerous tax payments undermined any attempt to stop child dealing.[80] In an unexpected turn, frustrated about how such pressure affected children's well-being, the women of Southeastern Nigeria became a vocal constituency against mounting fiscal burdens. Consequently, by the end of the second decade of the twentieth century, a new fervor arose from the least anticipated quarter when Nigerian mothers demanded that their voices be heard. And the West listened.

CHAPTER 4
The *1929* Ogu Umunwaanyi *(Women's War)*

The number of those killed in rioting in Southeast Nigeria, British West Africa, has now grown to at least forty-three women and one man. The exact cause of the riots has not been definitely ascertained.

—New York Times, *December 24, 1929*

In 1929, Southeastern Nigeria erupted in a violent insurrection led by thousands of militant women. The event so challenged assumptions about African women's lack of political sophistication that for the past fifty years scholars have been investigating the deep-seated causes of what Igbo women entitled the Ogu Umunwaanyi ("women's war") and what others erroneously called the "Aba Riot."[1] Fortunately, we have access to the voices of those women who gave eloquent testimony in the subsequent commission summoned to examine the Ogu Umunwaanyi.[2] In reading the testimonies, it is immediately evident that the personal accounts provided during the hearings underscore the reality that women from all the major ethnic groups in Southeastern Nigeria experienced economic hardships amid the political disorder unleashed by colonial policies in the first two decades of the twentieth century.[3]

Although the idea that African women could conceptualize grievances and organize a response that threatened the local foundations of the entire colonial project was unimaginable, the women voiced their concerns through the performance of their protest and, even more clearly, in the public hearings of the investigative commission that followed. At the top of their list of complaints was their suffering at the hands of the corrupt warrant chief system and the economic crisis of 1929. Their formidable remonstration forced a total reorganization of the warrant chief system, though it did not cause the colonial state to rethink its assumptions about the alleged political naïveté of Igbo and other African women.[4]

The revolt, perhaps the most famous and extensively examined example of African women's political activism, is usually attributed to the rumor of the then imminent taxation of women. This chapter examines women's involvement in the 1929 Women's War as a way to get a glimpse of the disruption that women experienced as a result of the economic and political transformations that characterized the opening decades of the twentieth century. Moreover, we can identify how the breakdown of women's political power and their decreasing economic solvency threated their children's well-being and brought about social upheaval.

By the conclusion of the Aba Commission of Inquiry (1930), it was clear that women rose up against the warrant chiefs, court clerks, court messengers, tax collectors, and those who defrauded them in their trade dealings, causing the erosion of their wealth and political status in society.[5] The testimony reveals that the economic conditions and the fines assessed by native courts resulted in child pawning, child stealing, and dubious court cases that involved nefarious child marriage arrangements and coerced or stolen bride-price payments. In putting together the 1930 testimony, including oral histories and colonial documents, we acquire a critical portrayal of what women and children experienced. Moreover, the simple and often-made argument that attempts to describe tensions in African colonies, that is, between Africans and Europeans, does not suffice. An array of reasons caused the social and political dislocation suffered by women.

That women participated in the 1929 uprising because their children had succumbed to financial stress brought on by colonialism is one aspect of the motivation for the war that scholars have yet to fully explore. Therefore, examining the inquiry testimony illuminates the historical connection between the internal slave trade, women's collective protests, and child trafficking. As mentioned in previous chapters, the domestic slave trade in Nigeria increased with the decline of the transatlantic slave trade, which subsequently affected the trade in children during the early twentieth century. One of the most salient examples comes from testimony given by a woman named Nwachi, who expressed that should women be taxed in addition to men and boys, they "would have no children left." She explained that her people, the impoverished Nguru, had to borrow money to pay taxes, lest they be subject to imprisonment and further abuse by the warrant chiefs. Noting the distinct continuities between the end of the transatlantic trade and the contemporary conditions under British rule, Nwachi lamented: "In the old days there were tribal fights, and men carried on slave dealing, but since the advent of Government we have been told to stop these old customs. Since the introduction of taxation, people have sometimes gone to bed, and their children have been stolen, owing to poverty. We want to make a report about the children who were stolen. We make reports to Chiefs, but if it is a girl who is stolen it takes nearly all the money that would be paid for her dowry to trace her. If your child is stolen, in the first place the Chief would make no effort to get it back, and if the parents found out where the child was and the culprits were arrested, they would pay money to the Chiefs not to punish them, and in the end there would be no justice at all. The Chiefs are always harsh to us."[6] This statement clearly illustrates the link between the local and colonial economies and the resulting consequences for children. The advent of colonialism transformed child dealing as colonial labor, moneylending, and governance policies caused new forms of servile labor to develop. The movement of children, through which individuals acquired funds to pay their court fines and taxes, became a point of contention, especially when warrant chiefs demanded the payment of erroneous fines and acted as moneylenders.[7] And while the analysis herein is focused on the use of children for monetary gain as a method to avoid colonial penalties, it is worth reviewing the ways in which the Women's War has been treated by other scholars and why it is still written about today.

FIFTY YEARS OF WOMEN'S WAR SCHOLARSHIP

Formal scholarship on the women's uprising began with British historian Margery Perham's recognition of the women's "vigor and solidarity" and anthropologist Sylvia Leith-Ross, who argued that women's independence led them to take matters into their own hands when they encountered economic hardship during the late 1920s. Leith-Ross, one of the first anthropologists, recognized that Igbo women played a major role in the fiscal development of Nigeria and that the newly established native court system and the warrant chiefs negatively affected women's trade activities. This connection seems to have gone unnoticed by the colonial authorities before 1929. The British, drawing on their own patriarchal notions of women's political backwardness, lacked an in-depth understanding of women's rights in the southeast and based their assumptions on previous knowledge they had about women in Islamic societies in northern Nigeria.[8]

Judith Van Allen, then a graduate student in political science at the University of California at Berkeley, came across a reference to the Women's War and in 1972 penned the renowned article "'Sitting on a Man': Colonialism and the Lost Political Institutions of Igbo Women." This article immediately captured the interest of feminist scholars. Van Allen's scholarly revision of previous analyses by Leith-Ross and Perham claimed that women who participated in the 1929 Women's War transformed a practice sometimes used in their polygamous society to force men to treat all wives equally. She argued that women who participated in the 1929 Women's War used an accepted "traditional" process called "sitting on a man" or "make war on a man" through which they expressed their discontent with an individual man who they felt had violated social norms or traditions regarding women.[9]

Subsequently, anthropologist Caroline Ifeka-Moller disagreed with Van Allen's assessment and argued that "sitting on a man," a far cry from what actually happened in the war, needed further examination. The women who "destroyed property, looted factories, dressed in the garb of war, sang of death and blood, gestured most obscenely and became spirit obsessed on occasion" behaved more militantly than those who engaged in the traditional method of "sitting on a man."[10] Ifeka-Moller viewed "sitting on a man," as a domestic practice that equalized the relations between the sexes, whereas Van Allen highlighted the political aspects of the Women's War as a case of African feminism.[11] Both scholars recognized that women in Southeastern Nigeria saw a deterioration of their traditional political institutions after the onset of the new political regime in which colonial authorities largely marginalized women in deference to men. Women felt disenfranchised by newly implemented colonial laws, especially the appointment of non-customary warrant chiefs and the decline in income caused by decreasing palm product prices—the women's major source of income.

Ten years after Van Allen's intervention, anthropologist and dance historian Judith Lynne Hanna offered an examination of "dance-play" as an integral part of the Women's War. Hanna explains that important life moments, such as "birth, death, harvest, markets, visiting dignitaries, and religious celebrations," incorporated singing and dancing while bringing people together. Dance-play, a ritual process whereby conflicting parties sought resolution, centered opposing parties' efforts on finding a resolution. Alternatively, in instances where dance-play did not peacefully mediate conflict, women "violently waged war," as seen in the 1929 protest.[12]

Whether offered as a central theme or as a limited analysis in published texts, Women's War scholarship expanded as the focus on women's and gender histories and feminist studies developed in tandem with Nigerian history. Notable among these books is the scholarship by Harry A. Gailey, A. E. Afigbo, Elizabeth Isichei, Nina Mba, Ekwerre Otu Akpan and Violetta L. Ekpo, Ifi Amadiume, and Gloria Chuko.[13]

With each new examination of the Women's War, scholars continue to highlight the movement's importance. For example, the work by Marc Matera, Misty L. Bastian, and Susan Kingsley Kent prioritizes the recognition and close anthropological examination of precolonial Igbo lifeways, outlines how the influx of Europeans challenged and changed cultural norms, and documents the women's physical and intellectual response to those changes. This assessment is, however, in conflict with that of Gailey, who suggests that "women were in no position to analyze these events philosophically" and claims that the women believed that the British conspired "to impoverish them."[14] His analysis of the Ibibio and Igbo women's inability to intellectualize their financial disfranchisement leaves much to be refuted. In any case, the uprising continues to garner attention to the extent that Adam Paddock and the celebrated Nigerian scholar Toyin Falola took on the task of publishing a collection that consists of archival materials, pedagogical tools, and a description of the women's movement that undoubtedly serves as an excellent resource in the classroom in 2011.[15]

More recently, the *Journal of West African History*'s fall 2017 issue dedicated six out of its twenty articles to Van Allen's "Sitting on a Man" and its significant influence on Igbo history. And even with the growing scholarship, Judith A. Byfield argues that "the analysis of tax protests during the colonial period must move beyond resistance for these protests also provide insights into African conceptualizations of taxation."[16] When the colonial government moved forward in 1921 with census taking for the purpose of taxation, it encountered stern opposition. Resistant to census taking, Igbo believed that counting men, women, and especially children was taboo and would result in "misfortune and even death." In addition, for mothers who struggled to pay their husbands' and sons' taxes, and for entire communities wherein poor people lost children to disreputable warrant chiefs and moneylenders, it is no wonder that women fought against the threat of a woman tax. Therefore, it is essential that we analyze the use of children as an economic strategy for personal and political survival in the colony.[17]

The articles, book chapters, and other writings dedicated to the war are numerous, but the intent of this chapter is not to delineate the uprising events in intricate detail. Rather, I offer a brief look at the years leading up to 1929 and to give a general overview of the women's movement and its importance. Most significant, this chapter will show how the events of 1929 can be used as a lens through which we examine how the social economy of children factors into the abuses brought forth by the native courts, warrant chiefs, and others as they dealt with the devastating effects of the economic downturn.

FACTORS LEADING TO THE WAR

The women of Igboland practiced long-standing traditions whereby they demonstrated against mistreatment and social ills. In the years preceding the 1929 movement, women created and practiced songs and dances at meetings that only women attended. In 1925, the women participated in the Nwaobiala (Dancing Women's movement) as a way to express their opposition to economic and political changes born by colonial rule. They sang and danced while sweeping public spaces to demonstrate their desire to cleanse their environment from negative influences. They called this practice "making *egwu*." As they danced, they sang their grievances while traveling the pathways that led townspeople to the marketplace. Along the way, women unfamiliar with the songs and dances spontaneously joined in and sometimes accompanied the original dancers when they moved to demonstrate at the warrant chiefs' compounds, also expressing displeasure with the chiefs' abuses. For several weeks the women traveled from town to town singing their dissatisfaction and soliciting support. They began their demonstration at Okigwe (also known as Okigwi) in the center of the Palm Belt, moved between the Okigwe and Bende Divisions, and eventually arrived in Umuahia, located along the rail lines. We now know the women chose this route to condemn the influx of people and goods that symbolized westernization.[18] These towns were major commercial centers and core collection and sale points for slaves and pawns. The women's public performances revealed the deep frustration they experienced with the literal and figurative pollution in the "compounds and markets."[19]

Igbo mothers, wives, and daughters had many complaints. In particular, fertility and childbearing issues concerned the women. They feared declining fertility rates and unsuccessful pregnancies. Bearing a dead baby or dying during birth represented the wrath of Ala/Ani (earth and fertility deity).[20] In addition, the colonial state disrupted their domestic spheres by interfering with the customary division of labor based on gender. They were particularly concerned that administrators had imposed their "Western conceptions of state, family, and gender roles on the Igbo—notions that were prejudiced against women."[21] They also protested the incursion of men into their space and did not want men to operate in the marketplace. Other concerns included the chiefs' exploitation of men, especially poor men involved in litigation, and the demonetization of native currencies, with women arguing that bride-prices should be paid in cowries, a currency in which women invested.[22] These were only some of their concerns.

The women also considered new forms of labor and governance, along with Nigeria's growing global engagement, as main causes for distress. Misty L. Bastian explains that women believed "the roads built by the colonialists with the labor of the colonized people 'go missing,' through death, servitude, or complete alienation from Igbo values; they did not bring people together for marriage or trade, as the women's pathways did." Worse, people who used these new roads returned to their towns, bringing a host of afflictions. Some of their anxiety can be attributed to the spread of the Spanish influenza (1918–20), which killed 512,000 Nigerians overall and 250,000 in the southern provinces alone. As the pandemic killed so many young and otherwise healthy people, the Igbo believed that the illness was a "by-product of colonial modernity." The chief sanitation officer found that the disease in fact spread because of modern transportation, mainly the railways.[23] While the 1925 protest focused on returning to core Igbo values, sanitation, fertility, and maintaining long-standing gendered norms, the 1929 uprising focused more heavily on the weak economy, taxation, warrant chief abuses, and loss of children through child stealing and pawning.

Concerns about warrant chiefs, women's declining political and economic solvency, and the fear that direct taxation would extend to women are generally noted as the main reasons for women's participation in the 1929 uprising. Women's income from trade decreased during the late 1920s.[24] For example, palm kernel revenues fell 33 percent between 1911-13 and 1929. Male encroachment on their trade activities and the subsequent loss in income contributed to the women's distress.[25] The warrant chiefs' activities as judges and tax collectors brought them into conflict with increasingly impoverished women. Initially, Frederick Lugard instituted taxes on all Nigerians except for those in the southeast in 1916, where he rightly anticipated objections and lacked sufficient troops to enforce the tax plan. Lord Harcourt, governor of the southern provinces, thought it best to wait until his troop strength increased before trying to collect local taxes; in 1926, colonial authorities decided to commission the warrant chiefs to collect taxes from men in the southeast.[26]

In 1927, the British government began the process of increasing government revenues by having Nigerian authorities, mainly warrant chiefs, carry out a census of the property that belonged to adult males in Owerri and Calabar Provinces.[27] In 1927 and 1928, colonial representatives traveled throughout all of the southeast to persuade warrant chiefs that the new tax policy would provide the resources to pay Nigerians to work on public projects rather than depending on forced labor, a practice British antislavery groups had championed to end. Colonial officials, eager to make this change, believed that the Igbo "would accept the alternative with little or no resistance." However, an Igbo elder refuted this idea and argued: "We prefer strong boys being made to work on the roads to paying tax. We want tax abolished."[28] This statement expresses the expectation that elders in the community held the power to appropriate the labor of young males. It also shows that the indigenous population felt that paying tax to a colonial government was unacceptable, and the imposition of direct taxation triggered resistance. Frederick Cooper explains that "caught between political and ideological limitations on the use of coercion and their limited ability to do without it—trying to hitch their authority to the continued existence and legitimacy of African modes of authority—colonial officials could not directly pose the labor question."[29] As much as the Igbo detested compulsory labor policies, the elders preferred them to paying tax and the British were content to benefit from both.

Soon after the government took account of men's possessions, including animals and other property, officials demanded tax payments. When the 1927 census began, British authorities increased the number of police and colonial troops at their disposal. By 1928, families had already begun to pawn children at increasing rates to pay the new taxes placed on men.[30] Predictably, in the same year, the resident of Calabar feared backlash to the new policy because the people of Calabar did not want to endure further financial hardship brought on by taxation.

THE WAR

In 1929 the Colonial Office commissioned a census of women, children, and livestock, in addition to men. The events that followed in the Calabar and Owerri Provinces are detailed in the testimony of 486 witnesses, including 103 women, during the Aba Commission of Inquiry (February 7, 1930, to March 10, 1930). The testimonies, oral histories, and archival documents highlight the prevalence of child pawning, child stealing, and chiefs' abuses relating to court cases, and child marriage and bride-price payments. Even though most scholars point to loss of income, increased import prices, and warrant chief abuses, it is clear that women touted children's welfare as the reason they sought to shed light on child pawning and stealing practices. A deeper look into the testimony reveals that at the core of women's private and public domestic spheres was coming undone, which implicitly decreased their power within and outside the home. Above all else, bearing children legitimated marriages, provided comfort and care for parents in their old age, and secured women's identities as fully functioning members of society.

On November 23, 1929, Warrant Chief Okugo Ekuma Okezie instructed Mark Emeruwa, a schoolteacher, to count the number of men, women, children, and animals in each compound in the town of Oloko.[31] When he arrived at a local compound of a woman called Nwanyeruwa, Emeruwa explained that he intended to count all her family's belongings.[32] Nwanyeruwa immediately expressed outrage that he had come to conduct the census. It was not customary to count the belongings of Igbo women, and she later testified that "I was in my house pounding palm nuts in the morning. I was then squeezing oil. He [Emeruwa] asked me to count my goats, sheep and people. I turned around and looked at him. I said: 'Are you still coming last year my son's wife died [sic]. What am I to count? I have been mourning for the death of that woman. Was your mother counted?' He held me by the throat. One's life depends on her throat. With my two hands covered with oil I held him also by the throat. I raised an alarm, calling a woman . . . I asked her to raise an alarm as I did not know what I had done. In the meantime Emeruwa ran away. As he ran away I followed him shouting."[33] In Owerri Province, a series of events followed this initial encounter. The day after the incident, a group of women traveled to the local mission house to ask Emeruwa why he wanted to count women. He suggested that they raise their questions with Warrant Chief Okugo. When they approached the chief's compound, they placed leaves on the ground, insulted him, and demanded that he relinquish his warrant cap. The women were clearly upset by the planned census. On November 25, nine women accused Chief Okugo of beating them with sticks, and on November 26, the protesting women rushed the Bende District Office. The protests continued, and on December 2, ten thousand women gathered at Bende to demand the conviction of Chief Okugo for his assaults on the nine women, and on December 4 a native court heeded their demand. Women continued their uprisings despite their success in having Chief

Okugo's warrant cap removed, which ultimately stripped him of power. Subsequently, over a series of days and weeks, the protests expanded to other locations, drawing in hundreds of new recruits.[34]

Dissatisfied with economic conditions brought on by colonialism, other women joined the protest. By December 6, the news of the census had reached the Aba Division of the Owerri Province, the location of a large, important market town. Women met in the village of Amapu in the Owerrinta Native Court area two days later. Throughout the region, women sacked courthouses and European factories, destroyed documents, freed prisoners, and blocked trains. The protest continued, and within days, three to four thousand women convened in the district of Owerrinta, where they stoned the state magistrate's home and looted three factories on December 11. One day later at Imo River, the women used similar tactics and burned down native courts, after which women's activities against the government multiplied. From December 15 to December 28, they continued to meet in Bende, Aba, and Owerri. Over twenty-five hundred women carried sticks and palm fronds, symbols of the women's protest, calling for the removal of warrant chiefs. The women continued to loot the property of native court members and demanded that their grievances be heard.[35]

When women protested in the districts located in Calabar Province on December 14, machine gun platoons had confronted the thousands of women in the village of Ikot Ekpene. A government intermediary briefly succeeded in pacifying the group, but the protest escalated soon after. In other villages, particularly at Utu Etim Ekpo and Utu Etim Abak, women faced severe repression when they burned numerous court buildings and trading houses and destroyed local markets. Unrestrained authorities opened fire and killed up to nine unarmed women, citing the Ordinance of the Magistrate that permitted the colonial government "to do all things necessary for preventing riots."[36]

The protest quickly spread to the eastern Delta, and in the early morning of December 16, over two thousand women convened at Opobo's district office. They chanted and shouted their grievances. They smeared their faces with red and yellow clay and dressed themselves in palm and fern leaves. Women carried sticks as they marched along singing, "*Ihe putra anyinge me*," (Whatever comes, we will face it). As representatives of Opobo Town, Bonny, Andoni, and Kwa, the women demanded that the district officer prepare and distribute a document that, among other things, promised not to tax women. Impatient, they began to pound their pestles and sticks on a fence. Lieutenant Hill, who was with the District Officer, panicked and ordered his soldiers to shoot the protesting women. Madam Adiaha Edem was the first shot. In the end, colonial authorities acknowledged twenty-six deaths, whereas local people claimed five hundred.[37]

The Commission of Inquiry testimonies reveal protest leaders' motivations: The chairman asked a local woman, Nwugo Enyidie, to explain "why they danced all night for a matter like that?" She responded, "We danced like that for some people who have wronged us. Okugo brought about all this trouble, and so we sang and danced. We sang: 'Who ordered this thing? Who ordered that we should pay tax?'"[38] While in Okigwe, women signaled that "they were at war with the government" by marking themselves with black chalk and ashes, symbolizing their "unbearable economic reality."[39]

The Women's War represented a fight against the loss of land, taxation of women, postwar economic hardship, oppression by warrant chiefs and court clerks, and the continued loss of children to pawnship and trafficking. At the hearing, some colonial officials described the burden that taxation placed on families already struggling with inflation and the postwar depression. Both colonial officers and Nigerian witnesses testified that in Southeastern Nigeria taxation exacerbated kidnapping and pawning children in the late 1920s. One witness lamented, "We are dependent on men;

we have no money to maintain our children, how much more can we afford to pay tax?" As such, the prominent Archdeacon George Thomas Basden, of the Church Missionary Society, explained why the families could not pay the taxes: "In some bush places there is very little money at all. They live on the land, and they do not work [for wages], as cash is limited. In many cases in order to raise the cash for the tax, they have had to borrow; none of them can pay back and they pawn their children in order to pay their debts."[40] As children vanished, leaving no way to redeem them, women lost all trust in the warrant chief system. They desperately needed the help of the colonial administration to check warrant chief abuses. Abraham Okolo of Amoriji, Nike (Enugu), recalls how the Igbo and Ibibio responded to direct taxation during the late 1920s and early 1930s:

> *We were paying three shillings or three dollars in modern language. Money was hard to get. Somebody who has no such money will have worked for four pence a day and paying three shillings in a year. If people don't pay tax they will harass him. Someone who is poor will now pawn the child. They were seeing the court messenger as the colonial master. He will use his staff and yell, "Stop! Stop! Stop!" If you don't pay the tax they will beat you like a beast. Then somebody who was poor would run to his neighbor and ask him to lend him three shillings to avoid them coming to his compound or destroy his belongings. The court class will come to your house and make an announcement . . . All villagers will assemble at the village square. Clerk will come and talk to them. The chief and servants will also be there. They will call roll. Those who didn't pay they will carry the person to court in Aba. When the clerk finishes the job in that community the community will contribute yams for him. The community will also give him a goat, then they will select people from the community to carry the yams to his own town. People will be selected to carry goods*

and yams to his house. You don't doubt the court clerk because he can send you to jail. Then the warrant chief would give an order that nobody could challenge him. He will just say he will send you to prison.[41]

Avoiding penalties and public humiliation created a communal response in some instances where fellow villagers helped relieve the debtor's burden. On other occasions, if someone could not evade the tax collectors, they had to find a way of securing the funds. The fear of public prosecution was enough to provoke increasing numbers of people to seek out loans. Evidence shows that those who could not secure a loan from a friend or family member would approach a known moneylender and suffer the egregious interest rates.

As Nigerians struggled to pay taxes, they borrowed as a last resort, even when exorbitant interest caused further financial stress. For example, Olenga of Umuakpara in Aba claimed that she borrowed money from Nkwerre moneylenders, a group known for slaving, who many described as "oppressors" because they mercilessly compounded interest on loans.[42] Other women claimed that they borrowed money from their *esusu* subscriptions (rotating credit associations) and paid interest at 100 percent. For instance, Ejiohu of Owerrinta borrowed twelve shillings to help her husband with his taxes and promised to pay an additional twelve shillings in interest. In the worst of cases, one colonial official claimed that he had witnessed cases where people paid 200 percent in interest.[43] Pawning oneself or a child had the potential to alleviate borrowers of the additional financial burden because the pawn's labor would pay the interest on the loan.

The manner in which parents pawned and sold children varied. Okolo claims that Nike people always gave a female rather than male in pawn. If a man did not have a female child to lend, then he would pawn himself and farm the lender's land. Desperate taxpayers might even sell a child. Chief Ugwuefi Reuben recalled stories from his childhood, revealing that selling children was rampant during the 1920s and 1930s: because of "financial problems—because of dickheadness among children—you sell them."[44] In general, the people of Igboland believed that pawning children with character "defects" to avoid the challenge of trying to correct them was an acceptable solution. Moreover, doing so in a time when taxation became more onerous proved beneficial. Nevertheless, pawned children, regardless of their personal characteristics, experienced a new set of circumstances during the 1920s.

Insightful oral testimonies from Enugu residents provide a glimpse into the customs shared by Igbos. Some accounts suggest that child pawns went to live with chiefs, who as "strong men," mainly men of wealth and status, could protect them. Some parents pawned children to European officials in lieu of tax payments, and in such a case one resident claimed that colonial officials treated these children "as beasts of burden," using them to carry heavy loads ranging from building materials to bicycles. Another claimed that colonial staff made children carry the "white man . . . on the[ir] shoulder[s]," causing the deaths of some child pawns due to the oppressive weight.[45] Similarly, Anthony Nwadinko, born in Owerri in 1914, remembers that as a young man his parents told cautionary tales about the children from his village who had been given to wealthy men in lieu of loan payments. Severe abuse provoked early death in some, who perished before the loan was paid.[46]

Taking into consideration the legacy of the transatlantic slave trade and the measures whereby forced labor continued as a custom in Nigeria in its aftermath, it is not surprising that some children suffered abuse by both Nigerians and the British. Peter Kirby argues that it is necessary to "explore the extent to which violence against children arose from specific workplace factors or was indicative of broader customs and practices." His argument largely emphasizes

that cultural norms that normalized violent behaviors created conditions within which children suffered physical abuse.[47] In this
context, the child's dislocation from his or her kin and their associated subordinate status as pawns created the environment in which
others abused children's bodies. A child's death at the hands of a
moneylender (or another guardian) is what I describe as "corporeal
depreciation," a process whereby the risk of a child's death under
strenuous labor circumstances outweighs the risk of loss in potential
labor, income, profit, etc. Parents had to consider the cost-benefit
analysis when deciding whether to pawn a child.

When parents pawned children, they could not prevent moneylenders from selling them into slavery. Colonial records suggest that
the Abajas and the Nkanus (Enugu's Udi Division), two clans with
deep historical roots in the slave trade as both victims and slavers,
used the "dowry" system to obtain girl pawns to avoid criminal conviction.[48] Chief Anthony Chibueze Agubaram of Calabar explained
that when cash was in particularly short supply, the enslavement
of child pawns increased to the extent that the people of Calabar
who had suffered the loss of a child labeled moneylenders "devil
merchants."[49] Without significant appreciation for the nuance of
pawning customs, Mr. T. B. Dew, district officer of Enugu, claimed
that the majority of child pawns were already classified as "unfree"
at birth; however, surely it was difficult for Dew to prove such a
claim. Nevertheless, in instances where children had been stolen
or sold into slavery, colonial authorities observed that prosecuting
offenders was particularly difficult because warrant chiefs refused
to assist their efforts.[50]

Testimonies accounted for numerous warrant chief abuses. A
woman, Igbeauku from Nchara, Oloko, complained that if someone took a debt case to court, the chief would take £3 in addition
to the 15s summons fee. A male witness described these actions as
"extortion" against the women. Akulechula of Obowo claimed that
she heard one chief claim that he had "twelve bags of money"—an

inordinate sum for a chief to own. In fact, testimony reveals that bribery ruled court decisions, and whoever could offer the chief the largest sum won the case. Chiefs had a variety of other methods to extort money from their constituents. A reoccurring complaint during the inquiry highlights concerns about child stealing. District Officer Fergus Ferguson of Bamenda testified that he had heard rumors that if taxation continued, "there would be more child stealing and more crop stealing than formerly." Once a child disappeared, a parent had to pay a prohibitive £15 to £20 to a warrant chief to gain assistance.[51] Left in an untenable position, how could parents afford the fee when they could not afford to pay taxes? Moreover, if authorities caught the kidnappers, they could easily bribe the warrant chiefs to avoid prosecution.

The warrant chiefs also used the native courts to interfere in marriage and divorce cases that involved money. Ahudi, a woman from Nsidimo, explained that "women are very much annoyed. If I had a case with another in the Native Court, that case would not be heard until I kept borrowing money, about £10 in all. If I do not borrow the money, the case would be kept waiting for six months That is what chiefs do. If I had a daughter and a chief came to me to say he wanted to marry my daughter, he would only pay £5. He would not complete the proper dowry."[52] Prior to the 1920s, a man in Amorji-Nike, Enugu, could pawn his daughter to a rich man and repay the loan when the girl decided to marry. The female pawn's future groom would then pay the bride-price to the moneylender, not the father.

As witnesses testified about the various warrant chief abuses, they raised the issue of marriage and bride-prices. Eredo of Inyishi, Enugu, lamented that warrant chiefs divided bride-price payments among themselves rather than allowing the girl's family to enjoy the full payment. In other cases, men paid equal amounts of the bride-price to the girl's parents and the local chief. Given that many men performed extra work to raise funds for such payments, giving additional sums to the warrant chiefs became an untenable burden.

CHAPTER 4

Though he did not believe the allegations, Ferguson testified that chiefs had been accused of failing to pay proper bride-prices themselves, marrying their wives for "free." One witness attributed the chiefs' ability to obtain "20 or 25 or 100" wives to the practice of stealing refunded bride-prices.[53] This behavior is significant because the offering of a bride-price signified the worth of the daughter and represented the loss of her labor when she left her natal home. The breakdown of cultural norms had real consequences for those whose daughters were taken by warrant chiefs. Another witness, China, explained that "in the end there would be no justice at all. The chiefs are always harsh to us."[54]

While Nigerians faced economic hardships that tore at their families, British colonial officials treated child pawning in an ambiguous manner during the first quarter of the twentieth century. In 1923, one colonial authority acknowledged that the issue of child pawning in Southern Nigeria had been investigated once under Sir Walter Egerton and again under Lord Lugard. Under Egerton, officials decided to postpone any forceful action against pawning, and Lugard did not want any additional distractions in the face of the First World War.[55] Moreover, in December 1924, Governor Hugh Clifford (1919–25) defended pawnship as a practice that was not "vicious or liable to abuse . . . that it did not entail any prolonged infringement of the personal liberty of the pawn . . . that it was a very essential feature of the fiscal, economic and social system." Abolishing pawning altogether would "plunge innumerable families into financial embarrassment."[56] Administrators understood that pawning was essential to economic and social systems; what they may not have realized is the emotive connection between parents and the pawned children who were lost to nefarious lenders. The continual loss of children provoked the women to rise up.

By the 1930 Commission of Inquiry, Alan Lorimer Weir, district officer of Okigwe, conceded in testimony that women touted taxation as "one of their planks in their platform, the other was the high price of produce, and another was the iniquities of their warrant chiefs." Women cited these issues in conjunction with their concern about the welfare of their children.[57] Nigerian mothers protested in the war because indigenous forms of receiving loans had failed to protect their children. As a matter of law, the British attempted to punish those who took part in child selling, but depending on warrant chiefs made this difficult because they refused to help prosecute those who pawned children and often themselves received children as pawns in lieu of loans. It is reasonable to deduce warrant chiefs did not readily prosecute individuals for child pawning when the colonial tax structure demanded that parents raise funds. These actions rendered significant consequences.

Women rebelled when indigenous men, local leaders, and European administrators infringed on their customary rights or when they were denied certain privileges. At times, women employed European tropes to increase access to resources, manipulated colonial courts to end unwanted marriages, protested unbearable taxation policies, and fought to maintain or reclaim land that had been stolen from their families. African women also confounded Europeans by adhering to or reshaping gender norms not easily understood by non-Africans. Simply put, African women befuddled European men.

Historians of the 1929 Women's War rarely look to novels to seek a better understanding of the women's movement. T. Obinkaram Echewa's novel *I Saw the Sky Catch Fire* tells the story of a young boy who on the eve of his departure from Nigeria to attend university in the United States is held captive by his grandmother's stories. Nne-nne, Ajuziogu's grandmother, recounted the details of the Women's War. She described how women moved from one village to another, lurking in the bushes, spreading the news that women had been shot and killed over disputes about taxation. The tumultuous exchanges between the women, African soldiers, and

British officials birthed an unstoppable expression of frustration. This work of fiction strays little from documented historical events relating to the Woman's War. Published in 1993, the novel enters into the historiography without reference to formal historical publications about the war. Nevertheless, the account is historically based. The main protagonists are Chief Alaribe (Warrant Chief Okugo Ekuma Okezie); Sam-el (Mark Emeruwa, the schoolteacher); and Akpa-Ego (Nwanyeruwa).[59] My interest in the novel led me to interview the author.

During the interview with Dr. Obi (his preferred title), I asked what had led him to write about the Woman's War. His answer had several components. He explained that as a child, he lived in the Ngwa area in Southeastern Nigeria (the same area that Susan Martin conducted her research in for *Palm Oil and Protest*.) Geographic proximity and shared history linked his village to Chief Okugu's, which was located less than eight miles away. He was not born until several years after the Women's War but relayed the everlasting impression the women's movement had on his village. All major natural disasters, social and political events, significant historical moments, and births were described in reference to the 1929 Woman's War. He called the war "a time marker."[60] Neither his mother nor his grandmother participated in the movement, but his grandmother's acquaintances did. It was not uncommon to hear the women in his household and throughout the community detail the events of the war in casual conversation.

The production of literary fiction is one method by which scholars and other writers can push back against particular historical interpretations. Dr. Obi claimed that memory, "the most treasured possession," is the best archive and that storytelling is a significant way to make history come alive. He refuted the notion that the production of fiction should be disregarded as substandard histories or irrelevant to ethnic studies, that is, Igbo studies. His conviction is best summarized by his claim that "a fiction writer is more important than the economist."[61] Perhaps he meant that understanding history through storytelling is a meaningful and thought-provoking experience that stirs the imagination more than studying in scientifically ordered academic paradigms. Ultimately, the vivid details of his childhood memory, coupled with his desire to produce a history about his own people, gave birth to *I Saw the Sky Catch Fire.*

The development of feminist studies and conversations with his daughter serve as two significant factors that led Dr. Obi to write the novel. He claimed that by the late 1980s he had observed feminism creating "artificialities" and "false categories" for African women. With what seemed like sheer annoyance, he proclaimed, "*The Vagina Monologues* ain't nothing, just sheer bawdiness, compared to the Igbo crotch dance!" He spoke about the importance of motherhood and described how women performed the crotch dance in groups, raising their arms, swinging them down, and slapping their crotches. This birth ceremony, even if seemingly bawdy, had spiritual and social importance. He recounted that women became even more bawdy with age, and often those depicted in historical accounts of the Women's War are said to have flaunted their naked bodies and rubbed up against the leaders they were protesting. He conceded that he had never heard of Judith Van Allen, Caroline Ifeka-Moller, Judith Hanna, and others involved in the overall debate about the Women's War but claimed that, whatever it meant to be a feminist in the United States, feminism had nothing to do with the Women's War in Nigeria. He exclaimed that "Igbo women went to war. This was an actual war, not an intellectual debate."[62]

All too often, we as scholars attempt to find the defining reason "why" the women revolted. Was it taxes, the faltering economy, or the like? Dr. Obi reasoned that the basis of such questions is faulty because *one* definitive reason does not exist. Just like the climax of a novel, a multilayered trajectory led up to the Women's War. The social hierarchies had been turned upside down. People who originated from lands with less fertile soil and had once been looked down upon as travelers became wealthy traders. Women reacted to the social inversion that had occurred. He went on to explain that "the women had had enough, and like an earthquake, they linked themselves to the spiritual and they heaved." The ripple effect of the uprising shook all that existed in the colonial order.[63]

The issue of donning warrants upon nontraditional leaders came to the fore, and Dr. Obi explained that the natural leaders hesitated to claim their rightful place under colonialism owing to their inherent coyness, as communicating in parables was very common among Igbos. Dr. Obi noted that "Igbos did not offer information in a straightforward manner, but they liked to be found out."[64] This is one of the reasons why the colonial administration entered into hasty contracts with illegitimate rulers, men who claimed ruling status (without much immediate objection from rightful leaders) and proceeded to abuse Igbos and others, resulting in the violent uprising.

The novel addresses some of the questions that scholars still ask today, one of them being, "Were men the *real* leaders of the revolt?" During the inquiry, women were asked if men were the true leaders of the protest, but women denied this allegation. The novel reads, "Everywhere women. Not many men. The men I saw were standing in groups and shaking their heads at things they did not seem to believe." When I asked Dr. Obi about the accusation that the men were the ones behind the scenes pulling strings, he laughed, saying, "The observer finds whatever he needs." The administration wanted to believe that men were responsible for this social outburst, but the claim is untrue.[65]

The novel referenced various colonial laws, such as the Riot Act and the bill that required approval for public assemblies or processions. The latter states: "Any person who is desirous of convening or collecting any assembly or of tormenting any procession in any public road or place of public resort shall first make the application for a license to a superior police officer, and if such superior police officer is satisfied that the assembly or procession is not likely to cause a breach of the peace, he shall issue a license specifying the name of the license and defining the condition on which the assembly or procession is permitted to take place." This particular bill is significant because it limited the movement of women in groups. The Riot Act was an ordinance that allowed the colonial government to shoot and kill the protesting women.[66] When I asked Dr. Obi which archive he drew the information from, he explained that when he was a young boy these acts, bills, and ordinances were displayed in public on posts for all to see. Many did not change over the years. This, he explained, is how he and his childhood friends mastered their reading skills. The words of the various laws had been etched in his mind. There was no need for the archive.[67]

Dr. Obi had a political agenda when he wrote *I Saw the Sky Catch Fire*. He resisted the categorization of African women within feminist frameworks, the tendency for Igbo histories to exist without any checks and balances against factual evidence, and the development of early "Africanist theory" as written by Westerners. But his work does not exist without criticism. Igbo women have criticized him because he is a man. Others have claimed that his work is too suggestive and bawdy, and to this he replied, "Every man has a right to his mother's story."[68]

CONCLUSION

The 1925 and 1929 women's movements are significant because they show why women responded to the social and economic changes brought on by colonialism. The consequences of the implementation of indirect rule, especially the appointment of warrant chiefs, encroached on their social and economic rights. Changes in currency usage, taxation, and indebtedness decreased their capacity to maintain their economic responsibilities. Women participated in both movements to express their collective grievances and demand reform. After the 1929 war, one man said: "They have shown it in this rising that they are a kind of power in this country"[69]

Some scholars have undermined the intellectual and philosophical integrity of the Nigerian women's protests as an "unconscious cultural protest." On the contrary, Igbo women testified that their protest was a direct consequence of continuous social and economic decline.[70] The new political institutions, such as the installation of warrant chiefs and the native court system, categorically disregarded indigenous social institutions. Igbo women clearly understood their waning economic, social, and political power. Even Igbo men acknowledged the women's social awareness. Ikeja, son of a local Ezeala (chief), stated that "if everything was peaceful, then there would have been no need for women to come forward and make use of bad expression and for some people to be taken away."[71]

Child pawning often required children to leave their homes and live with the moneylender, exposing them to the risk of being sold into domestic slavery. The safety net of kinship networks, which during the precolonial period had assisted in preventing the sale of family members, had begun to fail. As an addition to existing scholarship, the analysis of the Women's War presented herein shows that at the core of the women's uprising was an unwavering desire to maintain women's security in children. The social economy of a child is most evident when analyzing family economic (in)security in the wake of taxation and moneylending.

Inquiry testimony provides evidence of women's understanding that their children's lives were at risk under the colonial taxation system. Even though the immediate exchange (debt collateral) may have provided a temporary solution, the institution had shortcomings. Above and beyond economic ruin, when women lost access to pawned children, their social status declined and long-term security decreased. The British failed to acknowledge "traditional female autonomy" and were oblivious to the various strains shouldered by Igbo communities. As a result, the most vulnerable dependents within the region suffered. As Harry Gailey notes, "The imposition of taxes merely served as the focal point for a whole series of dissatisfactions within the society."[72] A. E. Afigbo commented, along with many other scholars, that "it is indeed a limited view which portrays the Riot as a response to a passing economic crisis. British administration, especially through the Warrant Chief System, had struck and undermined indigenous society at many vital points."[73]

In the decade following the war, child trafficking did not decrease. Many Nigerian communities continued to practice child pawning in order to obtain loans under dire economic circumstances. As a perpetual practice, child dealing in its various forms continued to endure. In the next chapter, I discuss how colonial investigations during the 1930s shifted their focus from child pawnship to child slavery. The exploration of the postwar decade continues to expose the difficulties of ending the incorporation of impoverished children into unfree labor systems.

CHAPTER 5
Child Trafficking after the War

About two weeks ago I borrowed from one Nwachiku Ocho of Inyishi the sum of 3/-
that I used in paying taxation and the brother of my wife by name of Osuji Egbubuza
[to] whom I owed £2.10/- [a] part of dowry . . . [When] I see all these troubles I said
within myself that I will take my daughter by name Ukacho and sell her in order to
obtain the money so as to pay the man whom I can borrow money from.

—*Okpala Eheakandu, Statement, March 18, 1934*

In 1934, Okpala Eheakandu of Umuahia Township struggled to
pay multiple debts. According to his testimony, he owed creditors
for money borrowed to pay taxes and to settle the remaining bride-
price balance for his wife. Okpala and his wife decided that selling
his daughter was the most efficient way to deal with his debts and
agreed to offer their two-year-old to an Aro child dealer in the same
town. However, when Okpala's wife attempted to deliver the girl to
the Aro child dealer, police arrested her.[1] Personal accounts such as
this speak to the harsh economic realities that continued to persist
in the aftermath of the 1929 Women's War.

In the previous chapter I noted that the investigations into pawning mainly focused on children. Colonial administrators wanted to
know how pawning cases related to other systems of unfree labor.
They also wanted to ascertain how pawning contracts transformed
into marriages between adults and children. It is not a coincidence
that the 1929 Women's War occurred during the same decade that
these investigations launched. Much of the incorporated inquiry
testimonies and oral histories unveil Igbo and Ibibio economic

desperation under the colonial taxation scheme, as well as detailed accounts of warrant chief abuses and others who worked for the native courts. What became most apparent is that the women protested because they lost their children in pawn and outright theft with nearly no recourse to redeem them. The women of the southeast lost economic and political power under colonial rule, and by 1929, the threat of a woman tax proved too much to bear.

What came in the following decade opened a series of possibilities as it relates to child trafficking. The choices administrators made speak volumes about their priorities, their misconceptions of slave-dealing networks, and their lack of understanding about the socioeconomic value of children. In this chapter I argue that despite humanitarian efforts and anemic efforts by colonial officials to investigate and end domestic slavery, the underlying economic condition of the colony prevented any measurable decrease in child trafficking. The importance of the social economy of children continued to exist as it related to the local and colonial economies. Moreover, the participation of children and women in child trafficking ploys further thwarted investigations on account of gendered assumptions that women and children were victims and should be considered protected groups during the 1930s.

The Great Depression (1929–39) presented many challenges for Europeans and Africans alike. The British enacted cost-saving measures in the colony, one of which included the withdrawal of currency, further weakening the Nigerian economy. Moses Ochonu argues that "imperial solidarity and colonial outposts became fulcrums of economic recovery," as a way to deal with the Depression, not to intentionally and severely exploit Nigerians. Britain relied on the colonies as a way to buttress its own economy by envisioning the economies of each as deeply dependent and intertwined. The main point, for the purpose of this chapter, is not to delineate the complete course of action taken by the British but rather to show that the policies implemented focused mainly on the economic recovery of Britain itself while relying on Nigeria's "existing productive capacity."[2] It is within this context that the colonial state struggled to end domestic slavery and appease antislavery proponents.

The Colonial Office moved from investigating primarily pawning cases to slavery cases. Although the administrators carried out a long investigation into the causes of the 1929 Women's War, the prevailing economic conditions led Nigerians to continue trafficking children in the southeast. Assistant Commissioner of Police S. P. George believed that male taxation continued to be a major cause, but the Great Depression also contributed to the disastrous economic conditions that fostered an increase in child trafficking. Consequently, just as in the 1920s, Western women continued to inundate colonial administrators throughout the empire to end slavery. A. E. Afigbo describes this era as the "third phase" (1933–50), during which administrators no longer waited for its "civilizing mission" to end slavery. Rather, they decided to combat the internal slave trade head-on.[3]

Antislavery proponents continued to organize committees that solidified efforts to persuade British administrators in Nigeria to end slavery. In 1930, Eleanor Rathbone and her counterparts in the League of Nations Advisory Committee on Child Welfare pressed the British government to allow women to join the Colonial Office and the Slavery Commission of the League of Nations.[4] In 1930 Maria Ogilvie Gordon submitted a memorandum to the League of Nations asserting that she intended to bring a deputation of women to the next League meeting to consider the issue of slavery in the colonies.[5] Like Rathbone, Gordon had long been committed to improving the condition of women and children. In 1916 she served as the president of the National Council of Women and then became the first vice president of the International Council of Women in 1920.[6] She also formed the Council for the Representation of Women in the League of Nations in 1919 and served as chair of the Mothercraft and Child Welfare Exhibition Committee between 1919 and 1921 and again in 1930.[7]

The delegation Gordon led consisted of some of Britain's most prominent women activists, including Lady Mary Gertrude Emmott, who convened the Parliamentary and Legislation Committee of the National Council of Women and was a member of the African Society.[8] Gordon also invited Chrystal Macmillan, a suffragist and the first female barrister-at-law to plead a case in front of the House of Lords; Macmillan was also known for championing women's marital rights.[9] Marjorie Chave Collisson, a cofounder of British Commonwealth League, who sought to promote "citizenship throughout the Empire," also joined.[10] In addition, Margery Corbett Ashby, a longtime British suffragist and liberal politician, sought out ways to fund their campaigns through donations.[11] These women all worked to improve women's welfare, uphold the rights of women and children, and advance reforms for women and children across the empire. The delegation was especially eager to have the League reform the Slavery Commission and appoint a female representative to the Colonial Office to oversee the well-being of British and indigenous women throughout the colonies. In 1929, the women had attempted to persuade the League to reconstitute the Slavery Commission and investigate all forms of slavery. Their endeavor to amend the 1926 Slavery Convention's definition of slavery highlighted pawning practices as they related to bride-price payments and made illegal the selling or pawning of girls and women, because the delegation believed that each engendered the "status or condition of a person over whom any or all of the powers attaching to the right of ownership" were "exercised."[12] For the women of the League, a female pawn's status was no better than that of a slave.

As with some male colonial representatives, it is evident that League women did not recognize Nigerian women's social position nor their decision-making power to make choices regarding marital arrangements. That is not to say that child marriage did not mask trafficking in girls or that a woman generally agreed to a marriage without her family's input. As I have shown in previous chapters, most freeborn women exercised free will, and as such, League women's assumptions about Nigerian women's lack of autonomy likely stemmed from projection and prejudice. Rathbone claimed that Nigerian fathers and husbands considered women to be their property and that, "while no doubt 'bride price' often operates as an inducement to the husband to treat his wife properly, it in fact leads to abuses of the most revolting character." She suggested that providing educational services would counteract what she deemed to be the unfair treatment of women and children, though it is not readily apparent what she had in mind. While outwardly sympathetic, Secretary of State Sidney Webb (known as Lord Passfield), a Fabian socialist and "reformist humanitarian," explained that any forceful attempt to change indigenous marriage practices would be costly and that it would be "impossible" for any British officer to "regulate the daily lives and customs of the people in detail." Webb claimed that native law rather than colonial law regulated marriage practices and argued that changes would occur over time. However, in March 1930, his office received numerous letters from the various women's associations belonging to the council requesting an audience to discuss the condition of Nigerian women throughout the colony.[13]

Other women's groups also registered their concerns about the welfare of children in the colonies. Invited to suggest methods to implement protective measures for children, government representatives, educators, welfare workers, and business operators who worked in various capacities with children on the continent convened in June

1930 at the Save the Children International conference in Geneva to discuss the fate of the African child. While at the conference, conveners discussed options for ending child labor and pawning practices in Africa, developing proposals that would charge colonial governments to take child welfare seriously.[14] The continued pressure from this and other international groups spawned yet another investigation into the long-standing trade in children and slaves. It is noteworthy that evidence does not indicate any significant effort to include Nigerian women, or West African women in general, in organizations that focused on the trafficking of women and children in Africa during the 1930s. It seems reasonable to question whether efforts to end child trafficking would have been more effective had these groups insisted on the inclusion of African women. Thus, it is important to consider Jessica Cammaert's suggestion, in her work on Ghanaian children and international humanitarian efforts during the colonial era, that calls for a reconsideration of *who* was "the best trustee" of African children.[15]

On the one hand, colonial authorities prioritized their economic agenda during an era when most of the world experienced a financial crisis. On the other hand, League members and other humanitarians focused on the very factor that had the potential to improve economies: unfree labor systems, which financially supported some Nigerian families and the British colonial state. In the 1932 Owerri Province annual report, Senior Resident O. W. Firth reported that: "In Okigwi Division there has been a considerable increase in the number of cases of slave-dealing and child-stealing. These crimes are particularly common in the Obowo area where there appears to be gangs who carry on a steady trade in stolen children."[16] With rising cases and constant pressure by League women, British representatives had little other choice but to acquiesce to their request.

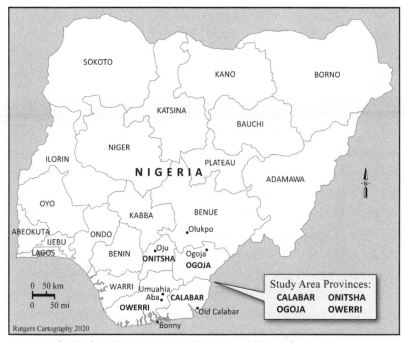

FIGURE 3. Study Area Provinces, 1930s. Created by Michael Siegel.

THE INVESTIGATION INTO CHILD-DEALING NETWORKS

In 1933, the Secretary for the Southern Provinces of Nigeria ordered a formal investigation into child stealing and slave dealing in the provinces of Owerri, Onitsha, Ogoja, and Calabar that lasted twenty-seven months. British officials already knew that Igbo-speaking populations continued to engage in child trafficking, therefore the goal of the investigation was to develop a comprehensive understanding of child-dealing networks and their primary actors, in addition to identifying reasons why parents and child dealers pawned, stole, and sold children. In the cases that follow, it becomes evident that the frail economy, new forms of transportation, tendencies toward double-crossing, violence, and children's and women's search for economic opportunities created the environment wherein children continued to be trafficked during the 1930s.

As colonial development projects refined the transport system, child traffickers utilized the infrastructure to move children in a number of ways. During the 1920s, child dealers frequently made use of railways as a central form of transportation, drawing larger numbers of children to major market centers.[17] The use of canoes and increased access to bicycles and motorized vehicles facilitated the proliferation of long-distance trade, allowing coastal traders to travel farther inland, with middlemen informing them about the various labor shortages in agriculture or the need for tailors or brick makers for which children might be trained.[18] As the colonial development projects refined the transport system, they also facilitated the continued movement of enslaved children. However, by the early 1930s, traffickers had decreased their use of railways as police began to inspect trains.[19]

As early as 1915, colonial officials recognized that the old slave trading centers, such as the Uzuakoli market in the Bende District and the Uburu market in Afikpo District, gave shelter to child trafficking.[20] By transporting children under the cloak of darkness, claiming them as sons and daughters when necessary and using middlemen to inform willing buyers at market centers, many who dealt in children successfully evaded police detection. Modernity and masquerade, in this sense, allowed for the continuation of past practices in the most efficient way possible.

The slave-dealing and child-stealing investigation from November 1933 to May 1936 revealed that increasingly more children were stolen and sold.[21] Yet, even while launching various inquiries into child trafficking, colonial officials had conflicting views on whether young girls suffered as a result of pawning or marriage.

In a statement submitted to the Council for the Representation of Women in the League of Nations, J. E. W. Flood, the Colonial Office administrator in charge of Nigerian affairs, claimed that the office had always discouraged pawning practices and that by 1930 "no children [were] taken as pawns," and that "native custom never permitted the pawning of a girl." He denied the existence of abuses suffered by some pawned children, while acknowledging that "the payment of a bride price" did "not suggest that the woman is thereby sold into slavery"; rather, the bride-price represented the promise of the man to "treat his wife properly."[22] Maintaining that the penalty of imprisonment for up to seven years deterred people from pawning children, he did not agree that parents continued to pawn girls. As the same time, he incongruously insisted that girls and women never suffered any abuse as a result of pawning. However, other officials openly admitted the ills of pawning children, especially those instances where a child pawn fell victim to slavery.

The district officer at Bende, a core area for slave trading, rightly noted that even though a girl might be pawned while she was quite young, she could always marry if her future husband repaid the debt. In the case of boys, he argued that although the practice was considered a "criminal offence," it was "not always detrimental to the child's happiness." The officer alleged that he observed "several instances in which this has been done and [I] have usually found that the boy is better treated than he would have been had he lived with his impecunious parents."[23] Those concerned primarily with the colonial economy frequently expressed such sentiments. Responsible for generating revenue, the district officer understood that some parents could pay taxes only if they pawned their children. To criticize and prosecute the practice would thwart his goal of tax collection.

By the fall of 1933, Assistant Inspector-General of Police of the Southern Provinces G. N. Faux-Powell appointed Assistant Commissioner of Police Major J. W. Garden to oversee the investigation into slave dealing in the southeast in the aforementioned provinces. District officers and residents investigated how traffickers acquired children, identified the routes traveled, and discovered how traffickers disposed of children.[24] The resulting reports illuminate many aspects of child dealing that prevailed during the 1930s. Reports on child trafficking included child testimonies, such as the following:

TESTIMONY ONE

I came to market "ORIE UGURE" a man called Ukuebula [told] me that I should come and look [at] nice beads and earrings that he would present me. I was then tied in a sack and carried away on [a] cycle to Oguta and from there to Okugba in a house of one Ogidebo, a middle man of slave dealer.

TESTIMONY TWO

I was on top of a tree in the station, [and] one Jack of Umunze of Awka Division came and told me that the Police man said that I should go with him . . . to bring tobacco. I agreed and followed him to Umunzo town [where] he kept me in the house[.] When night come . . . Jack put me into the basket and carried me to a certain woman called Mbeko at Uga town in Awka Division.

TESTIMONY THREE

About 5 years ago one Ume Ogarakwe of Lokpa and one Kaluku of Aro Chuku residing in Agwa that time came to our place when all the people had gone to farm. Ume told me [Oduomyenma of Okigwe] to come and join them to go and visit a woman of my father's relative at Ngodo. I followed them passed Ngodo to a place called Uburu. We slept two nights on the way to Uburu. We entered in the house of a certain chief . . . and the chief paid them some money dowry on my head. They left me there and went away but after 5 months Ume alone came one night and met me where I was playing with other girls and took me away . . . He took me to New Calabar to the house of one chief . . . He received £10 from him and left me there for 7 months.[25]

Even though parents continually warned their children to be wary of child stealers, these stories illustrate how easily traffickers manipulated children into following them.[26] The testimonies include references to several familiar elements: the role of the Aro, the use of bicycles, the invocation of fear of police, and the sale of a child to a chief. The ethnic groups who profited from slave trafficking in the earlier decades continued to do so during the 1930s. These narratives highlight child dealers' double-crossing natures, selling someone a child, only to steal the same child back again. The child-dealing business in Southeastern Nigeria exposed the enterprising and ruthless nature of those involved.

In 1933, Mr. E. Dickinson, district officer of Owerri Province, claimed that most child dealing occurred in Isu in Orlu Division and Ekwereazu (also known as Ekwerazu), in the Owerri Division, located east of Bende and south of Onitsha. People who kidnapped children found markets in the northeast area of the Owerri Province as well. Traffickers took the children north to Amachara, which served as a clearing station for the Okigwe Division (north of Obowo).[27] One Obowo man testified that "I am the father of the girl-child stolen by the accused. Ihenwenwa is about three years old. About two weeks ago when rain had finished falling, we all went to bed. I was alone in my room. In the middle of the night

I was awakened by the sound of a dog barking. I came out and saw two men carrying [a] child. I recognized the child as my own and raised the alarm." Fortunately, with the help of his son, the father retrieved his daughter.[28] In other instances, once traffickers kidnapped a child, they took the child from Obowo and traveled several miles to their destination. They crossed the Imo River, either by bridge or canoe, and then traveled by foot to Umuahia and Amachara. An Igbo man named Ubendu operated as the main intermediary in the area during the early 1930s and employed messengers to inform buyers, mainly Aro agents, when he was in possession of an available child. While some parents traveled the terrain "by foot or by lorry" in order to sell their own children, the circuitous journey made it nearly impossible for parents to search for children who landed throughout the southeast and beyond without their consent.[29]

The district officer of Degema urged Major Garden to begin his investigation in the Degema Division in Owerri Province because it was a key location for trafficking girls. Aro agents usually collected girls from Agbiam, Umuahia, Kwale, and Owerri for the purpose of selling them in Degema.[30] During their patrol of the market, officers often discovered and retrieved a number of women and children who had been captured and brought to Degema.[31]

Okigwe, particularly the villages located in Egodo, Isu, and Obowo, was a primary hub where slave dealers bought children.[32] Dealers sold Okigwe children predominantly in the Isu and Obowo areas.[33] Officials cited Obowo as a well-known location to find stolen children and those who had been sold by their parents.[34] Once in receipt of the children, traffickers transported them by railroad and then sailed south down the Imo River to the creek region or to the southeast in Umuahia. The district officer of Ahoada confirmed that along with the Aro, Okigwe traders dominated the kidnapping rings in the area. Their conspicuously large homes made obvious their wealth acquired from the trade in children.[35]

Child dealers also took captives from the northeastern Owerri Province to Obowo and transferred them through Umuokpara, east to Umuahia through Achara, and north to Uzuakoli (located slightly northwest of Bende).[36] Again, with the help of local informants, colonial investigators identified the homes of slave dealers located in Umuahia and Uzuakoli.[37] According to the investigators, child dealers also traveled south from Oguta to Ahoada and sold children along the creeks as far as the North Brass area.[38]

Situated on the coast, the Brass area had historically incorporated large numbers of slaves into the canoe houses and continued to employ slave labor to facilitate trade with the Palm Belt region, enhancing the size and power of their trade corporation.[39] Traffickers transferred slaves through Mbidi, traveled through Oguta, and crossed the Niger River, where they eventually sold their captives to the Ijaws or southward to the Abonnema people.[40] The Ijaws, neighbors of the Igbo in the Eastern Delta, ventured into an even more heinous form of trafficking. They bought Igbo children for the purpose of breeding and sold the resulting offspring to dealers in the north who operated in Oguta in Owerri Division.[41] The Ijaws also transported children east to the Obowo area of the Okigwe District.[42]

The investigation uncovered the persistent operation of the trading systems that the Aro had first developed during the transatlantic slave trade. Parents in Owerri Province claimed that they preferred "to deal" with the Aro because they paid "a higher price than that offered by the local people."[43] The Aro paid £9 to £12 for girls who ranged in age from five to ten years old. When parents decided to sell a child, they accompanied the child and the Aro dealer to the child's final destination. In one instance, when police approached parents and a child travelling with an Aro man, the parents claimed that the child was going to work as a caregiver for the Aro man's younger children.[44] When challenged by authorities regarding the true nature of the exchange, the parents took the child home. Even though officials did not arrest the parents or the Aro man, they described the incident as an obvious slave-dealing case.[45] In other incidents, Major Garden claimed that parents admitted to district officers and police that they established a written marriage agreement in order to avoid prosecution, but it is unlikely that parents would have explained how they avoided prosecution. Garden may have assumed this to be the case when parents argued that they had received payment for the child in the context of an arranged marriage. In any event, the existence of a tangible marriage contract complicated matters for those who sought to end child dealing.

Other child-dealing routes saw a variety of methods employed by traffickers throughout the southeast. When dealers transported children south to the Niger Delta creeks region, an adult usually traveled with the child by train from Uzuakoli to Umukoroshe (now called Rumukoroshe), near Port Harcourt. According to some reports, women often fulfilled this role of transporting children on foot to Okrika and other towns located along the creeks. If at any point authorities questioned a woman about the child in her care, she claimed to be the mother. If a man accompanied a "more fully grown girl," he claimed to be her husband. In other instances, the Okigwe district officer claimed that child dealers took the children to the Aro capital at Arochukwu and sold them to plantation owners at Akpabuyo or Creek Town. Dealers also sold girls to brothels located along the coast.[46]

Major Garden produced a report listing all cases of child stealing and slave dealing brought to the attention of the court in December 1933 for the west-central part of Igboland. In all, the court reviewed the cases of sixteen boys and eighteen girls.[47] It spanned the previous twenty-two months and showed the data presented in table 4.

TABLE 4. Slave dealing cases, December 1933

DIVISION	NUMBER OF CASES TRIED	GUILTY	NOT GUILTY
Owerri	14	6	8
Okigwe	11	5	6
Bende	8	5	3
Ahoada	2	1	1
Degema	0	0	0
Aba	0	0	0
Totals	35	17	18

Source: Garden, *Slave Dealing Report: Report for December 1933.*

Understanding that thirty-five child-stealing and slave-dealing cases might seem minimal, Major Garden warned that the "figures merely show the cases which have been before the Courts and cannot be taken to indicate that slave dealing is not being extensively carried on." He explained that a large number of acquittals resulted from parents' and relatives' participation and the percentage of "not guilty" verdicts was "undoubtedly an incentive" for them to "carry on in the traffic."[48] His statement highlights the reality that colonial officers handled cases of child stealing differently when strangers stole and sold children versus when parents participated in the exchange of a child, because then prosecution proved too difficult.

The investigations into eastern Igboland unveiled its supply-and-demand needs as well as unique trafficking routes. The Ogoja Province had high demand for women and children's agricultural labor since its population was lower than many of the other towns in Southeastern Nigeria.[49] Numerous slaves came from throughout Igboland and from Bamenda, Cameroon. For instance, British officials did not believe that the children originated from Afikpo Division on the Cross River but that Afikpo, an Aro enclave, operated as a main location where dealers bought and sold children. Middlemen from the Cross River traveled to Afikpo to assess the need for children by speaking with agents from the Bende and Okigwe Divisions. Evidence suggests that some children traded in Afikpo came from the historic slave source areas of Udi District near Enugu and Awka near Onitsha. Dealers chose to negotiate the terms of exchange at the Uburu market, which was held every twenty-four days, allowing time for the middlemen to communicate with parents and others who sold children. Often, they agreed to deliver children to the Obubra and Ikom Divisions for pickup. In many cases, once a dealer located a "suitable" child, buyers claimed the child at night so as to avoid detection.[50]

Children served a variety of purposes in the Obubra and Ikom Divisions in Ogoja Province. Secret societies and social clubs continued to create a large demand for child slaves. A specific demand for girls arose from dealers who forced them into prostitution. As Ben Naanen noted, "by the 1920s prostitution had become a substantially developed trade in the area," and by the "mid-1930s the level of prostitution in Obubra Division became a major concern to both the colonial administration and the local elders."[51] However, remittances from prostitution ensured a continuous influx of income to Obubra family members even when the prostitute worked outside the Ogoja Province.

Dealers transported children in caravans to the Cross River region of Calabar Province as well. Traffickers avoided police detection by working in teams and colonial authorities believed that women claimed to be the children's mothers or sisters when they traveled with the dealer and the children.[52] In addition, scouts on bicycles and armed men who traveled by foot led the groups and warned the perpetrators if they saw authorities on the path. The Cross River people received just as many boys as girls, paying up to £35 for both. The children were usually bought to work on palm farms in Ediba and Ugbun. To avoid detection as "foreign" children, the new guardians renamed the children, sequestered them, and made them learn the local language before allowing them to socialize with children outside of their immediate compound.[53] In addition to the process by which children assimilated to their destination environments, child dealers disguised children as apprentices as they traveled and conducted trade carrying their wares from one town to another. By operating child-dealing schemes in conjunction with legitimate business, the traders made it extremely difficult for authorities to identify them as traffickers.[54]

The March 1934 slave-dealing report does not reflect the actual number of children transported between regions in Southeastern Nigeria, and likely severely underestimates the numbers. In fact, during his investigation, Major Garden received seventy-six complaints about child stealing that occurred between 1932 and 1934.[55] In November 1934, Assistant Commissioner of Police C. R. Bell reported that he received complaints that sixty-eight children had been kidnapped over the past fifteen years from Okigwe, Owerri, Aba, and Bende, all main locations of the Women's War. But for any case to be brought forth and successfully prosecuted, authorities needed willing parties to testify. In most cases, not even the child would testify against his or her captor.[56]

TABLE 5. Slave-dealing report, March 1934

TOWN	CASES	NUMBER OF PERSONS CHARGED	NUMBER OF PERSONS CONVICTED	NUMBER OF PERSONS ACQUITTED
Afikpo	5	15	5	10
Obubra	8	25	15	10
Ogoja	1	3	2	1
Abakiliki	1	0	0	0
Ikom	0	0	0	0
Total	**15**	**43**	**22**	**21**

Source: Garden, *Slave Dealing Report: Report for March 1934.*

After 1929, child stealing had become a lucrative and increasingly violent business. During the 1930s, child traffickers frequently committed murder to obtain a child. For example, in February 1935, a young man named Dick Wogu stole his five-year-old stepsister from her hometown of Owerrinta, Owerri. With the assistance of two associates, he took the girl to Okigwe, where they hid in a home during the day. Joined by another man, they traveled again by night to Obowo where a known slave dealer, Akwukwaebu, met them. After agreeing on a price, Akwukwaebu took the girl to Uzuakoli, where she was passed off two more times. At some point during the transaction, Wogu's accomplices killed him, presumably to gain a larger portion of the profits from selling the girl. Fortunately for her, the police raided the home of her final kidnapper and she likely returned home. After a thorough investigation, the authorities were able to convict twelve of the fourteen people who participated in her abduction and sale.[57]

In another instance, authorities apprehended a known Aro child dealer, Lemadim of Ibom, and noticed a bullet wound in his neck.[58] It is likely that another child trafficker shot him during a transaction. And in a case similar to Wogu's story, child dealers killed one mother to obtain her two children, who were found twelve miles from Umuahia with two unrelated men and two women. Police officers approached child dealers in plain clothes to avoid scaring them off and then held them for questioning. The dealers in this case accused someone else of the murder and pleaded with authorities to continue their investigation to prove their innocence. Colonial records do not provide the accused dealers' explanation of how they had acquired the children, but clues do exist as to why men engaged in such acts.[59]

Pervasive child-dealing practices, spurred by economic hardship, prevailed because cultural expectations could not be achieved otherwise. In the midst of the Great Depression, many Nigerian men lost access to wage labor and suffered financial loss in palm products and other farming industries. This financial decline prevented men from paying bride-prices in addition to taxes. This caused a deep crisis in village society because marriage was the precondition for a man's social maturity and participation in village government. Furthermore, remaining unmarried decreased men's capacity to survive as farmers. So despised was bachelorhood that the word for an adult unmarried man was *oko okporo*, meaning "male woman." This distressing environment created conditions wherein family members betrayed each other for the purposed of gaining access to cash. For example, a police constable testified about one man, who could not afford a bride-price, stole his female cousin and sold her to earn the funds necessary to marry. The desire to acquire the bride-price for a wife superseded his allegiance to kin. Such crises resulted from earlier years when young men decided to no longer depend on assistance from their fathers for bride-price funds—a change advanced by wage labor practices. As many opted to participate in wage labor employment, they paid the bride-price on their own, subverting gerontocratic norms. Young men no longer had to yield to the will of the village elders.[60]

WOMEN AND CHILDREN: VICTIMS OR PERPETRATORS?

The international community and colonial officials wanted to ascertain how and why human traffickers dealt in women and children; however, in an attempt to survive Nigeria's economic decline, both groups also participated in human trafficking that mainly victimized other women and children. They traveled the same trade routes as men and informed agents when children were available for purchase.[61] Women claimed that the accompanying child was a son or daughter or some other family member when they countered authorities on a footpath, train, or canoe. In addition, women scouted children for the purpose of having them sway their counterparts away from the safety of their homes.

League of Nations members concerned themselves with the well-being of Nigerian women and children, but they did not take into account that women and children also participated in child stealing and slave dealing. This reality presented a particular kind of problem for humanitarians when they classified women and children as potential victims and protected groups. Women and children may have been the minority of those involved in human trafficking, but their participation should not be underestimated. Some children, mostly sons, assisted their fathers by transporting younger children to the destination. As for women, there is evidence that they participated in the sale, buying, and transport of children. Some acted as routine child dealers, whereas others participated only if the opportunity presented itself, such as when a child dealer persuaded a woman to participate by paying her to "pass this child off as her own if questioned" during transport.[62] Many women likely participated in this manner when in need of money.

The 1930s investigative reports provide a trove of information about how women contributed to the traffic in children through the institutions of slavery, pawnship, and prostitution in Southeastern Nigeria. Women's involvement in certain types of child-dealing schemes was not new, but by the mid-1930s, women were known as "habitual dealers" as senior women often bought and sold young girls for the purpose of prostitution.[63] At times, a number of prominent women traders and moneylenders offered their homes as a meeting place for a fee.[64]

In the decades following the 1920s, some impoverished families sold daughters into prostitution as easily as they could have pawned them.[65] Moreover, as Saheed Aderinto has noted in his work on child prostitution in Lagos, when girls fell victim to pawning, child marriage arrangements, and kidnapping, they were defenseless again sexually exploitative practices, mainly prostitution. Prostitution itself was a product of colonial urban policies that discouraged family life and made factory centers, sites of railroad construction, and coal and tin labor camps into prostitution havens for single men. In her study of female prostitutes in Nairobi, Kenya, Luise White notes that prostitution resulted from the development of capitalist society in Africa as women attempted to make rational economic choices. However, unlike the women who chose sex work in Nairobi, children in Igboland were generally forced into prostitution by older women. Mfom Umoren Ekpo-Otu argues that the rise of prostitution in colonial Nigeria resulted from the "socio-economic dislocations" of imperialism, underscoring that economic hardship intensified throughout the southeast for many Nigerians.[66]

One of the most prominent areas associated with colonial prostitution was the Akunakuna region of the Cross River. Women controlled the trade of young girls between Akunakuna (south) and Ediba (north). Assistant Commissioner C. R. Bell alleged that women "who have been harlots and have no children of their own" were the main purchasers of young girls and that girls from Okigwe often ended up in the Cross River region: "A case occurred where a woman named Obia Ogum Anum living at Umon on the Cross River was found in possession of four girls from Umunga, Okigwi Division. The four girls were repatriated to Okigwi by the District Officer, Okigwi Division, who has the matter in hand." It is clear that retired prostitutes acquired girls for the purpose of prostitution, but, in a twisted application of gendered inheritance preferences, they also bought or informally adopted boys so that they could become their heirs.[67]

Madams also recruited girls from Degema, and 1933 court records reveal how one madam, who had in her possession two young girls, attempted to sell them to a French commercial agent for the purpose of sexual exploitation. The two marriage certificates in her possession, which noted that the girls were betrothed to an Okrika man, did not provide sufficient evidence to avoid conviction for illegally selling the children. Luckily, the marriage certificates noted their natal villages, which allowed authorities to reunite them with relatives in the Owerri and Okigwe Divisions.[68]

Authorities discovered that the majority of the girls, sixteen to twenty years old, taken from Owerri to Brass seemed "old enough to look after themselves," remarking that the girls claimed to have left their homes on their own volition.[69] Colonial reports do not state whether the girls knew that they would engage in sex work. It is likely that some young women who wanted to leave home or delay marriage willingly left with older prostitutes who promised them lucrative employment of some kind, however dubious. In addition to prostitution, "big women," meaning women with wealth and social standing, adopted and fostered children for other economic reasons.

Some women achieved great success as they extended their economic endeavors through trade and control of the sexual relations of other women. Omu Okwei (1872–1943), known as "the merchant queen of Ossomari," is one example. The lawless coastal town of Ossomari, located on the eastern side of the Niger River, was a major center of the slave trade. Okwei had developed her trade business in Onitsha as an agent for the Royal Niger Company, a charter business that controlled commerce on the Niger River.[70] She traded palm products for imported wares and was part of a larger population of wealthy women who earned income transporting goods inland. She also lent funds with very high interest rates, from 60 to 90 percent, to farm owners and young traders. Okwei presided over a workforce comprised of "beautiful girls—mostly 'adopted,' presumably women who as children were pawned to her by debtors." She raised the children and offered them as "mistresses or wives to influential business men and others."[71] Okwei's use of marriage to cement alliances and develop clients was a time-honored pattern of commerce in Igboland and throughout Africa. Once the foreign traders left Nigeria, the women were expected to return to Okwei with any "children or property" they acquired while with the trader. Okwei's sons assisted with her local global enterprises and she became so successful that in 1935 she was given the title Omu, meaning "queen."[73] Okwei's story highlights how women acquired capital through their use of child pawns and trafficked children, who when grown functioned as petty and commercial traders, accumulating wealth on Okwei's behalf.[74]

The League of Nations and other humanitarian groups sought out the cooperation of colonial officials to end the trafficking of children during the Great Depression.[75] But fear of further reducing Nigeria's economic capacity must have led Southeastern Nigerians and colonial officials to recognize the personal cost of ending the institutions of child pawnship and trafficking.[76] By April 1935, the Assistant Commissioner of Police George admitted that he agreed with Residents O. W. Firth and Major H. C. Stevenson that is was "impractical to prosecute all the cases of pawning, quasi-slave dealing, and quasi-marriages which come to light. Only those cases that involve definite ill-treatment of the children should be proceeded with." He acknowledged that individuals against whom complaints were lodged should be investigated but argued that returning the children to their natal homes had to be the priority.[77] This proved to be a difficult task especially because parents were unlikely to welcome home a pawned child for whom the debt had not been repaid.

The decision to end the investigative campaign opened officials to criticism from international humanitarian organizations. In the end, the Secretary of the Southern Provinces E. J. G. Kelly acknowledged that the League of Nations Advisory Committee of Experts on Slavery would be appalled at their decision to end the campaign against child trafficking. He admitted that there would be "opinion in England which will hardly be convinced of the justification for discontinuing this special campaign." Even at the risk of criticism and potential disagreement, he did not believe that the results up to that point justified the continued cost and effort.[78]

CONCLUSION

At the end of the campaign to end the trade in slaves and children, little had been accomplished. In April 1936, the resident at Owerri wrote to the secretary of the Southern Provinces requesting the termination of the campaigns against slave dealing and child stealing. He stated: "I agree with the Inspector General of Police that the results of the campaign have not recently been such as to justify the retention of a Police Officer on this special duty. The number of cases investigated and the convictions obtained in the first half of the year 1935 had a salutary effect and made people realise that they could not sell children with impunity, it may be that this check to the activities of those engaged in the traffic is the cause of the meager results which have since been obtained."[79] The resident of Ogoja Province also agreed that the appointment of a special investigator to inquire about child-dealing cases should end. This decision was based on the assumption that child dealers often worked independently and therefore were difficult to detect. Authorities doubted that large organized gangs dominated the trade in children, as they had done previously.[80] However, as A. E. Afigbo aptly explains: "The fact of the matter was that the government soon found out that in mounting a special campaign it had bitten off more than it could chew and so had to beat a dignified retreat. This, in our view, was perhaps the single most important reason for the ending of the campaign . . . There were gangs involved within trade but not gangs with the kinds of institutional structures which the government could easily identify and deal with using police methods or any other known formal methods for that matter."[81]

Defining women and children as "protected groups" suggested that the international community and the Colonial Office did not understand that women and children also participated in human trafficking. Some children kept watch along the trade routes and fooled other children into being caught. In addition, women were intricately involved in producing exports for the global economy. They provided the majority of the labor for processing palm oil and had a recognized monopoly in the marketing of palm kernels. Thus, as trade declined and the price of exports plummeted during the 1930s, women sought out other ways to earn income, often turning to the same options as men did. Prominent traders offered loans with high interest rates, employed pawned labor, and sexually exploited young girls. Some women in Igboland were just as involved in the trade in children as were men and could often disguise the sale by claiming that the girls were their daughters. Nevertheless, the international effort to protect women and children continued in the 1930s.

The investigators lacked an understanding of the complexity of the economic and transport dimensions of the intricate child-dealing network and did not work in earnest to truly comprehend it.[82] Nevertheless, the administration's failure to end the trafficking of women and children seemed to have had more to do with its desire to avoid weakening the colonial economy, arguing that it did not want to interfere with indigenous labor customs. Consequently, the investigation into child stealing and other forms of human trafficking so eagerly championed by members of the League of Nations and other humanitarian groups resulted in negligible results. By the fall of 1936, the League of Nations Advisory Committee of Experts on Slavery turned its attention to the "economic and social situation of emancipated slaves in Nigeria."[83] This, however, did little to stop the pawning of children, child stealing, and slave dealing in Southeastern Nigeria.

As part of larger networks, child traffickers transported children from one part of Southeastern Nigeria to another (or outside the country) when they identified destination markets. By visiting marketing centers in advance and by discussing the need for children with other agents, they made sure that they would be able to hand off the child quickly.[84] Children were hidden in houses and were often transported at night, making the transaction virtually impossible to detect. Children often ended up in locations far from their homes, making it difficult for them to return.[85] Moneylenders, chiefs, family members, long-distance traders, and the "occasional helper" created a large network through which children were trafficked. If a child was stolen, parents found it challenging to find him or her given the child dealers' swift and efficient actions. This was the case for thousands of children who never returned home during the first few decades of the twentieth century.

As the special committees of the League of Nations, Save the Children Fund, and the International Labor Organization (among others) campaigned against the exploitation of children and women throughout the British Empire, the conditions on the ground blocked their goals. Women and children did not fight for their own protection as much as they sought out ways to survive, however dangerous, in an economic environment that challenged their incomes, traditions, and existence.[86]

CONCLUSION

In 2016, the International Labour Organization (ILO) estimated that there were nearly two million modern-day child slaves (forced labor and forced marriage) in Africa. In the same year, the Nigerian government funded 1.69 billion naira ($5.56 million) to the National Agency for the Prohibition of Trafficking in Persons in an effort to combat child trafficking. Many international and national agencies have conducted studies in order to stem the traffic in persons. In Nigeria, the governor of Edo State created the Edo State Task Force, a committee that brings together nongovernmental organizations (NGOs), national agencies focused on youth and immigration, police and government executives, and other organizations to combat trafficking and slavery. However, while some Nigerian government officials are committed to finding solutions to this problem, the United States Department of State's *Trafficking in Person's Report 2018* concluded that "there were continued reports of, and negligible efforts to address, government officials complicit in human trafficking offenses."[1] This statement shows that even when large-scale efforts are in process to stop child trafficking, top-level officials exacerbate the criminal acts. As in other regions of the globe, the illicit movement and guardianship of children continues to be multifaceted and difficult to curtail.

Child trafficking in West Africa has gained increased scrutiny in the last few decades.[2] In 2002 the United Nations International Children's Emergency Fund (UNICEF) Innocenti Research Centre concluded that child trafficking "is one of the gravest violations of human rights today." In its effort to eliminate all forms of child trafficking, UNICEF commissioned a study to uncover the main agents of trafficking and their networks, as well as develop possible solutions to the problem.[3] Solution-based policies often describe poverty as one of core reasons for child dealing and, therefore, demand an inquiry into the interplay between local and global economics, as well as a full understanding of the region's economic and cultural history.[4] International geopolitics, global trade, and the interdependency of Global South resource extraction, industrialized manufacturing, the sex industry, and childlessness all influence trafficking patterns. Political scientist Alison Brysk argues that we cannot underestimate the importance of "globalization's structural pressures on decision making in households." Consequently, development inequities produce an environment of exploitation wherein children are trafficked.[5] Paying attention to these international phenomena is important but doing so has limitations.

Identifying globalization processes and resulting poverty norms as main factors for trafficking is helpful, but this narrow conclusion requires expansion. Benjamin N. Lawrance asserts that exploring the historical legacy of child trafficking in West Africa during the Great Depression and World War II shows us that modes of transferring children increased during times of economic strain. However, child labor and trafficking are often discussed as "problems" and as a result deny children and parents any agency in their decision-making processes.[6] Child trafficking can produce negative consequences for the child, but describing all child traffickers as nefarious actors does not allow for a comprehensive consideration of family dependencies worldwide.[7] To understand the transformation and reinvention of slavery in Nigeria, it is essential to consider the country's history and involvement in the transatlantic slave trade, as well as internal methods of appropriating a child's body and labor across time.

In the research presented herein, I have provided a chronological outline of child trafficking from the nineteenth century to the 1930s in Southeastern Nigeria. By explaining where, how, and why child trafficking extended beyond the transatlantic slave trade, we better understand the use of child labor in Nigeria today. Analyzing the motivations that families, child dealers, moneylenders, and colonial authorities had in the deployment of child labor further demonstrates that an account of Nigeria's economic history necessitates a discussion of the *social economy of children*. Exploring the modality of children's labor and the porosity of their subjugated statuses allows historians of Nigeria, slavery, and children and childhood to reimagine the importance of placing children front and center in colonial histories. There is, however, a need for further analysis of child trafficking practices after the 1930s.

New approaches to monitoring Nigerian children and youth developed during the 1940s and 1950s. After World War II, the Nigerian Colonial Welfare Office increasingly focused on children's activities in public spaces, especially those they deemed illegal, which led to the enactment of the Children and Young Persons Ordinance of 1943.[8] The *Nigerian Eastern Mail* reported that the purpose of the ordinance was "to provide constructive treatment for young offenders, rather than more punishment; to provide proper care and treatment for young people found to be in need of it and to prevent some of the evils which constantly threaten these young people, such as prostitution and begging." The legislation prioritized identifying children in need of care and protection, decreasing juvenile delinquency, and ending prostitution. It also formalized the juvenile justice system in Lagos, Nigeria, and was the catalyst for the development of social welfare services in the southeast.[9]

Further historical study that would extend the history of child trafficking in Southeastern Nigeria and the international efforts to end it can best be done by analyzing the development of the British Social Welfare Office (BSWO) in Calabar during the late 1940s and 1950s. The work of BSWO members F. W. J. Skeates and Margaret Laurie Belcher would offer unique insight into how British and Nigerian officers continued to seek out and reform juvenile delinquents and provide for those in need of care at the Calabar Remand Home.[10] Perhaps most importantly, just as in the 1920s–1940s, child stealing is evidenced by the number of articles published in local Nigerian newspapers that warned children to be wary of kidnappers. For example, in 1956, one children's article warned, "You must have been startled by the recent cases of kidnapping. Perhaps that reminds you of the days of the slave trade when life was unsafe. But as if this dirty business had not been finally uprooted, we find in our midst today living memories of those evil days. They roam about in the garb of decent folks see[k]ing for whom to enslave. I do not have to mention the names of the children whom Providence has delivered from the dreadful clutches of the modern slavers. Cases of kidnapping are still pending in court. All these events double stress the importance of a note of warning. And pray God you heed the warning." The article highlights the fact that child traffickers continued to abduct children at alarming rates during the 1950s, many of whom ended up on palm oil farms in the Spanish colony Fernando Pó.[11] The author also alludes to the fact that traffickers continued to be members of unsuspecting communities, rendering their participation in child dealing invisible.

By the early 1960s, Nigerian politicians had begun to address human trafficking more intensely, touting the 1948 Universal Declaration of Human Rights. The belief in the existence of inherent human rights was a significant development in the attention paid to women and children believed to be victims of sex trafficking. Articles 1–5 of the declaration state that:

1. All human beings are born free and equal in dignity and rights. They are endowed with reason and conscience and should act towards one another in a spirit of brotherhood.
2. Everyone is entitled to all the rights and freedoms set forth in this Declaration, without distinction of any kind, such as race,

colour, sex, language, religion, political or other opinion, national or social origin, property, birth or other status. Furthermore, no distinction shall be made on the basis of the political, jurisdictional or international status of the country or territory to which a person belongs, whether it be independent, trust, non-self-governing or under any other limitation of sovereignty.

3. Everyone has the right to life, liberty and security of person.

4. No one shall be held in slavery or servitude; slavery and the slave trade shall be prohibited in all their forms.

5. No one shall be subjected to torture or to cruel, inhuman or degrading treatment or punishment.[12]

In an attempt to end the sex trafficking of young girls and women, Nigeria established the Immigration Act of 1963, addressing two important issues. The act put measures into place that required noncitizens to provide documentation about the reason for and length of the visit. It also called for the deportation of any noncitizen who owned and operated a brothel, "which permit the defilement of young girls on its premises, persons, encouraging the seduction or prostitution of girls under thirteen years of age, person trading in prostitution or a procurer."[13] The heavy focus on prostitution sprouted from concerns about sex abuse suffered by children during the mid-1960s to early 1970s, when social unrest erupted in the southeast.

The Nigerian Civil War (July 6, 1967–January 15, 1970) between the Biafran secessionist state, dominated by the Igbo, and the newly independent Nigerian government presented a new challenge for children. The war, which primarily unfolded in Igboland–Southeastern Nigeria, subjected children to new forms of trauma as violence erupted, food supplies disappeared, and they experienced physical dislocation from their homes. Some children survived their participation in the war, while others lost their lives as a result of it.[14] Male children on the Biafran side fought without protective combat uniforms and weapons, cloaked in rags and in possession of machetes. As for women and girls, sex abuse and other forms of exploitation proliferated within and outside military zones. Federal soldiers were known to abduct girls *"en masse,* with some seizures ending in forced marriages."[15] The attempt to separate Southeastern Nigeria from the rest of the country resulted in approximately 3.5 million deaths, many of whom were children. Countless Nigerians struggled to recover from the war and its aftermath during the 1970s. In the next decade, however, Nigeria experienced intense global financial intervention that is now blamed for the current proliferation of child trafficking.[16]

The 1980s were characterized by the structural adjustment programs (SAPs) meant to prevent "impending economic disaster" on the African continent. The International Monetary Fund and the World Bank stepped in to relieve African countries of their postindependence debt with a neoliberal approach. The World Bank's 1981 Agenda for Action and subsequent Sustainable Growth Plan, among other strategies, aimed to improve civic services and infrastructure. The sentiment was that if sub-Saharan Africa received outside economic investment, an "absolute poverty reduction" could be achieved. Conversely, by the end of the 1980s and into the 1990s, Africans and world economists alike recognized SAPs' shortcomings.[17] The failure of SAPs is highlighted by the fact that African governments cut social programs and human development efforts instead of decreasing military funding or eliminating corrupt tendencies within the government. Scholars fault SAPs for what they describe as new, "disturbing" patterns of child labor and trafficking.[18] Similarly, NGOs claim that contemporary child labor (mining, agricultural work, etc.) and prostitution are a direct consequence of SAPs. Other historical factors, like those discussed in this study, should be also be taken into consideration. In any case, it is evident that postindependence Nigeria and its corresponding SAPs produced an environment for the proliferation of child labor and prostitution.

Broad public attention to human trafficking in Nigeria did not develop until the mid-1990s. The rise of Nigerian sex trafficking in the Middle East and Europe became evident as deportation cases of accused prostitutes made headlines. By 2005, anti-trafficking activists had launched awareness campaigns in secondary schools by introducing curricula that highlighted the prevalence of sex trafficking and detailed the propensity of young girls to be tricked by promises of legitimate employment abroad. Siddharth Kara reflected on his 2010 research about child sex trafficking victims who were deported or returned from Europe on their own accord and explained, "I documented the stories of these children, one painful tale at a time. The shelter [TREM Redeemed Evangelical Mission in Lagos] was striving to give them hope, healing, and a chance at a decent future, but there was no mistaking the brutalities they had endured. The stories they told of arduous journeys to Europe, the tortures of men and madams, and their fears of failing to repay their debts were identical to the narratives of the Nigerian sex trafficking victims I had documented in shelters across Europe several years earlier."[19] Documenting the children's experiences made obvious the abuse they experienced and the challenges they continue to face in recovery.

In addition to traffickers transporting girls and women across national borders for prostitution, cases also develop where insurgent groups kidnap children as an act of terrorism. This type of assault on a community highlights "economic, religious, ethnic, and political tensions" that exist in diverse regions.[20] For example, in April 2014 Boko Haram, an Islamic militant organization, kidnapped over 250 girls from Chibok (located in the northern state Borno) while they were at school. After taking to taking the girls as wives, the fighters coerced them to denounce Christianity. When the girls were unwilling to do so, militants forced them to conduct suicide bombing missions against non-Muslim believers.[21] The main goal of this insurgency group was and is to revive a "medieval Islamic caliphate," which has led to a significant amount of devastation in northern Nigeria as Boko Haram continues to target political and religious opponents.[22] Whether it be a national or international trafficking ring, evidence reveals that children and women continue to be pursued for various reasons.

As recently as July 2019, Nigeria's Home Office reported that "Nigeria is a source, transit and destination country for the trafficking of women and girls for forced labour and sexual exploitation" and "that 6,993 potential victims of modern day slavery were referred in 2018, an increase from 5,142 in 2017."[23] In particular, girls and women tricked or forcibly trafficked are assumed to be part of what some now call Italy's "foreign mafia." Nigerian affiliates dominate a region spanning from Palermo to Turin and are responsible for trafficking women, who, in addition to engaging in sex work, also smuggle illicit substances. The attention drawn to Nigerian sex workers in Italy has incited Italian nationalists to call for a "lock-the doors-order," arguing that Nigerian nationals should be prevented from entering Italy, not as a way to save children from harm but to remove the scourge of scandalous and immoral behavior from the country.[24] Sex trafficking is one of the most written-about illicit phenomena both inside and outside of Nigeria, but another practice is on the rise.

Baby farms, also called baby factories or child harvesting, and illegal adoptions are other forms of child dealing in Southeastern Nigeria that have garnered media attention.[25] A baby farm is where child harvesting occurs: young girls are housed in a closed facility for the purpose of giving birth to children who are then put up for adoption outside the purview of the state. In 2011, Nigerian police stormed the Cross Foundation in Aba, where human traffickers stole newborns from mothers. Some of the thirty-two school-age girls whom the traffickers forcibly held claimed that "the hospital owner gave them $192 (£118) for newborn boys and $161 for newborn girls after they were sold." In May 2013, authorities rescued seventeen teenage girls and eleven babies from a home located in Imo state where one man had impregnated all of the girls. The woman who held the girls captive intended to sell the babies on the black market for up to $6,400 before authorities intervened. Touting the legitimacy of orphanages, a police officer in Rivers State explained that baby farms can be distinguished from orphanages because pregnant women do not reside in orphanages.[26] It is critical to emphasize that the number of instances reported and the amount of money people are willing to pay for children signals how important children are to Nigerians. Women seek to obtain children from baby farms because of the cultural taboos associated with childlessness and adoptions, as well as religious beliefs that stigmatize surrogacy.[27]

As we can see from the data above, human trafficking, sex slavery, and forced child labor practices continue to exist in Nigeria. International groups and humanitarians whose purpose is to end human trafficking will benefit from historical research that exposes the social and economic underpinnings that initiated trafficking and allow it to continue. However, the broad consensus given to the declaration that prompted legal practitioners, social scientists, and human rights activists focused on Nigeria to reframe human trafficking as "new slavery" or "modern-day slavery" remains problematic when it is assumed that contemporary slavery "reemerged" directly from transatlantic slave trade.[28] It is crucial that scholars and humanitarians recognize that slavery, in all of its various forms, has evolved over time. There existed neither a pause and reengagement in slaving practices from two hundred years ago to today nor an absolute reconfiguration of practices stemming from the same historical moment. The movement of bodies and use of labor has always depended on immediate economic, social, and political circumstances, as well as the reiteration and application of force and control. It is only in this nuanced manner that we can truly understand the persistence of slavery as it relates to child trafficking in Southeastern Nigeria today.

NOTES

Preface

1. "African Riot Toll," 5.
2. Matera, Bastian, and Kent, *Women's War of 1929*, 159, 164, 168.
3. Van Allen, "'Sitting on a Man,'" 165–81.
4. Aba Commission of Inquiry, *Notes of Evidence*.
5. I. Tribal Customs and Superstitions of the Southern Province of Nigeria; II. Practice of Pawning Children as Security for Debts of Parents, and S. P. George, *Slave Dealing and Child Stealing Investigation*. "Child dealing" loosely refers to child pawning, stealing, selling, panyarring, and marriage.
6. Jeremy Slack, Daniel E. Martínez, and Prescott Vandervoet, "Methods of Violence: Researcher Safety and Adaptability in Times of Conflict," in Slack, Martínez, and Whiteford, *Shadow of the Wall*, 63–71.

Introduction

1. Rex v. Mbakwe of Avutu and three others, OkiDist 4/11/46.
2. Rex v. Mbakwe of Avutu and three others, OkiDist 4/11/58.
3. United Nations, *Convention against Transnational Organized Crime*, 43.
4. Elodie Razy and Marie Rodet, introduction to Razy and Rodet, *Children on the Move*, 3.
5. Grier, "Child Labor and Africanist Scholarship," 3.
6. Dessy and Pallage, "Worst Forms of Child Labour," 68.
7. Grier, "Child Labor and Africanist Scholarship," 3.
8. Children's Bureau, U.S. Department of Labor, "Child-Welfare News Summary."
9. Sharp, *African Child*, 76–77.
10. "Republic of Liberia: Slavery Does Exist," 10.
11. Sundiata, *From Slaving to Neoslavery*, 7; King, A Proclamation; Christy, Johnson, and Barclay, "1930 Enquiry Commission to Liberia," 277–78.
12. DeMause, *History of Childhood*.
13. Ariès, *Centuries of Childhood*.
14. King, M. "Concepts of Childhood."
15. Stearns, *Growing Up*, 5.
16. Graff, "Review."
17. Ryan, "Social Study of Childhood," and Fass and Mason, *Childhood in America*.
18. Fass and Mason, *Childhood in America*, 2.
19. Heywood, *History of Childhood*; Stearns, *Growing Up*, 15; Cunningham, "Histories of Childhood."
20. Nearing, *Child Labor Problem*, 1–6; quotation on 6.
21. Nardinelli, *Child Labor and the Industrial Revolution*.

22. Diptee and Klein, "African Childhoods," 5; Ndukwe, "Age Grade Practices in Nigeria," 177; U. Dike, "Role of Age Grade," 83–84.

23. Gailey, *Road to Aba*, 16; Ndukwe, "Age Grade Practices in Nigeria," 177, 182; McNee, "Languages of Childhood," 25; Rich, "Searching for Success."

24. Campbell, Miers, and Miller, *Children in Slavery*.

25. Campbell, Miers, and Miller, *Child Slaves in the Modern World*.

26. Lawrance and Roberts, *Trafficking in Slavery's Wake*, and Razy and Rodet, *Children on the Move*.

27. George, *Making Modern Girls*.

28. Aderinto, *Children and Childhood*, 7–12; quotation on 7.

29. Aderinto, *Children and Childhood*.

30. Nwokeji, *Slave Trade and Culture*, 178–79.

31. Duane, *Child Slavery before and after Emancipation*, 5.

32. David Eltis and David Richardson, "New Assessment of the Transatlantic Slave Trade," in Eltis and Richardson, *Extending the Frontiers*, 46–47; Miers, *Slavery in the Twentieth Century*.

33. Anderson, "Human Trafficking Increase"; Young, "Time to Raise the Bar"; Wozniak, "Inmates Rights Groups Protest.

34. League of Nations, "Slavery Convention."

35. Miers, *Slavery in the Twentieth Century*, 47–48; Allain, "Legal Definition of Slavery," in Allain, *Legal Understanding of Slavery*, 255–56.

36. Miers, *Slavery in the Twentieth Century*, 19–21.

37. Martin, *Palm Oil and Protest*, 46–47, 52.

38. Elisée Soumonni, "The Compatibility of the Slave and Palm Oil Trades in Dahomey, 1818–1858," in Law, *Slave Trade to "Legitimate" Commerce*, 82.

39. Robin Law, introduction to Law, *Slave Trade to "Legitimate" Commerce*, 1, 7.

40. Kristin Mann and Richard Roberts, introduction to Mann and Roberts, *Law in Colonial Africa*, 27–28.

41. Miers, *Slavery in the Twentieth Century*, 2–3.

42. Mann and Roberts, introduction, 28.

43. Stilwell, *Slavery and Slaving*, 21.

44. Miers, *Ending of the Slave Trade*, 145; Lawrance, *Amistad's Orphans*, 5–7.

45. Duane, *Child Slavery before and after Emancipation*, 3–4; Miers, *Ending of the Slave Trade*, 118–34; M. Klein, introduction to Klein, *Breaking the Chains*, 4–5, and see also Patterson, *Slavery and Social Death*, and Miers and Kopytoff, *Slavery in Africa*; Lovejoy, *Transformation in Slavery*, 1.

46. Mann and Roberts, introduction, 28.

47. Lovejoy and Falola, *Pawnship, Slavery, and Colonialism*, 3, 6.

48. Allina, *Slavery by Any Other Name*, 127–28, and Naanen, "'Demanding Tax from the Dead,'" 71–72.

49. Lovejoy, "Pawnship, Debt, 'Freedom,'" 59. See also Ekechi, "Pawnship in Igbo Society," 175, and H. Klein, *Atlantic Slave Trade*, 5. Furthermore, clients, serfs, and subjects were people who lacked wealth and usually offered to work in return for sustenance and protection.

50. Lovejoy and Falola, *Pawnship, Slavery, and Colonialism*, 16.
51. Lovejoy and Falola, *Pawnship, Slavery, and Colonialism*, 33.
52. Chanock, "A Peculiar Sharpness," 84; Coe, "How Debt Became Care," 306; Falola, *Pawnship in Africa*; Paul E. Lovejoy and Toyin Falola, "Pawnship in Historical Perspective," in Lovejoy and Falola, *Pawnship, Slavery, and Colonialism*, 3. See also Judith Byfield, "Pawns and Politics: The Pawnship Debate in Western Nigeria," 357–86; Paul E. Lovejoy and David Richardson, "'Pawns Will Live When Slaves Is Apt to Dye': Credit, Risk and Trust at Old Calabar in the Era of the Slave Trade," 71–96; and Felix Ekechi, "Pawnship in Igbo Society," 165–86, in Lovejoy and Falola, *Pawnship, Slavery, and Colonialism*.
53. Guyer, *Marginal Gains*.
54. Ezinna, interview, August 29, 2012. Ezinna was born in Aba in 1929 and offered in-depth knowledge about pawning during the 1930s and 1940s.
55. Latham, "Currency, Credit and Capitalism," 599–605; Ekechi, 165; Lovejoy and Falola, *Pawnship, Slavery, and Colonialism*, 3.
56. Falola and Heaton, *A History of Nigeria*, 97.
57. Law, *Slave Trade to "Legitimate" Commerce*, 66–69.
58. Afigbo, *Warrant Chiefs*, 39.
59. K. Dike, *Trade and Politics*, 126.
60. Isichei, *History of Nigeria*, 100, and Law, *Slave Trade to "Legitimate" Commerce*, 72. A partnership among nine of the most prominent firms in the Niger Delta region by 1889, the African Association Ltd., formed the Oil Rivers Protectorate (ORP) in 1891. The creation of the ORP established comprehensive control over the interior trade and was allotted governing power by the British government.
61. As cited in Uche, "Foreign Banks, Africans, and Credit," 688.
62. Afigbo, *Warrant Chiefs*, 56.
63. Carland, *Colonial Office and Nigeria*, 2.
64. Lugard, *Amalgamation of Nigeria*, 4.
65. Brown, "Testing the Boundaries of Marginality," 62–63.
66. Lugard, *Amalgamation of Nigeria*, 6.
67. Afigbo, *Warrant Chiefs*, xiii.
68. Seddon, "Class Struggle in Africa," 62; Miers and Roberts, *End of Slavery in Africa*, 42–43; Brown and van der Linden, "Shifting Boundaries," 4–6.
69. Carland, *Colonial Office and Nigeria*; Lugard, *Diaries of Lord Lugard*, 4:11, 18–19, 26–27. Lugard was born to a British army chaplain who worked in Madras, India, and whose mother was a missionary of the Church Missionary Society. He served as a British soldier in India and then traveled to East Africa, where he worked as a British administrator in 1897. He worked on behalf of the Royal Niger Company as well. In West Africa he also commanded the West African Frontier Force.
70. Afigbo, *Warrant Chiefs*, 16, 6–7.
71. Sharp, *African Child*, 12.
72. Miers and Roberts, *End of Slavery in Africa*, 42–43.

Chapter 1: Politics, Social Relations, and Trade in the Bight of Biafra

1. Eltis and Engerman, "Slave Trade Dominated by Men," 237–57; see also Afigbo, *Abolition of the Slave Trade*, and Paul E. Lovejoy, "The Demography of the Bight of Biafra Slave Trade, ca. 1650–1850," in Falola and Njoku, *Igbo in the Atlantic World*, 146–54.
2. Ofonagoro, "From Traditional to British Currency," 626.
3. Laird and Oldfield, *Narrative of an Expedition*, 102–3, 105.
4. Roberts, "French Colonialism, Imported Technology"; Gadio and Rakowski, "Farmers' Changing Roles," 733; Judith Byfield, "Women, Marriage, Divorce."
5. Korieh, "Commercial Transition in West Africa," 591. See also Roberts, "French Colonialism, Imported Technology," who argues that "any relationship which regularly brought the men's and the women's tasks together, such as slavery, pawnship, and even cooperative relations, could set production in motion" (465). Roberts offers an analysis of production within the African context and genders it by way of looking at how and when men and women are forced to interact economically.
6. Gwyn Campbell, Suzanne Miers, and Joseph C. Miller, introduction to Campbell, Miers, and Miller, *Children in Slavery*, 1–2.
7. Lovejoy, "Olaudah Equiano or Gustavus Vassa," 165. There exists an ongoing academic debate about where Equiano was born, whether in Africa or in Carolina, and how that fact should determine the name used to refer to him; see Afigbo, *Ropes of Sand*, 156. While historians have not been able to identify his exact village, Afigbo, the eminent Igbo scholar, believed that Equiano was born in Nsukke, in northern Igboland.
8. Equiano, *Interesting Narrative*, 46–49. Equiano's biography is well-known and is often taught in colleges and universities throughout the United States. It is popular because it tells the history—a sort of success story—of a freeborn child from the Bight of Biafra who was enslaved and who eventually gained his freedom.
9. Laird and Oldfield, *Narrative of an Expedition*, 287–88. Peter's father was a Bimbia trader who operated in the Cameroons, which was then a part of Southeastern Nigeria. There is no record of the time that passed between his father initially leaving him in pawn with the canoe trader and the subsequent transaction when the slaver stole Peter.
10. Behrendt, Latham, and Northrup, *Diary of Antera Duke*, 237. According to Antera Duke, a slave trader, Calabar slave traders spent up to nine months out of the year in Cameroon.
11. Martinez, *Slave Trade*, 99–100.
12. Laird and Oldfield, *Narrative of an Expedition*, 288.
13. Lovejoy and Richardson, "Business of Slaving," 72.
14. Lovejoy and Richardson, 68–69. Lovejoy and Richardson note the use of human pawns did not dominate slave trade transactions in every city-state, particularly Bonny.

15. For a full discussion on slavery in Igboland, see Oriji, "Igboland," 121–31.

16. Isichei, *Ibo People and the Europeans*, 2; Uchendu, *Igbo of Southeast Nigeria*, 39. The absence of a unified state to coordinate the trade is discussed in David Northrup's *Trade without Rulers* (1978), where he explains how a group of the Igbo, the Aro, were able to link these villages in a trade grid.

17. A. E. Afigbo, "The Aro and the Bight of Biafra," in Falola and Njoku, *Igbo in the Atlantic World*, 71–75.

18. Afigbo, 75.

19. Curtin, *Cross-Cultural Trade*, 48, 217; K. Dike, *Trade and Politics*, 30–31.

20. Nwokeji, *Slave Trade and Culture*, 173; K. Dike and Ekejiuba, *Aro of South-Eastern Nigeria*, 2–3.

21. Isichei, *Igbo Worlds*, 68; Afigbo, "Aro and the Bight of Biafra," 75. See also Nwokeji, *Slave Trade and Culture*, 6, 178–79; K. Dike, *Trade and Politics*, 2; and Nwokeji, *Slave Trade and Culture*, 131.

22. "A Journey to Nsugbe and Nteje, 1897 (S. R. Smith)," in Isichei, *Igbo Worlds*, 204; Nwokeji, *Slave Trade and Culture*, 51, 66.

23. K. Dike, *Trade and Politics*, 1–2, 133–35.

24. Chuku, *Igbo Women*, 43.

25. Hodder, Hodder, and Ukwu, *Markets in West Africa*, 136; Afigbo, "Eclipse of the Aro Slaving Oligarchy, 9.

26. Basden, *Among the Ibos of Nigeria*, 28.

27. Hodder, Hodder, and Ukwu, *Markets in West Africa*, 138–39.

28. Uchendu, *Igbo of Southeast Nigeria*, i.

29. Nwokeji, *Slave Trade and Culture*, 178.

30. Noo Udala, age ca. 102, in Umuaga, 1973, in Isichei, *Igbo Worlds*, 73.

31. Afigbo, *Warrant Chiefs*, 28.

32. K. Dike, *Trade and Politics*, 30–31.

33. Kenneth Morgan, "The Trans-Atlantic Slave Trade from the Bight of Biafra: An Overview," in Falola and Njoku, *Igbo in the Atlantic World*, 89; Doro, letter, 1–2.

34. Forde, *Efik Traders of Old Calabar*, 4, viii.

35. Behrendt, Latham, and Northrup, *Diary of Antera Duke*, 16.

36. Latham, *Old Calabar*, 43–45.

37. Law, *Slave Trade to "Legitimate" Commerce*, 47.

38. Lovejoy and Richardson, "'This Horrid Hole,'" 371–72. Lovejoy and Richardson claim that Bonny's trade was largely due to its ability to secure credit with Europeans and inland traders.

39. Laird and Oldfield, *Narrative of an Expedition*, 341; Lovejoy and Richardson, "'This Horrid Hole,'" 365.

40. K. Dike, *Trade and Politics*, 31.

41. Dike, 183.

42. Martin, *Palm Oil and Protest*, 11; Martin Lynn, "The West African Palm Oil Trade in the Nineteenth Century and the 'Crisis of Adaptation,'" in Law, *Slave Trade to "Legitimate" Commerce*, 57–77.

43. Latham, *Old Calabar*, 90.
44. Johnston, "Journey up the Cross River," 438; Latham, *Old Calabar*, 86, 96; and Forde and Jones, *Ibo and Ibibio-Speaking Peoples*, 91. Though much of their wealth and power depended on the success of the trading houses, the Efik also invested in working the land. Unlike the trading firms at Bonny and Opobo, the Efik turned arable land into palm oil plantations and other types of produce farms at Duke Town and Creek Town, increasing the need for slave labor.
45. Lugard, "Memorandum."
46. Nworah, "Aborigines' Protection Society," 89, 79.
47. Miers and Roberts, *End of Slavery in Africa*, 24.
48. Harris, "Native House Rule Ordinance," 8.
49. Okonkwo, "Lagos Auxiliary," 423–24; "Formation of the Lagos Auxiliary," 4–5.
50. "Native House Rule Amendment Ordinance," 5.
51. Lovejoy and Falola, *Pawnship, Slavery, and Colonialism*, 3.
52. Dennett was an employee of the trading firm Thomas Wilson, Sons & Co. He worked and lived in Kingston upon Hull in England during the 1870s, then becoming employed by Hatton & Cookson trading company in 1879 in the Congo. Dennett was born in Valparaiso, Chile, and educated at Marlborough, an institution that catered to ministers' sons. Cadbury, "Trader in Central Africa," 109.
53. Dennett, "Development of Native Governments," 3.
54. Dennett, 3; Marie Rodet, "Under the Guise of Guardianship and Marriage," in Lawrance and Roberts, *Trafficking in Slavery's Wake*, 86, 95. Rodet argues that children's social mobility increased (moving from one home to another) as a result of the end of the slave trade and that pawnship was one way through which child labor was mobilized during the colonial period.
55. Dennett, *Black Man's Mind*, 40–41.
56. Dennett, "Development of Native Governments"; "Native House Rule Ordinance in Southern Nigeria," 2.
57. Lynn, *Commerce and Economic Change*, 128–70.
58. F. S. James, letter, 3.
59. K. Dike, *Trade and Politics*, 36; Layton, letter.
60. F. E. G. Johnson, letter. from District Commissioner F.E.G. Johnson to the High Provincial Commissioner," November 13, 1911, CSE 8/7/39 : Slave Dealing : Extension of Jurisdiction of D.C.'s to hear and determine cases sitting with Native Court or with selected Assessors-Requests, 1912–1914, NNAE.
61. Punch, *Slave Dealing*; Statement by chiefs to the commissioner of Warri. Even though these were chiefs from the Western Province, their opinions mirrored those of the eastern chiefs; Isichei, *History of Nigeria*, 259.
62. Numa, *Slave Dealing*.
63. A Chief, "Concerning the House Rule Ordinance." In the newspaper article, he calls himself a chief. It is likely that he acquired status within the canoe house through successful trade ventures.

64. A Chief, "Concerning the House Rule Ordinance." Jealous of Joseph, his brothers captured him and threw him in a cistern in the middle of the Canaan desert. Ishmaelites, Midianite traders (nomadic peoples related to Israelites), discovered Joseph, took him to Egypt, and sold him to one of Pharaoh's officers. Joseph would become a powerful man, second to Pharaoh, even though he was a slave.
65. A Chief, 4–5.
66. C. Brown, "Testing the Boundaries of Marginality."
67. A Chief, "Concerning the House Rule Ordinance."
68. C. Johnson, "Editor's Response," 5.
69. Slave Dealing: Precis.
70. Roberts, *Litigants and Households*, 105–9.
71. Miers, *Ending of the Slave Trade*, 301–2; Slave Dealing: Precis.
72. Grant, *Civilised Savagery*, 141–42.
73. Afigbo, *Warrant Chiefs*, 15.
74. Lovejoy and Richardson, "'This Horrid Hole.'"
75. Law, *Slave Trade to "Legitimate" Commerce*, 1; Ekechi, "Pawnship in Igbo Society"; A Chief, "Concerning the House Rule Ordinance."
76. Naanen, "Economy within an Economy."
77. Ofonagoro, "From Traditional to British Currency," 626.

Chapter 2: Colonial Policies and Coercive Labor

1. *Owerri Province Annual Report for 1921*, 12; Isichei, *History of Nigeria*, 424–25.
2. District Officer at Bende, letter.
3. Toyin Falola and Paul E. Lovejoy, "Pawnship in Historical Perspective," in Lovejoy and Falola, *Pawnship, Slavery, and Colonialism*, 4.
4. Miers, *Ending of the Slave Trade*, 301–2.
5. Sir Claude Macdonald of the Foreign Office Protectorate and his successor, Sir Ralph Moor (1896), began the work of instituting the warrant chief system under indirect rule; see Afigbo, *Warrant Chiefs*, 151, 6, 7.
6. Brown, "Testing the Boundaries of Marginality," 52.
7. Law, *Slave Trade to "Legitimate" Commerce*, 66–69.
8. Glover to Newcastle, and Glover to Administrator in-Chief, Sierra Leone.
9. Afigbo, *Warrant Chiefs*, 16, 88–89. Cases in each court could be appealed at the highest level in the district court.
10. Afigbo, 84–85.
11. Afigbo, 90, 14–15.
12. Harneit-Sievers, "Igbo 'Traditional Rulers,'" 60.
13. Paul E. Lovejoy and David Richardson, "Trust, Pawnship, and Atlantic History: The Institutional Foundations of the Old Calabar Slave Trade," 335, 337, 349.
14. German traders were extremely popular in Southeastern Nigeria because they offered higher prices for oil and because the main processing plants were in

Hamburg. The sudden disappearance of this market brought hardship to most Nigerian palm producers when the global economic downturn resulted in a significant decrease in shipments to Germany.

15. Afigbo, *Warrant Chiefs*, 147, 154. Legal practitioners were barred from the Provincial Court, leaving appeals to be heard in the Supreme Court.

16. *Owerri Province Annual Report for 1921*, 131. The court ruled on offenses related to slavery, firearms, wild animals, witchcraft, the murder of twins, etc.

17. *Owerri Province Annual Report for 1921*, 109, 162, 170.

18. *Owerri Province Annual Report for 1921*, 6.

19. Afigbo, *Warrant Chiefs*, 107.

20. Afigbo, 185.

21. Afigbo, 308.

22. Ugwu, interview.

23. *Owerri Province Annual Report for 1821*, 9.

24. Ugwu, interview; *Owerri Province Annual Report for 1921*, 10, 3.

25. Asawalam, interview; *Owerri Province Annual Report for 1921*, 5.

26. Heathcote, memorandum, 153.

27. Afigbo, *Warrant Chiefs*, 189–91.

28. District Officer of Okigwi, letter.

29. In January 1914, all native courts were abolished and replaced by one native court assigned to each district; see Afigbo, *Warrant Chiefs*, 138.

30. Mwalimu, *Nigerian Legal System*, 2:416. The bill was also referred to as the "Money Lenders Bill"; "Pawnbrokers Bill," 1.

31. "Pawnbrokers Bill," 4.

32. Ojo, "Yoruba Credit and Debt Mechanisms Adjusted." 4.

33. "Pawnbrokers Bill," 4–5.

34. "Moneylender's Bill," 2.

35. "News of the Week," 1.

36. Slave Dealing: Extension.

37. Falola, "'My Friend the Shylock,'" 408.

38. "Pawnbrokers Order in Council," 1.

39. *Calabar Province Slave Dealing*, 1–3.

40. Provincial Commissioner at Calabar, letter, 2.

41. *Sessional Papers.*

42. "Register of Freed Slaves," in *Owerri Province Annual Report for 1921*, 43.

43. I. Enactment of Slavery Ordinance, 1916; II. The Slavery (Amendment) Ordinance, 1916.

44. Letter from Lord Lugard to L. G. S., December 25, 1915, in I. Enactment of Slavery Ordinance, 1916; II. The Slavery (Amendment) Ordinance, 1916.

45. Letter from Lord Lugard to L. G. S., January 13, 1916, in I. Enactment of Slavery Ordinance; II. The Slavery (Amendment) Ordinance, 1916.

46. Austin, *Labour, Land, and Capital*, 205; Whyte, "'Freedom but Nothing Else,'" 236.

47. "Native House Rule Amendment Ordinance," 5.
48. For an in-depth discussion of changes in currency usage in Nigeria, see Ekundare, *Economic History of Nigeria*, 85–86, and Jones, *Annual Reports of Bende Division*, 31.
49. Naanen, "Economy within an Economy," 425–28; Ofonagoro, "From Traditional to British Currency"; *Colonial Currency*, 8.
50. Jones, *Annual Reports of Bende Division*, 31, 434–36; Ofonagoro, "From Traditional to British Currency."
51. Southern Provinces, Nigeria, *Annual Report on the Prison Department*, 2; *Owerri Province Annual Report for 1921*, 16, 7.
52. Usoro, *Nigerian Oil Palm Industry*, 2–3.
53. "Report on Native Court Cases in Owerri Province," in *Owerri Province Annual Report for 1921*; *Owerri Province Annual Report for 1921*, 25; Southern Provinces, Nigeria, *Annual Report on the Prison Department*, 2, 5.
54. *Owerri Province Annual Report for 1921*, 8.
55. Southern Provinces, Nigeria, *Annual Report on the Prison Department*, 2. From 1924 to 1928, some Nigerians enjoyed a reprieve from the economic downturn when the prices of palm products recovered, permitting access to additional income.
56. *Owerri Province Annual Report for 1921*, 29, 32.
57. *Owerri Province Annual Report for 1921*, 29.
58. Campbell and Stanziani, *Debt and Slavery*, 2013.
59. Hives, Report on the Pawning of Children, 54.
60. Uzor-Eghelu, letter, May 26, 1925.
61. Okanu of Ochida, letter.
62. Uzor-Eghelu, letter, May 29, 1925.
63. Uzor-Eghelu, letter, May 26, 1925; Chief Ezeonyodu vs. Okanu.
64. Okanu of Ochida, letter.
65. I. Tribal Customs and Superstitions of the Southern Province of Nigeria; II. Practice of Pawning Children as Security for Debts of Parents, 2.
66. Afigbo, *Warrant Chiefs*, 89, 58.
67. *Owerri Province Annual Report for 1922*.
68. *Calabar Province Slave Dealing*, 4; Okeke, *History of Onitsha*, 1–3.
69. Hodder, Hodder, and Ukwu, *Markets in West Africa*, 133–34.
70. *Owerri Province Annual Report for 1921*, 7; K. Dike, *Trade and Politics*, 39; Afigbo, "Eclipse of the Aro Slaving Oligarchy," 4.
71. Murphy, "Pawning of Children," 88.
72. Ashley, "Pawning of Children," 89.
73. Resident of Owerri Province, letter to the Secretary of the Southern Provinces at Lagos, 77.
74. McDaniel, "An Igbo Second Burial," 31–32.
75. The British often conflated the statuses of slaves and pawns/pledges. *Owerri Province Annual Report for 1921*, 43.
76. Oral history by L. O. Nwahiri of Nguru, "Five Nguru Elders, in Chief G. A. Waturuocha's Conference Hall, 9 September, 1972," in Isichei, *Igbo Worlds*, 83. The

five chiefs included Chief G. A. Waṭụrụọcha, age 75; Onuoha, age 90; Edmund I. Waṭụrụọcha, age 70; Chief I. Erege, age 70; and Chief Oparaocha Anyamele, age 65. Ebubedike, interview.

77. Okolo, interview.
78. I. Tribal Customs and Superstitions of the Southern Province of Nigeria; II. Practice of Pawning Children as Security for Debts of Parents, 6. Kwa of the Cameroons spilled over into Calabar and/or engaged in moneylending practices with the Efik and others.
79. The Orsu were located between Enugu and Port Harcourt.
80. I. Tribal Customs and Superstitions of the Southern Province of Nigeria; II. Practice of Pawning Children as Security for Debts of Parents, 5.
81. Hives, Report on the Pawning of Children, 52.
82. Okolo, interview.
83. District Officer at Bende, letter.
84. District Officer at Okigwi, memorandum.
85. District Officer in Awka, letter, 35.
86. I. Tribal Customs and Superstitions of the Southern Province of Nigeria; II. Practice of Pawning Children as Security for Debts of Parents, 95–96.
87. Clifford, letter, 123.
88. Ormsby-Gore, letter, 126–28.
89. Hives, Report on the Pawning of Children, 53; Ezinna, interview, August 29, 2012; Asawalam, interview.
90. Not all pawns suffered at the hands of their master. Some pawns achieved economic success. The most famous example is King Jaja of Opobo. Additionally, there were many pawns who were sent on behalf of their masters to Britain to obtain an education or to learn a trade.
91. Ebubedike, interview.
92. Ebubedike, interview.
93. Ibgocheonwu, interview.
94. Falola and Lovejoy, "Pawnship in Historical Perspective," 2.
95. I. Tribal Customs and Superstitions of the Southern Province of Nigeria; II. Practice of Pawning Children as Security for Debts of Parents, 13; Falola and Lovejoy, "Pawnship in Historical Perspective."

Chapter 3: International Debate on the Welfare of Children, 1920s

1. Snow, "Committee on the Traffic in Women," 414. United States representative William F. Snow served as the chair of the committee. Other members included an Englishman, a Frenchman, a Belgian, a Swede, a Uruguayan woman who was a physician and professor, an Italian woman, and a Japanese man.
2. See Aderinto, *When Sex Threatened the State*, and George, *Making Modern Girls*.
3. Chief Inspector, letter.
4. Copy of minutes by H. E., April 26, 1916, in Lugard, letter to L. G. S.; Chief Inspector, letter.

5. Copy of minutes by H. E.
6. Gorham, "Maiden Tribute of Modern Babylon,'" 353–54. See also Ellis, Juvenile Delinquency.
7. Hendrick, Children, Childhood and English Society, 1. In 1833, the Factory Act banned children under the age of nine from working in steam- or water-powered textile mills; it also limited the workweek of nine- to twelve-year-olds to forty-eight hours. The 1844 act dictated that children could work half days but also had to attend school half days; it lowered the age limit to eight as well. The 1874 Factory Act changed the age limits to ten to thirteen years old.
8. Galbi, "Early English Cotton Mills," 358; Nardinelli, "Child Labor and the Factory Acts," 739–55. See also Nardinelli, Child Labor and the Industrial Revolution, and Hendrick, Children, Childhood, and English Society.
9. Stead, "Maiden Tribute of Modern Babylon"; Badran, Feminists, Islam, and Nation, 192–93.
10. "Turning from Child Labor."
11. "Labor Shortage Forcing Children"; Marland, Health and Girlhood in Britain, 155–88.
12. Pusey, "June 3, 1918."
13. "Labor Shortage Forcing Children."
14. "Child Labor," 834–35; Morrison, Childhood and Colonial Modernity, 53–54; Aderinto, "Empire Day in Africa," 732–34.
15. Huberman and Meissner, "Riding the Wave of Trade," 664; Samson, "ILO," 32. The ILO was established by the Treaty of Versailles.
16. "International Convention for the Suppression of the Traffic"; Traffic in Persons, chap. 7. Previous iterations of this convention were ratified in 1904 and 1910 as the Convention for Suppression of White Slave Trade.
17. Snow, "Committee on the Traffic in Women," 411–17.
18. "Health and Social Questions Section"; Weindling, International Health Organisations and Movements; Lauren, Evolution of International Human Rights, 110; "Geneva Declaration"; Sharp, African Child, 4.
19. Lauren, Evolution of International Human Rights, 120. Jebb's mission had long-lasting effects and motivated the 1931 conference on "the African child." Sharp, African Child.
20. Lauren, Evolution of International Human Rights, 103; Byfield, Bluest Hands, 136.
21. Burrill, States of Marriage, 32.
22. Miers, "Contemporary Forms of Slavery," 716.
23. National Industrial Conference Board, International Labor Organization, 1–2. Early iterations of the ILO included the Second Internationale, the International Conference for Labor Protection, and the International Association for Labor Legislation. The early creation of these institutions resulted directly from the Industrial Revolution (1750–1850) and its associated labor demands.
24. Weindling, International Health Organisations and Movements, 163. Organizations included the International Council of Women and the International Women's

Suffrage Alliance. Lathrop, "International Child Welfare Problems"; National Industrial Conference Board, *International Labor Organization*, 1–2.

25. Morris, "Statutory Marriage Law," 37.

26. Olomojobi, "Marriage in Nigeria," 7–8.

27. I. Tribal Customs and Superstitions of the Southern Province of Nigeria; II. Practice of Pawning Children as Security for Debts of Parents.

28. Grosz-Ngaté, "Social Relations," 59.

29. Mann, *Marrying Well*, 35; Lindsay, *Working with Gender*, 36, 46; Esther Goody, "A Framework for the Analysis of Parent Roles," in Alber, Martin, and Notermans, *Child Fostering in West Africa*, 37.

30. "Covenant of the League of Nations," 12.

31. Agbo, interview.

32. Afigbo, *Abolition of the Slave Trade*, 56. See also Meillassoux, *Maidens, Meal, and Money*, 61–62.

33. Amadiume, *Male Daughters, Female Husbands*, 60–79.

34. Jones, *Annual Reports of Bende Division*, 91.

35. Basden, *Among the Ibos of Nigeria*, 70–71; Jones, *Annual Reports of Bende Division*, 91.

36. Ibeawuchi, interview.

37. Allman, "Rounding up Spinsters," 201–3; Rattray, *Ashanti Law and Constitution*.

38. Ibgocheonwu, interview; Agu, interview; Agbo, interview.

39. Azuka, interview.

40. I. Tribal Customs and Superstitions of the Southern Province of Nigeria; II. Practice of Pawning Children as Security for Debts of Parents, 92–93.

41. Nwadinko, interview; Ezeji, interview.

42. Van den Bersselaar, "In Search of Igbo Identity," 178. District Officer of Owerri Reginald Hargrove compiled and edited the responses.

43. Afigbo, *Abolition of the Slave Trade*, 72–73; I. Tribal Customs and Superstitions of the Southern Province of Nigeria; II. Practice of Pawning Children as Security for Debts of Parents; Tribal Customs and Superstitions of Southern Nigeria.

44. Memorandum, "Pawning of Children," from the Resident of the Benin Province to the District Officers of Benin, Ishan, Auchi, Asaba and the Assistant District Officer of Agbor, in the file I. Tribal Customs and Superstitions of the Southern Province of Nigeria; II. Practice of Pawning Children as Security for Debts of Parents, found on page 43 of file.

45. Azuka, interview.

46. Marcellenus, interview.

47. F. Ferguson, Report: Pawning of Children, in I. Tribal Customs and Superstitions of the Southern Province of Nigeria; II. Practice of Pawning Children as Security for Debts of Parents, March 1, 1923, 1–2.

48. H. T. B. Dew, letter, 37–39.

49. Nmah, "Land Identity Crisis," 140–41.

50. Okolo, interview.

51. Okolo, Interview.
52. Nwadinko, interview.
53. *Owerri Province Annual Report for 1921*, 42; Ibeawuchi, interview; Okolo, interview.
54. Okolo, interview. It is important to note that while many societies in Southeastern Nigeria pawned sons and daughters, Abraham of Nike claims that the Nike people never pawned boys.
55. Horton, "Ohu System of Slavery." Horton claims that many of the children came from Agbaja.
56. Falk, letter, 107.
57. Stevenson, letter.
58. *Owerri Province Annual Report for 1921*, 27.
59. Reuben, interview.
60. I. Tribal Customs and Superstitions of the Southern Province of Nigeria; II. Practice of Pawning Children as Security for Debts of Parents, March 5, 1923, page 74 in file.
61. Letter from the District Officer in Awka to the Senior Resident of Onitsha Province, (February 15, 1923), in I. Enactment of Slavery Ordinance, 1916; II. The Slavery (Amendment) Ordinance, 1916, 35.
62. Reuben, interview.
63. McKenzie, "A Few Words of Interest," 126; Lovejoy and Richardson, "Business of Slaving."
64. Pedersen, *Guardians*, 5.
65. Archival and primary sources, as well as informants, suggest that there were no fixed time limits for a girl pawn to be held before she was taken as a wife. In each case, the prevailing personal situation of both the moneylender and the debtor determined the outcome of the pawning transaction.
66. Hives, Report on the Pawning of Children.
67. Brown, "Testing the Boundaries of Marginality," 53.
68. M. Green, *Ibo Village Affairs*, 158.
69. Report by Mr. O. W. Firth, District Officer in Charge of Okigwi Division, Pawning of Children, January 31, 1923, in I. Tribal Customs and Superstitions of the Southern Province of Nigeria; II. Practice of Pawning Children as Security for Debts of Parents, 73; I. Tribal Customs and Superstitions of the Southern Province of Nigeria; II. Practice of Pawning Children as Security for Debts of Parents.
70. Chanock, *Law, Custom and Social Order*, 4.
71. Mr. Butler, District Officer of Warri, letter, in I. Tribal Customs and Superstitions of the Southern Province of Nigeria; II. Practice of Pawning Children as Security for Debts of Parents, 93.
72. Ross, letter.
73. Davidoff and Hall, *Family Fortunes, 18–19*.
74. Pitman, "Treatment of the British West Indian Slaves," 616.
75. Nwadinko, interview.
76. *Owerri Province Annual Report for 1921*.

77. I. Tribal Customs and Superstitions of the Southern Province of Nigeria; II. Practice of Pawning Children as Security for Debts of Parents.
78. Schwelb, "Marriage and Human Rights," 338.
79. Olatunji Ojo, "Forced Marriage, Gender, and Consent in Igboland, 1900–1936," in Bunting, Lawrance, and Roberts, *Marriage by Force?*, 77–80.
80. Afigbo, "Revolution and Reaction," 551.

Chapter 4: The 1929 *Ogu Umunwaanyi* (Women's War)

1. M. Green, *Ibo Village Affairs*.
2. Aba Commission of Inquiry, *Notes of Evidence* (hereafter cited as *Notes*). See also Akpan and Ekpo, *Women's War of 1929*.
3. Matera, Bastian, and Kent, *Women's War of 1929*, 132.
4. Falola and Paddock, *Women's War of 1929*, 98–99.
5. *Notes*.
6. *Notes*, 221–22.
7. Rasheed Olaniyi, "Economic Crises and Child Trafficking in Nigeria: A Comparative Analysis of the 1930s and 1990s," in Agbu, *Youth in the Labour Process*, 38; Afigbo, *Abolition of the Slave Trade*, 119; Gloria Chuku, "Gender Relations in Nineteenth- and Early Twentieth-Century Igbo Society," in Falola and Njoku, *Igbo in the Atlantic World*, 22.
8. Perham, *Native Administration in Nigeria*, 30, 211; Leith-Ross, *African Women*, 20–22.
9. Van Allen, "'Sitting on a Man.'"
10. Ifeka-Moller, "Reply to Judith Van Allen," 318.
11. Caroline Ifeka-Moller, "Female Militancy and Colonial Revolt: The Women's War of 1929," in Ardener, *Perceiving Women*, 143; Leith-Ross, *African Women*; Uchendu, *Igbo of Southeast Nigeria*.
12. Hanna, "Dance and the 'Women's War,'" 25–27.
13. See Gailey, *Road to Aba*; Afigbo, *Warrant Chiefs*; Elizabeth Isichei, *A History of the Igbo People* (New York: St. Martin's Press, 1976); Mba, *Nigerian Women Mobilized*; Akpan and Ekpo, *Women's War of 1929*; Amadiume, *Daughters of the Goddess*; and Chuku, *Igbo Women*, among others.
14. Gailey, *Road to Aba*, 100; Matera, Bastian, and Kent, *Women's War of 1929*, 15–77.
15. Falola and Paddock, *The Women's War of 1929*.
16. Matera, Bastian, and Kent, *Women's War of 1929*; Falola and Paddock, *Women's War of 1929*; Byfield, "Becoming Classic," 143.
17. Van den Bersselaar, "Establishing Facts," 87; Gailey, *Road to Aba*, 90.
18. Matera, Bastian and Kent, *Women's War of 1929*, 113; Misty L. Bastian, "Dancing Women and Colonial Men: The Nwaobiala," in Hodgson and McCurdy, *"Wicked" Women*, 110–12.
19. Bastian, "Dancing Women," 116–19.
20. Matera, Bastian, and Kent, *Women's War of 1929*, 119–20, 126. Ala/Ani is the deity of fertility, earth, and morality and considered the mother of the Igbo.

21. Chuku, "Igbo Women and Political Participation," 88.
22. Matera, Bastian, and Kent, *Women's War of 1929*, 116–17.
23. Matera, Bastian, and Kent, 100, 124; Beringer, *Influenza Epidemic of 1918*.
24. Chuku, *Igbo Women;* Martin, *Palm Oil and Protest*, 106.
25. Martin, *Palm Oil and Protest*, 107.
26. Nigerian Correspondent, "Disturbances in S.E. Nigeria," 1450.
27. Nigerian Correspondent, "Disturbances in S.E. Nigeria."
28. F. Cooper, *Decolonization and African Society*, 44; Falola and Paddock, *Women's War of 1929*, 45; Commission of Inquiry Appointed to Inquire into the Disturbance in the Calabar and Owerri Provinces, December, 1929, *Notes of Evidence*, 279–80.
29. Falola and Paddock, *Women's War of 1929*, 45; F. Cooper, *Decolonization and African Society*, 17.
30. Kaplan, *Democracy*, 73; Falola and Paddock, *Women's War of 1929*, 46; Afigbo, "Revolution and Reaction," 551.
31. *Notes*, 6.
32. See Perham, *Native Administration in Nigeria*, 208. Perham offers an explanation about the implication of counting a woman's animals. The animals that belong to a compound are most often considered the personal belongings of a wife. Hence, if the chiefs attempted to count these possessions, women might conclude that they would be taxed.
33. *Notes*, no. 363, 24–25, 11–18; Report of the Commission of Inquiry into the Disturbances in the Calabar and Owerri Provinces, December 1929 (January 1930), 11–18.
34. Akpan and Ekpo, *Women's War of 1929*, 26, 62, 27.
35. Falola and Paddock, *Women's War of 1929*, 49–62.
36. Nigerian Correspondent, "Disturbances in S.E. Nigeria," 1437; *Notes*, no. 2039, 101.
37. Madam Adiaha Edem was the mother of the man who later served as the president of the Ibibio Union and judge, Sir Udo Udoma. Akpan and Ekpo, *Women's War of 1929*, 41–43.
38. Nwugo Enyidie was the twelfth witness to testify at the Commission of Inquiry. She was a participant of the Woman's War on Okugo's compound. *Notes*, no. 1184, 62.
39. *Notes*, 56.
40. *Notes*, 260, 201.
41. Okolo, interview.
42. *Notes*, 665; Afigbo, *Abolition of the Slave Trade*, 119.
43. *Notes*, no. 15470, 805; 516; 701.
44. Reuben, interview.
45. Ugwu, interview.
46. Nwadinko, interview.
47. Kirby, *Child Workers and Industrial Health*, 124–30; quotation on 125
48. Dew, letter, 37.
49. Okolo, interview; Agubaram, interview.

50. Dew, letter, 37–39.
51. *Notes*, no. 2759, 138; no. 3256, 166; no. 3443, 175; no. 12967, 679; no. 14626, 760; no. 3596, 186.
52. *Notes*, no. 2321, 114.
53. *Notes*, no. 5764, 297; 261; nos. 3540–41, 182; no. 16074, 842.
54. *Notes*, 233.
55. I. Tribal Customs and Superstitions of the Southern Province of Nigeria; II. Practice of Pawning Children as Security for Debts of Parents, 96.
56. Clifford, letter, 123.
57. *Notes*, no. 1025, 54; 221.
58. Dew, letter, 39.
59. Echewa, *I Saw the Sky Catch Fire*, 169, 161–64.
60. Echewa, interview.
61. Echewa, interview.
62. Echewa, interview; Eve Ensler, *The Vagina Monologues*. Ensler is a second-wave feminist whose work highlights women's voices.
63. Echewa, interview.
64. Echewa, interview.
65. Echewa, *I Saw the Sky Catch Fire*, 171; Echewa, interview.
66. *Notes*, no. 2039, 101. This act, also known as the Peace Preservation Ordinance, allowed the colonial government "to do all things necessary for preventing riots."
67. Echewa, interview.
68. Echewa, interview.
69. *Notes*, no. 5703, 294.
70. Perham, *Native Administration in Nigeria*, 218; Gailey, *Road to Aba, 100*.
71. *Notes*, no. 2098, 104.
72. Philomena E. Okeke, "Negotiating Social Independence: The Challenges of Career Pursuits for Igbo Women in Postcolonial Nigeria," in Hodgson and McCurdy, *"Wicked" Women*, 236; Gailey, *Road to Aba*, 97.
73. Afigbo, *The Warrant Chiefs*, 240.

Chapter 5: Child Trafficking after the War

1. Eheakandu, Statement.
2. Ochonu, 104–6.
3. George, *Slave Dealing and Child Stealing*, 153; Afigbo, *Abolition of the Slave Trade*, 85.
4. Weindling, *International Health Organisations and Movements*, 163; Pedersen, *Eleanor Rathbone*, 246–49.
5. *Council for the Representation of Women.*
6. "Dame Maria Ogilvie Gordon." As a specialist in geology and paleontology, Gordon was the first woman to receive a PhD from the University of Munich.
7. *Council for the Representation of Women.* Affiliated societies included the National Council of Women of Great Britain and Ireland, National Union of Societies

for Equal Citizenship, National Union of Teachers, National Women's Citizen's Association, Association of Assistant Mistresses, Association of Head Mistresses, Association for Moral and Social Hygiene, Association of Teachers of Domestic Subjects, Association of Post Office Women Clerks, Social and Political Alliance, Conservative Women's Reform Association, Women Civil Servants, Society for Women's Service, Mother's Union, Nursing Association, Open Door Council, Freedom League, and other groups; see "Dame Maria Ogilvie Gordon."

8. Slater, "Ladies of the Night," 541. Founded in 1901, the Royal African Society memorialized and celebrated Mary Kingsley, who as a writer-traveler throughout Africa during the 1890s encouraged the study of Africa in the United Kingdom. "Dinner of the Society," 359.

9. Macmillan, "Nationality of Married Women," 142–54.

10. Roe, "Collisson, Marjorie Chave." Collisson was born to English parents in 1887 in Indiana. She moved with her parents to Tanzania and then to South Australia on account of her father being a clergyman. In 1916 she attended the University of Sydney and won multiple honors for her historical research, becoming known as a "pestilential feminist." During the mid-1920s she worked on behalf of indigenous populations in India and Australia and was later a member of the International Alliance of Women and chair of its Equal Moral Standard Committee.

11. Simkin, "Margery Corbett Ashby." In 1900, at the age of 18, Ashby and her sister formed the group Younger Suffragists. It was in 1901, when she attended Newnham College in Cambridge, that she joined the National Union of Women Suffrage Societies, and a year later she became the Constitutional Suffrage Movement's secretary. She also served as the secretary for the National Union of Women Suffrage Societies in 1907, which united with the International Woman Suffrage Alliance in 1909. In the meantime, she had formed the Liberal Suffrage group with her sister and mother. In 1919, she attended the Versailles Peace Conference as a member of the International Alliance of Women and was elected president of the International Woman Suffrage Alliance in 1923.

12. *Council for the Representation of Women*, 30.

13. Flood, Notes on the position of women, 3–5; "Slavery: Slavery of Women"; Mark Bevir, *The Making of British Socialism*, 174–76, 180. As a British socialist organization, the Fabian Society touted democratic socialism and encouraged society to transform gradually. Influenced by his "liberal radical" father, Webb embraced utilitarian ethical principles and democratic socialism (Bevir, 175).

14. Sharp, *African Child*, 76.

15. Cammaert, *Undesirable Practices*, 192.

16. O. W. Firth, "Owerri Province Annual Report, 1932."

17. *Owerri Province Annual Report for 1921*, 11.

18. Okolo, interview.

19. Thomas, letter.

20. Provincial Commissioner at Calabar, letter, 2–4.

21. George, *Slave Dealing and Child Stealing Investigation*, 110.

22. Jacob, *Working Out Egypt*, 134; Flood, Notes on the Position of Women, 39–40.

23. George, *Slave Dealing and Child Stealing Investigation*, 127.
24. Assistant Inspector-General of Police, letter.
25. Obuta, "Statement," 6; Okofo, "Statement," 28; Oduomyenma, "Statement," 129.
26. Isichei, *Igbo Worlds*.
27. Dickinson, letter, 26.
28. Rex v. Wilson Edom," 3.
29. Bell, *Slave Dealing and Child Stealing: Monthly Report, September 1934*, 67, 71.
30. Garden, *Slave Dealing. Report for December, 1933*, 42; Naanen, "'Itinerant Gold Mines,'" 71.
31. Garden, *Slave Dealing. Report for December, 1933*, 43.
32. Garden, 41.
33. District Officer in Okigwi, letter, 34. Known aggressors in Obowo were Inyama of Alike, Ihemebere, Jeremiah Okafor (an Aro living in Amuzari), and Okpara Nwokeke.
34. Naanen, "'Itinerant Gold Mines,'" 71.
35. *Council for the Representation of Women.*
36. District Officer in Okigwi, letter, 35.
37. District Officer in Okigwi, letter.
38. Dickinson, letter.
39. Falola, *Colonialism and Violence in Nigeria*, 40.
40. District Officer in Okigwi, letter, 36.
41. George, *Slave Dealing and Child Stealing Investigation*, 110.
42. Dickinson, letter, 26.
43. Garden, *Slave Dealing: Report for December, 1933*, 41.
44. Garden, *Slave Dealing Report: Report for March 1934*, 60.
45. Garden, *Slave Dealing: Report for December, 1933*, 41.
46. District Officer in Okigwi, letter, 35.
47. Garden, *Slave Dealing: Report for December, 1933*.
48. District Officer in Okigwi, letter, 40.
49. Naanen, "'Itinerant Gold Mines,'" 63; Manton, "'The Lost Province,'" 327, 332.
50. Garden, letter, 54, 52, 50.
51. Garden, letter, 51; Naanen, "'Itinerant Gold Mines,'" 60.
52. Bell, *Slave Dealing and Child Stealing: Monthly Report, September 1934*, 68.
53. Garden, letter, 50.
54. Afigbo, *Abolition of the Slave Trade*, 124.
55. Garden, letter, 54; Garden, *Slave Dealing Report: Report for March 1934*, 59.
56. Bell, *Slave Dealing and Child Stealing: Monthly Report, November 1934*, 100; Garden, letter, 51.
57. Garden, *Slave Dealing: Monthly Report, February 1934*, 55–57.
58. Bell, *Slave Dealing and Child Stealing: Monthly Report, October 1934*, 93.
59. Bell, *Slave Dealing and Child Stealing: Monthly Report, September 1934*, 68.
60. George, *Slave Dealing and Child Stealing Investigation*, 110; Uchendu, *Igbo of Southeast Nigeria*, 86; Rex v. Mbakwe; Brown, "Construction of Working-Class Masculinity," 48.

61. Afigbo, *Abolition of the Slave Trade*, 125; Bell, *Slave Dealing and Child Stealing: Monthly Report, September, 1934*, 76.

62. Bell, *Slave Dealing and Child Stealing: Monthly Report, October, 1934*, 95, and *Slave Dealing and Child Stealing: Monthly Report, September, 1934*, 70.

63. George, *Slave Dealing and Child Stealing*, 146.

64. District Officer of Bende, letter, 11.

65. Ekpo-Otu, "Contestations of Identity," 75.

66. Aderinto, *When Sex Threatened the State*, 82–86, 74; White, *Comforts of Home*, 2, 13; Ekpo-Otu, "Contestations of Identity," 74.

67. Bell, *Slave Dealing and Child Stealing: Monthly Report, October 1934*, 90; George, *Slave Dealing and Child Stealing Investigation*, 110.

68. Garden, *Slave Dealing: Report for January, 1934*, 49.

69. Haydock-Wilson, *Slave Dealing and Child Stealing*, 212.

70. Ekejiuba, "Omu Okwei," 213. The Royal Niger Company (originally the National African Company) had dominated trade activities along the Niger River during the nineteenth and early twentieth centuries.

71. Isichei, *History of Nigeria*, 100. Ekejiuba, "Omu Okwei," 215. See also Emecheta, *Slave Girl*. Similar to Okwei's biography, Emecheta's novel offers the narrative of a successful female trader. It shows how women traders were common, especially in major market towns like Onitsha. The story features a young girl named Ogbanje Ojebeta, who after her parents' deaths was sold by her brother to a prominent female textile trader, for whom she worked as a seamstress.

72. This practice is strikingly similar to the practice of the eighteenth-century signares on the Senegal River, who married Portuguese and French men to gain special trade items; when the men returned to Europe, they contracted yet another "marriage."

73. Ekejiuba, "Omu Okwei," 216, 219.

74. Ugwu, interview. Adoption during the 1920s and 1930s referred to a type of fosterage. According to oral testimony, poor parents generally gave the child away, and the child would not know that he/she was adopted until old age; see Reuben, interview. According to Chief Rueben, formal adoption was not conducted until after World War II.

75. I. Tribal Customs and Superstitions of the Southern Province of Nigeria; II. Practice of Pawning Children as Security for Debts of Parents.

76. Ochonu, *Colonial Meltdown*, 2; Hardt and Negri, *Empire*, 322–28.

77. George, *Slave Dealing and Child Stealing Investigation: Monthly Report, March 1935*, 131.

78. Kelly, letter, 204.

79. Resident of Owerri Province, letter to the Secretary, Southern Provinces at Enugu," April 15, 1936, 202.

80. Kelly, letter, 202.

81. Afigbo, *Abolition of the Slave Trade*, 108.

82. Afigbo, 87.

83. Dickins, letter, 26.

84. Stevenson, letter.
85. Ezinna, follow-up interview, September 2012.
86. George, *Slave Dealing and Child Stealing Investigation*.

Conclusion

1. International Labour Organization, *Global Estimates of Modern Slavery*, 2; United States Department of State, *Trafficking in Persons Report 2017*, 313; United States Department of State, "Local Solutions to a Global Problem; United States Department of State, *Trafficking in Persons Report 2018*.
2. Howard, "Teenage Labor Migration," 125, and Lawrance, "Human Trafficking 'Crises,'" 71.
3. United Nations Children's Fund, *Child Trafficking in West Africa*.
4. Cullen-DuPont, *Human Trafficking*, 23.
5. Alison Brysk, "Rethinking Trafficking: Human Rights and Private Wrongs," in Brysk and Choi-Fitzpatrick, *Human Trafficking to Human Rights*, 74; Manzo, "Exploiting West Africa's Children," 394.
6. Lawrance, "Human Trafficking 'Crises,'" 66–67, 70–71, and International Labour Organization, *Combating Child Labour in Cocoa Growing*. Often, agencies mainly focus on ending the 'the worst forms of child labor' as opposed to ending all trafficking in children.
7. Joanne Westwood, "Unearthing Melodrama: Moral Panic Theory and the Enduring Characterization of Child Trafficking," in Cree, Clapton, and Smith, *Revisiting Moral Panics*, 86.
8. Fourchard, "Limits of Penal Reform," 517; Heap, "'Jaguda' Boys,'" 339–41.
9. "Welfare of the Young," 6; see Aderinto, *When Sex Threatened the State*, for a full discussion of prostitution in Nigeria; Abosede George, "Within Salvation: Girl Hawkers and the Colonial State in Development Era Lagos,' in Aderinto, *Children and Childhood*, 202.
10. "Announcements," 24; "Supplement," 26.
11. Uncle Mike, "Beware of Human Wolves," 4; Chapdelaine, "Marriage Certificates and Walker Cards."
12. Universal Declaration of Human Rights.
13. Kigbu and Hassan, "Legal Framework," 214.
14. Osakwe and Lipede, "Nigerian Child in War and Peace," 65.
15. Echendu, "Recollections of Childhood Experiences," 404, 408–9.
16. Aka, "Bridging the Gap," 11.
17. R. Green, "A Cloth Untrue," 209–11.
18. Geo-Jaja and Mangum, "Structural Adjustment," 31–32; Aderinto, "Problem of Nigeria"; Babatunde, "Human Trafficking," 62–64; Roger A. Tsafack Nanfosso, "Child Labor in Cameroon," in Hindman, *World History of Child Labor*, 251–53.
19. Women's Consortium of Nigeria, "Trafficking in Nigeria"; Omorodion, "Vulnerability of Nigerian Secondary School"; Kara, *Modern Slavery*, 51.

20. Adelaja, Labo, and Penar, "Root Causes of Terrorism," 37.
21. Mbah, "Nigeria's Chibok Schoolgirls."
22. Tim Cocks and Isaac Abrak, "Nigeria's Boko Haram Threatens to Sell Kidnapped Schoolgirls," Thomas Reuters, May 5, 2014. Boko Haram means "Western education is sinful."
23. Nigeria Home Office, *Country Policy and Information Note*, 7–8.
24. Harlan and Pitrelli, "Foreign Mafia."
25. Chapdelaine, "'He Remains a Second Person.'"
26. Smith, "Nigerian 'Baby Farm' Raided"; "Nigeria 'Baby Factory' Raided in Imo State"; Owolabi and George, "Nigerian Police Free Children."
27. Alabi, "Socioeconomic Dynamism," 1–9; Chapdelaine, "'He Remains a Second Person.'"
28. Okogbule, "Combatting the 'New Slavery,'" 58.

Bibliography

Secondary Sources

Adelaja, Adesoji O., Abdullahi Labo, and Eva Penar. "Public Opinion on the Root Causes of Terrorism and Objectives of Terrorists: A Boko Haram Case Study." *Perspectives in Terrorism* 12, no. 3 (June 2018): 35–49.

Aderinto, Saheed, ed. *Children and Childhood in Colonial Nigerian Histories.* New York: Palgrave Macmillan, 2015.

———. "Empire Day in Africa: Patriotic Colonial Childhood, Imperial Spectacle and Nationalism in Nigeria, 1905–1960." *Journal of Imperial and Commonwealth History* 46, no. 4 (April 2018): 731–57.

———. "The Problem of Nigeria Is Slavery, Not White Slave Traffic." *Canadian Journal of African Studies* 46, no. 1 (2012): 1–22.

———. *When Sex Threatened the State: Illicit Sexuality, Nationalism, and Politics in Colonial Nigeria, 1900–1958.* Champaign: University of Illinois Press, 2015.

Afigbo, A. E. *The Abolition of the Slave Trade in Southeastern Nigeria, 1885–1950.* Rochester, NY: University of Rochester Press, 2006.

———. "The Eclipse of the Aro Slaving Oligarchy of South-Eastern Nigeria, 1901–1927." *Journal of the Historical Society of Nigeria* 6, no. 1 (December 1971): 3–24.

———. "Revolution and Reaction in Eastern Nigeria, 1900–1929: The Background to the Women's Riot of 1929." *Journal of the Historical Society of Nigeria* 3, no. 3 (December 1966): 539–57.

———. *Ropes of Sand: Studies in Igbo History and Culture.* Oxford: Oxford University Press, 1981.

———. *The Warrant Chiefs: Indirect Rule in Southeastern Nigeria, 1891–1929.* London: Longman Group Limited, 1972.

Africa and the Americas: Culture, Politics, and History; A Multidisciplinary Encyclopedia. Santa Barbara, CA: ABC-CLIO, 2008.

Agbu, Osita. *Children and Youth in the Labour Process in Africa*. Dakar, Senegal: African Books Collective, 2009.

Aka, Philip C. "Bridging the Gap between Theory and Practice in Humanitarian Action: Eight Steps to Humanitarian Wellness in Nigeria." *Williamette Journal of International Law and Dispute Resolution* 24, no. 1 (2016): 1–52.

Akpan, Ekwere Otu, and Violetta I. Ekpo. *The Women's War of 1929: Popular Uprising in Southeastern Nigeria (Preliminary Study)*. Calabar, Nigeria: Government Printer, 1988.

Alabi, Oluwatobi Joseph. "Socioeconomic Dynamism and the Growth of Baby Factories in Nigeria." In "Reproductive Health in Sub-Saharan Africa." Special collection, *SAGE Open*, April–June 2018, 1–9.

Alber, Erdmute, Jeannett Martin, and Catrien Notermans, eds. *Child Fostering in West Africa*. Leiden, Netherlands: Brill, 2013.

Allain, Jean, ed. *The Legal Understanding of Slavery: From the Historical to the Contemporary*. Oxford: Oxford University Press, 2012.

Allina, Eric. *Slavery by Any Other Name: African Life under Company Rule in Colonial Mozambique*. Charlottesville: University of Virginia Press, 2012.

Allman, Jean. Rounding up Spinsters: Gender Chaos and Unmarried Women in Colonial Asanra." *Journal of African History* 37, no. 2 (1996): 195–214.

Allman, Jean, Susan Geiger, and Nakanyike Musisi, eds. *Women in African Colonial Histories*. Bloomington: Indiana University Press, 2002.

Amadiume, Ifi. *Daughters of the Goddess, Daughters of Imperialism: African Women, Culture, Power and Democracy*. London: Zed Books, 2005.

———. *Male Daughters, Female Husbands: Gender and Sex in African Society*. London: Zed Books, 1987.

Ampofo, Akosua Adomako, Josephine Beoku-Betts, Wairimu Ngaruiya Njambi, and Mary Osirim. "Women's and Gender Studies in English-Speaking Sub-Saharan Africa: A Review of Research in the Social Sciences." *Gender and Society* 18, no. 6 (December 2004): 685–714.

Ardener, Shirley, ed. *Perceiving Women*. London: Malaby Press, 1975.

Ariès, Philippe. *Centuries of Childhood: A Social History of Family Life*. New York: Vintage, 1965.

BIBLIOGRAPHY

Austin, Gareth. *Labour, Land, and Capital in Ghana: From Slavery to Free Labour in Asante, 1807–1956*. Rochester, NY: Boydell & Brewer, University of Rochester Press, 2005.

Babatunde, Abosede Omowumi. "Human Trafficking and Transnational Organized Crime: Implications for Security in Nigeria." *Peace Research* 46, no. 1 (2014): 61–84.

Badran, Margot. *Feminists, Islam, and Nation: Gender and the Making of Modern Egypt*. Princeton, NJ: Princeton University Press, 1995.

Basden, G. T. *Among the Ibos of Nigeria: An Account of the Curious & Interesting Habits, Customs & Beliefs of a Little Known African People*. Stroud, Gloucestershire: Nonsuch Publishing, 2006.

Behrendt, Stephen D., A. J. H. Latham, and David Northrup. *The Diary of Antera Duke, an Eighteenth-Century African Slave Trader*. New York: Oxford University Press, 2010.

Bevir, Mark. *The Making of British Socialism*. Princeton, NJ: Princeton University Press, 2011.

Bourdillon, Michael, and Georges M. Mutambwa, eds. *The Place of Work in African Childhoods*. Dakar, Senegal: Codesria, 2014.

Brooks, George E. *Eurafricans in Western Africa: Commerce, Social Status, Gender and Religious Observance from the Sixteenth Century to the Eighteenth Century*. Athens: Ohio University Press, 2003.

Brown, Carolyn. "Race and the Construction of Working-Class Masculinity in the Nigerian Coal Industry: The Initial Phase, 1914–1930." In "Working-Class Subjectivities and Sexualities." Special issue, *International Labor and Working-Class History*, no. 69: Working Class Subjectivities and Sexualities (Spring 2006): 35–56.

Brown, Carolyn A. "Testing the Boundaries of Marginality: Twentieth-Century Slavery and Emancipation Struggles in Nkanu, Northern Igboland, 1920–29." *Journal of African History* 37, no. 1 (January 1, 1996): 51–80.

———. *We Were All Slaves: African Miners, Culture, and Resistance at the Enugu Government Colliery, Nigeria*. Portsmouth, NH: Heinemann, 2003.

Brown, Carolyn, and Marcel van der Linden. "Shifting Boundaries between Free and Unfree Labor: Introduction." *International Labor and Working-Class History* 78, no. 1 (Fall 2010): 4–11.

Brysk, Alison, and Austin Choi-Fitzpatrick, eds. *From Human Trafficking to Human Rights: Reframing Contemporary Slavery*. Philadelphia: University of Pennsylvania Press, 2013.

Bunting, Annie, Benjamin N. Lawrance, and Richard L. Roberts, eds. *Marriage by Force? Contestation over Consent and Coercion in Africa*. Athens: Ohio University Press, 2016.

Burrill, Emily S. *State of Marriage: Gender, Justice, and Rights in Colonial Mali*. Athens: Ohio University Press, 2015.

Byfield, Judith A. "Becoming Classic: 'Sitting on a Man' at Forty-Five." *Journal of West African History* 3, no. 2 (Fall 2017): 139–45.

————. *The Bluest Hands: A Social and Economic History of Women Dyers in Abeokuta (Nigeria), 1890–1940*. Portsmouth, NH: Heinemann, 2002.

————. "Women, Marriage, Divorce and the Emerging Colonial State in Abeokuta (Nigeria), 1892–1904." *Canadian Journal of African Studies / Revue Canadienne des Études Africaines* 30, no. 1 (1996): 32–51.

Cadbury, Tabitha. "A Trader in Central Africa: The Dennett Collection at the Royal Albert Memorial Museum, Exeter." *Journal of Museum Ethnography*, no. 20 (March 1, 2008): 109–19.

Cammaert, Jessica. *Undesirable Practices: Women, Children, and the Politics of the Body in Northern Ghana, 1930–1972*. Lincoln: University of Nebraska Press, 2016.

Campbell, Gwyn, and Alessandro Stanziani. *Debt and Slavery in the Mediterranean and Atlantic Worlds*. New York: Routledge, 2013.

Campbell, Gwyn, Suzanne Miers, and Joseph C. Miller, eds. *Children in Slavery through the Ages*. Athens: Ohio University Press, 2009.

————. *Child Slaves in the Modern World*. Athens: Ohio University Press, 2011.

————. *Women and Slavery*. Vol. 1, *Africa, the Indian Ocean World, and the Medieval North Atlantic*. Athens: Ohio University Press, 2007.

————. *Women and Slavery*. Vol. 2, *The Modern Atlantic*. Athens: Ohio University Press, 2007.

Carland, John M. *The Colonial Office and Nigeria, 1898–1914*. Stanford, CA: Hoover Institution Press, 1985.

Chanock, Martin. *Law, Custom and Social Order: The Colonial Experience in Malawi and Zambia.* Cambridge: Cambridge University Press, 1985.

———. "A Peculiar Sharpness: An Essay on Property in the History of Customary Law in Colonial Africa." *Journal of African History* 32, no. 1 (January 1991): 65–88.

Chapdelaine, Robin P. "'He Remains a Second Person No Matter the Age': Historical and Contemporary Perceptions of Childlessness and Adoption in Nigeria." *Journal of West African History* 7, no. 1 (forthcoming March 2021).

———. "Marriage Certificates and Walker Cards: Nigerian Migrant Labor, Wives and Prostitutes in Colonial Fernando Pó." *African Economic History* 48, no. 2 (Autumn 2020).

"Child Labor: Federal Child Labor Law." *Monthly Labor Review* 8 no. 3 (March 1919): 217–22.

Children's Bureau, U.S. Department of Labor. "Child-Welfare News Summary." Washington, D.C: January 16, 1932.

Chuang, Janie. "Beyond a Snapshot: Preventing Human Trafficking in the Global Economy." *Indiana Journal of Global Studies* 13, no. 1 (Winter 2006): 137–63.

Chuku, Gloria. *Igbo Women and Economic Transformation in Southeastern Nigeria, 1900–1960.* New York: Routledge, 2004.

———. "Igbo Women and Political Participation in Nigeria, 1800s–2005." *International Journal of African Historical Studies* 42, no. 1 (2009): 81–103.

Cocks, Tim, and Isaac Abrak. "Nigeria's Boko Haram Threatens to Sell Kidnapped Schoolgirls." Thomas Reuters, May 5, 2014. https://www.reuters.com/article/us-nigeria-bokoharam/nigerias-boko-haram-threatens-to-sell-kidnapped-schoolgirls-idUSBREA440BJ20140505.

Coe, Cati. "How Debt Became Care: Child Pawning and Its Transformation in Akuapem: The Gold Coast, 1874–1929." *Africa* 82, no. 2 (2012): 287–311.

Cooper, Barbara M. *Marriage in Maradi: Gender and Culture in Hausa Society in Niger, 1900–1989.* Portsmouth, NH: Heinemann, 1997.

Cooper, Frederick. "Africa and the World Economy." *African Studies Review* 24, no. 2/3 (June 1, 1981): 1–86.

———. *Decolonization and African Society: The Labor Question in French and British Africa*. New York: Cambridge University Press, 1996.

Cree, Viviene E., Gary Clapton, and Mark Smith, eds. *Revisiting Moral Panics.* Bristol, England: Policy Press, an imprint of Bristol University Press, 2015.

Cullen-DuPont, Kathryn. *Human Trafficking.* New York: Infobase Publishing, 2009.

Cunningham, Hugh. "Histories of Childhood." *American Historical Review* 103, no. 4 (October 1998): 1195–208.

Curtin, Philip D. *The Atlantic Slave Trade: A Census.* Madison: University of Wisconsin Press, 1972.

———. *Cross-Cultural Trade in World History.* New York: Cambridge University Press, 1984.

Davidoff, Leonore, and Catherine Hall. *Family Fortunes.* London: Routledge, 2002.

DeMause, Lloyd. *The History of Childhood.* Lanham, MD: Jason Aronson, 1995.

Dennett, R. E. *At the Back of the Black Man's Mind.* Miami, FL: General Books, 2009.

Dessy, Sylvain E., and Stéphane Pallage. "A Theory of the Worst Forms of Child Labour." *Economic Journal* 115, no. 500 (January 2005): 68–87.

Dike, Kenneth Onwuka. *Trade and Politics in the Niger Delta, 1830–1885. An Introduction to the Economic and Political History of Nigeria.* London: Oxford University Press, 1962.

Dike, Kenneth O., and Felicia Ekejiuba. *Aro of South-Eastern Nigeria, 1650–1980: A Study of Socio-Economic Formation and Transformation in Nigeria.* Oxford: African Books Collective, 1995.

Dike, Uche A. "The Role of Age Grade in Ogba Land." *Journal of Religion and Human Relations* 1, no. 4 (2012): 83–89.

"Dinner of the Society." *Journal of the Royal African Society* 25, no. 100 (July 1, 1926): 359–62.

Diptee, Audra A., and Martin A. Klein. "African Childhoods and the Colonial Project." *Journal of Family History* 35, no. 1 (2010): 3–6.

Duane, Anna Mae, ed. *Child Slavery before and after Emancipation: An Argument for Child-Centered Slavery Studies.* New York: Cambridge University Press, 2017.

Echendu, Egodi. "Recollections of Childhood Experiences during the Nigerian Civil War." *Africa: Journal of the International African Institute* 77, no. 3 (July 2007): 393–418.

Echewa, T. Obinkaram. *I Saw the Sky Catch Fire.* New York: Plume Printing, 1993.

Ekechi, Felix K. "Pawnship in Igbo Society." In *Pawnship, Slavery, and Colonialism in Africa*, edited by Paul E. Lovejoy and Toyin Falola, 165–86. Trenton, NJ: Africa World Press, 2003.

Ekejiuba, Felicia Ifeoma. "Omu Okwei : The Merchant Queen of Ossomari." *Nigeria Magazine*, no. 90, 1966, 213–20.

Ekpo-Otu, Mfom Umoren. "Contestations of Identity: Colonial Policing of Female Sexuality in the Cross River Region of Southern Nigeria." *Journal of Human and Social Sciences* 5, no. 1 (2013): 72–80.

Ekundare, Olufemi. *An Economic History of Nigeria, 1860–1960.* London: Methuen, 1973.

Ellis, Heather, ed. *Juvenile Delinquency and Limits of Western Influence, 1850–2000.* New York: Palgrave Macmillan, 2014.

Eltis, David. *The Rise of Slavery in the Americas.* New York: Cambridge University Press, 2000.

Eltis, David, and David Richardson. *Extending the Frontiers: Essays on the New Transatlantic Slave Trade Database.* New Haven, CT: Yale University Press, 2008.

Eltis, David, and Stanley L. Engerman. "Was the Slave Trade Dominated by Men?" *Journal of Interdisciplinary History* 23, no. 2 (1992): 237–57.

Emecheta, Buchi. *The Slave Girl: A Novel.* New York: George Braziller, 1980.

Ensler, Eve. *The Vagina Monologues.* New York: Dramatists Play Service, January 1, 2000.

Equiano, Olaudah, and Vincent Carretta. *The Interesting Narrative, and Other Writings by Equiano, Olaudah.* New York: Penguin Classics, 1995.

Falola, Toyin. *Colonialism and Violence in Nigeria*. Bloomington: Indiana University Press, 2009.

———. "'My Friend the Shylock': Money-Lenders and Their Clients in South-Western Nigeria." *Journal of African History* 34, no. 3 (January 1993): 403–23.

———. *Pawnship in Africa: Debt Bondage in Historical Perspective*. Boulder, CO: Westview Press, 1994.

Falola, Toyin, and Adam Paddock. *The Women's War of 1929: A History of Anti-Colonial Resistance in Eastern Nigeria*. Durham, NC: Carolina Academic Press, 2011.

Falola, Toyin, and Matthew M. Heaton. *A History of Nigeria*. New York: Cambridge University Press, 2008.

Falola, Toyin, and Raphael Chijioke Njoku, eds. *Igbo in the Atlantic World: African Origins and Diasporic Destinations*. Bloomington: Indiana University Press, 2016.

Fass, Paula S., and Mary Ann Mason, eds. *Childhood in America*. New York: New York University Press, 2000.

Forde, Cyril Daryll, and G. I. Jones. *The Ibo and Ibibio-Speaking Peoples of South-Eastern Nigeria*. Oxford: Oxford University Press, 1950.

Forde, Daryll, ed. *Efik Traders of Old Calabar: Containing the Diary of Antera Duke together with an Ethnographic Sketch and Notes and an Essay on the Political Organization of Old Calabar*. London: Oxford University Press for the International African, 1956.

Fourchard, Laurent. "The Limits of Penal Reform: Punishing Children and Young Offenders in South Africa and Nigeria (1930s to 1960)." *Journal of Southern African Studies* 37, no. 3 (September 2011): 517–34.

Gadio, Coumba Mar, and Cathy A. Rakowski. "Farmers' Changing Roles in Thieudeme, Senegal: The Impact of Local and Global Factors on Three Generations of Women." *Gender and Society* 13, no. 6. (1999): 733–57.

Gailey, Harry A. *The Road to Aba: A Study of British Administrative Policy in Eastern Nigeria*. New York: New York University Press, 1970.

Galbi, Douglas A. "Child Labor and the Division of Labor in the Early English Cotton Mills." *Journal of Population Economics* 10, no. 4 (October 1, 1997): 357–75.

Geo-Jaja, Macleans A., and Garth Mangum. "Structural Adjustment as an Inadvertent Enemy of Human Development in Africa." *Journal of Black Studies* 32, no. 1 (September 2001): 30–49.

George, Abosede A. *Making Modern Girls: A History of Girlhood, Labor, and Social Development in Colonial Lagos.* Athens: Ohio University Press, 2014.

Gorham, Deborah. "The 'Maiden Tribute of Modern Babylon' Re-examined: Child Prostitution in Late-Victorian England." *Victorian Studies* 21, no. 3 (Spring 1978): 353–79.

Graff, Harvey J. "Review: The History of Childhood and Youth: Beyond Infancy?" *History of Education Quarterly* 26, no. 2 (April 1986): 95–109.

Grant, Kevin. *A Civilised Savagery: Britain and the New Slaveries in Africa, 1884–1926.* New York: Routledge, 2005.

Greene, Sandra E. *Gender, Ethnicity, and Social Change on the Upper Slave Coast: A History of the Anlo-Ewe.* Portsmouth, NH: Heinemann, 1996.

Green, M. M. *Ibo Village Affairs.* Westport, CT: Praeger, 1964.

Green, Reginald Herbold. "A Cloth Untrue: The Evolution of Structural Adjustment in Sub-Saharan Africa," *Journal of International Affairs* 52, no. 1 (Fall 1998): 207–32.

Grier, Beverly. "Child Labor and Africanist Scholarship: A Critical Review." *African Studies Review* 47, no. 2 (2004): 1–25.

Grosz-Ngaté, Maria. "Social Relations: Family, Kinship and Community." In *Africa*, 4th ed., edited by Grosz-Ngaté, Maria, John H. Hanson, Patrick O'Meara, 56–82. Bloomington: Indiana University Press, 2014.

Guyer, Jane I. *Marginal Gains: Monetary Transaction in Atlantic Africa.* Chicago: University of Chicago Press, 2004.

Hanna, Judith Lynne. "Dance and the 'Women's War.'" *Dance Research Journal* 14, no. 1/2 (1981–82): 25–28.

Hardt, Michael, and Antonio Negri. *Empire.* Cambridge, MA: Harvard University Press, 2000.

Harneit-Sievers, Axel. "Igbo 'Traditional Rulers': Chieftaincy and the State in Southeastern Nigeria." *Africa Spectrum* 33, no. 1 (January 1998): 57–79.

Hendrick, Harry, and Economic History Society. *Children, Childhood and English Society, 1880–1990*. Cambridge: Cambridge University Press, 1997.

Heywood, Colin. *A History of Childhood: Children and Childhood in the West from Medieval to Modern Times*. Cambridge: Polity, 2002.

Hindman, Hugh D., ed. *The World History of Child Labor: An Historical and Regional Survey*. Armonk, NY: M. E. Sharpe, 2009.

Hochschild, Adam. *King Leopold's Ghost: A Story of Greed, Terror, and Heroism in Colonial Africa*. Boston: Houghton Mifflin, 1999.

Hodder, B. W., M. A. Hodder, and U. I. Ukwu. *Markets in West Africa: Studies of Markets and Trade among the Yoruba and Ibo*. Ibadan, Nigeria: Ibadan University Press, 1969.

Hodgson, Dorothy L., and Sheryl A. McCurdy, eds. *"Wicked" Women and the Reconfiguration of Gender in Africa*. Portsmouth, NH: Heinemann, 2001.

Honeyman, Katrina, and Nigel Goose, eds. *Childhood and Child Labour in Industrial England: Diversity and Agency, 1750–1914*. New York: Routledge, 2013.

Horton, W. R. G. "The Ohu System of Slavery in a Northern Ibo Village-Group." *Africa: Journal of the International African Institute* 24, no. 4 (October 1, 1954): 311–36.

Howard, Neil. "Teenage Labor Migration and Antitrafficking Policy in West Africa." In "Human Trafficking: Recent Empirical Research," ed. Ronald Weitzer and Sheldon X. Zhang. Special issue, *Annals of the American Academy of Political and Social Science* 653, no. 1 (May 2014): 124–40.

Huberman, Michael, and Christopher M. Meissner. "Riding the Wave of Trade: The Rise of Labor Regulation in the Golden Age of Globalization." *Journal of Economic History* 70, no. 3 (September 2010): 657–85.

Ifeka-Moller, Caroline. "'Sitting on a Man: Colonialism and the Lost Political Institutions of Igbo Women': A Reply to Judith Van Allen." *Canadian Journal of African Studies / Revue Canadienne des Études Africaines* 7, no. 2 (1973): 317–18.

Inkori, Joseph, and Stanley Engerman, eds. *The Atlantic Slave Trade: Effects on Economies, Societies, and Peoples in Africa, the Americas, and Europe*. Durham, NC: Duke University Press, 1992.

"International Convention for the Suppression of the Traffic in Women and Children." In "Official Documents." Supplement, *American Journal of Law* 18, no. 3. (July 1924): 130–37.

International Labour Organization. *Combating Child Labour in Cocoa Growing.* International Programme on the Elimination of Child Labour (IPEC), Geneva, 2005. http://www.ilo.org/public/english//standards/ipec/themes/cocoa/download/2005_02_cl_cocoa.pdf.

———. *Global Estimates of Modern Slavery: Forced Labour and Forced Marriage,* Regional Brief for Africa. International Labour Organization and Walk Free Foundation, Geneva, 2017. http://www.ilo.org/wcmsp5/groups/public/@dgreports/@dcomm/documents/publication/wcms_575479.pdf.

Isichei, Elizabeth. *A History of the Igbo People.* New York: St. Martin's Press, 1976.

———. *History of Nigeria.* London: Longman, 1983.

———. *The Ibo People and the Europeans: The Genesis of a Relationship—to 1906.* London: Faber and Faber, 1973.

———. *Igbo Worlds: An Anthology of Oral Histories and Historical Descriptions.* Philadelphia: Institute for the Study of Human Issues, 1978.

Jacob, Wilson Chacko. *Working Out Egypt: Effendi Masculinity and Subject Formation in Colonial Modernity, 1870–1940.* Durham, NC: Duke University Press, 2011.

Johnson, Christopher Kumolu. "Editor's Response to 'A Cry from the Central Province of Old Southern Nigeria.'" *Nigerian Chronicle,* September 25, 1914.

Johnston, H. H. "A Journey up the Cross River, West Africa." *Proceedings of the Royal Geographical Society and Monthly Record of Geography* 10, no. 7 (July 1, 1888): 435–38.

Jones, G. I. *Annual Reports of Bende Division, South Eastern Nigeria, 1905–1912: With a Commentary.* Cambridge: African Studies Centre, University of Cambridge, 1986.

Kalu, Ogbu U. "Primitive Methodists on the Railroad Junctions of Igboland, 1910–1931." *Journal of Religion in Africa* 16, no. 1 (February 1, 1986): 44–66.

Kaplan, Temma. *Democracy: A World History.* New York: Oxford University Press, 2015.

Kara, Siddharth. *Modern Slavery: A Global Perspective.* New York: Columbia University Press, 2017.

Kigbu, S. K., and Y. B. Hassan. "Legal Framework for Combatting Human Trafficking in Nigeria: The Journey So Far." *Journal of Law, Policy and Globalization* 38 (2015): 205–20.

King, Margaret. "Concepts of Childhood: What We Know and Where We Might Go." *Renaissance Quarterly* 60, no. 2 (Summer 2007): 371–407.

Kirby, Peter. *Child Workers and Industrial Health in Britain, 1780–1850.* Woodbridge, U.K.: Boydell Press, 2013.

Klein, Herbert S. *The Atlantic Slave Trade: New Approaches to the Americas.* Cambridge: Cambridge University Press, 1999.

Klein, Martin A. *Breaking the Chains: Slavery, Bondage, and Emancipation in Modern African and Asia.* Madison: University of Wisconsin Press, 1993.

Korieh, Chima J. "The Nineteenth-Century Commercial Transition in West Africa: The Case of the Biafra Hinterland." In "On Slavery and Islam in African History: A Tribute to Martin Klein." Special issue, *Canadian Journal of African Studies* 34, no. 3 (2000): 588–615.

Latham, A. J. H. "Currency, Credit and Capitalism on the Cross River in the Pre-Colonial Era." *Journal of African History* 12, no. 4 (January 1, 1971): 599–605.

———. *Old Calabar, 1600–1891: The Impact of the International Economy upon a Traditional Society.* Oxford: Clarendon Press, 1973.

Lathrop, Julia C. "International Child Welfare Problems." *Proceedings of the Academy of Political Science in the City of New York* 12, no. 1 (1926): 418–23.

Lauren, Paul Gordon. *The Evolution of International Human Rights: Visions Seen*, 3rd ed. Philadelphia: University of Pennsylvania Press, 2011.

Law, Robin, ed. *From Slave Trade to "Legitimate" Commerce: The Commercial Transition in Nineteenth-Century West Africa.* Cambridge: Cambridge University Press, 1995.

Lawrance, Benjamin N. *Amistad's Orphans: An Atlantic Story of Children, Slavery, and Smuggling.* New Haven, CT: Yale University Press, 2014.

———. "From Child Labor 'Problem' to Human Trafficking 'Crises': Child Advocacy and Anti-Trafficking Legislation in Ghana." *International Labor and Working Class History*, no. 78 (Fall 2010): 63–88.

Lawrance, Benjamin N., and Richard L. Roberts, eds. *Trafficking in Slavery's Wake: Law and the Experience of Women and Children in Africa*. Athens: Ohio University Press, 2012.

Leith-Ross, Sylvia. *African Women: A Study of the Ibo of Nigeria*. London: Routledge and Kegan Paul, 1939; New York: AMS Press, 1978.

Lindsay, Lisa A. *Working with Gender: Wage Labor and Social Change in Southwestern Nigeria*. Portsmouth, NH: Heinemann, 2003.

Lovejoy, Paul E. "Olaudah Equiano or Gustavus Vassa—What's in a Name?" *Atlantic Studies: Literary, Cultural and Historical Perspectives* 9, no. 2 (June 2012): 165–84.

———. "Pawnship, Debt, 'Freedom' in Atlantic Africa during the Era of the Slave Trade: A Reassessment," *Journal of African History* 55, no. 1 (2017): 55–78.

———. *Transformation in Slavery: A History of Slavery in Africa*, 2nd ed. Cambridge: Cambridge University Press, 2000.

Lovejoy, Paul E., and David Richardson. "The Business of Slaving: Pawnship in Western Africa, c. 1600–1810." *Journal of African History* 42, no. 1 (January 1, 2001): 67–89.

———. "'This Horrid Hole': Royal Authority, Commerce and Credit at Bonny, 1690–1840." *Journal of African History* 45, no. 3 (January 1, 2004): 362–92.

———. "Trust, Pawnship, and Atlantic History: The Institutional Foundations of the Old Calabar Slave Trade." *American Historical Review* 105, no. 2 (April 1999): 332–55.

Lovejoy, Paul E., and Toyin Falola, eds. *Pawnship, Slavery, and Colonialism in Africa*. Trenton, NJ: Africa World Press, 2003.

Lynn, Martin. *Commerce and Economic Change in West Africa: The Palm Oil Trade in the Nineteenth Century*. Cambridge: Cambridge University Press, 2002.

Macmillan, Chrystal. "Nationality of Married Women: Present Tendencies." *Journal of Comparative Legislation and International Law* 7, no. 4 (January 1, 1925): 142–54.

Mann, Kristin. *Marrying Well: Marriage Status and Social Change among the Educated Elite in Colonial Lagos.* Cambridge: Cambridge University Press, 1985.

Mann, Kristin, and Richard Roberts, eds. *Law in Colonial Africa.* Portsmouth, NH: Heinemann, 1991.

Manton, John. "'The Lost Province': Neglect and Governance in Colonial Ogoja." *History in Africa* 35 (January 1, 2008): 327–45.

Manzo, Kate. "Exploiting West Africa's Children: Trafficking, Slavery and Uneven Development." *Area* 37, no. 4 (December 2005): 393–401.

Marland, Hilary. *Health and Girlhood in Britain, 1874–1920.* New York: Palgrave Macmillan, 2013.

Martin, Susan. *Palm Oil and Protest: An Economic History of the Ngwa Region, South Eastern Nigeria, 1800–1980.* New York: Cambridge University Press, 1988.

Martinez, Jenny S. *The Slave Trade and the Origins of International Human Rights Law.* Oxford: Oxford University Press, 2012.

Matera, Marc, Misty L. Bastian, and Susan Kingsley Kent. *The Women's War of 1929: Gender and Violence in Colonial Nigeria.* New York: Palgrave Macmillan, 2011.

Mbah, Fidelis. "Nigeria's Chibok Schoolgirls: Five Years On, 122 Still Missing." Aljazeera, April 14, 2019. https://www.aljazeera.com/news/2019/04/nigeria-chibok-school-girls-years-112-missing-190413192517739.html.

Mba, Nina Emma. *Nigerian Women Mobilized: Women's Political Activity in Southern Nigeria, 1900–1965.* Berkeley: University of California Institute of International Studies, 1982.

McDaniel, Lorna. "An Igbo Second Burial." *Black Perspective in Music* 6, no. 1 (1978): 49–55.

McNee, Lisa. "The Languages of Childhood: The Discursive Construction of Childhood and Colonial Policy in French West Africa." *Africa Studies Quarterly* 19, no. 1 (March 2014): 20–32.Meillassoux, Claude. *Maidens, Meal, and Money: Capitalism and the Domestic Community.* Cambridge: Cambridge University Press, 1975.

Miers, Suzanne. *Britain and the Ending of the Slave Trade.* New York: Africana Publishing, 1975.

———. "Contemporary Forms of Slavery." *Canadian Journal of African Studies / Revue Canadienne des Études Africaines* 34, no. 3 (January 1, 2000): 714–47.

———. *Slavery in the Twentieth Century: The Evolution of a Global Problem.* Walnut Creek, CA: AltaMira Press, 2003.

Miers, Suzanne, and Igor Kopytoff, eds. *Slavery in Africa.* Madison: University of Wisconsin Press, 1977.

Miers, Suzanne, and Richard Roberts. *The End of Slavery in Africa.* Madison: University of Wisconsin Press, 1988.

Morris, H. F. "The Development of Statutory Marriage Law in Twentieth Century British Colonial Africa." *Journal of African Law* 23, no. 1 (Spring 1979): 37–64.

Morrison, Heidi. *Childhood and Colonial Modernity in Egypt.* New York: Palgrave Macmillan, 2015.

Mwalimu, Charles. *The Nigerian Legal System*, vol. 2. Bern, Switzerland: Peter Lang, 2005.

Naanen, Ben. "Economy within an Economy: The Manilla Currency, Exchange Rate Instability and Social Conditions in South-Eastern Nigeria, 1900–48." *Journal of African History* 34, no. 3 (January 1, 1993): 425–46.

———. "'Itinerant Gold Mines': Prostitution in the Cross River Basin of Nigeria, 1930–1950." *African Studies Review* 34, no. 2 (September 1, 1991): 57–79.

———. "'You Are Demanding Tax from the Dead': The Introduction of Direct Taxation and Its Aftermath in Southeastern Nigeria, 1928–38." *African Economic History*, no. 34 (2006): 69–102.

Nardinelli, Clark. "Child Labor and the Factory Acts." *Journal of Economic History* 40, no. 4 (December 1, 1980): 739–55.

———. *Child Labor and the Industrial Revolution.* Bloomington: Indiana University Press, 1990.

National Industrial Conference Board. *The Work of the International Labor Organization*, Studies of International Problems. New York: National Industrial Conference Board, 1928. http://dds.crl.edu/CRLdelivery .asp?tid=15989.

Ndukwe, Cajetan. "Changes and Continuity in Age Grade Practices in Nigeria: A Study of the Igbo Traditional and Modern Administrative System." *Journal of Policy and Development Studies* 9, no. 3 (May 2015): 176–84.

Nearing, Scott. *The Solution of the Child Labor Problem.* New York: Moffat, Yard, 1911.

Nigeria Home Office. *Country Policy and Information Note. Nigeria: Trafficking of Women*, Version 5.0, July 2019. https://assets.publishing.service.gov.uk /government/uploads/system/uploads/attachment_data/file/821554/ Nigeria_-_Trafficking_-_CPIN_-_v5.0__July_2019_.pdf.

Nmah, P. E. "Spiritual Dimension of Land Identity Crisis in Igboland of Nigeria: An Ethical Reflection." *Unizik Journal of Arts and Humanities* 12, no. 2 (2011): 136–51.

Northrup, David. *Trade without Rulers: Pre-Colonial Economic Development in South-Eastern Nigeria.* Oxford: Oxford University Press, 1978.

Nwokeji, G. Ugo. *The Slave Trade and Culture in the Bight of Biafra.* New York: Cambridge University Press, 2010.

Nworah, Kenneth D. "The Aborigines' Protection Society, 1889–1909: A Pressure-Group in Colonial Policy." *Canadian Journal of African Studies / Revue Canadienne des Études Africaines* 5, no. 1 (January 1, 1971): 79–91.

Ochonu, Moses E. *Colonial Meltdown: Northern Nigeria in the Great Depression.* Athens: Ohio University Press, 2009.

———. "Conjoined Empire: The Great Depression and Nigeria." *African Economic History* 34 (2006): 103–45.

Oduwobi, Tunde. "Tackling Leprosy in Colonial Nigeria, 1926–1960." *Journal of Historical Study of Nigeria* 22 (2013): 178–205.

Ofonagoro, Walter I. "From Traditional to British Currency in Southern Nigeria: Analysis of a Currency Revolution, 1880–1948." *Journal of Economic History* 39, no. 3 (September 1979): 623–54.

Ojo, Olatunji. "Yoruba Credit and Debt Mechanisms Adjusted, c. 1850–1900." November 23, 2006. https://tubman.info.yorku.ca/activities /tubman-seminar-series/tubman-seminars-series-20062007/.

Okeke, Okechukwu Edward. *A Political and Administrative History of Onitsha, 1917–1970.* Trenton, NJ: Africa World Press, 2009.

Okogbule, Nlerum S. "Combating the 'New Slavery' in Nigeria: An Appraisal of Legal and Policy Responses to Human Trafficking." *Journal of African Law* 57, no.1 (April 2013): 57–80.

Okonkwo, Rina. "The Lagos Auxiliary of the Anti-Slavery and Aborigines Rights Protection Society: A Re-Examination," *International Journal of African Historical Studies* 15, no. 3 (January 1, 1982): 423–33.

Olomojobi, Yinka. "Marriage in Nigeria Across the Ages: Problems and Prospects," September 24, 2016. http://dx.doi.org/10.2139/ssrn.2858618.

Omorodion, Francisca Isi. "Vulnerability of Nigerian Secondary School to Human Sex Trafficking in Nigeria." *African Journal of Reproductive Health / La Revue Africaine de la Santé Reproductive* 13, no. 2 (June 1, 2009): 33–48.

Oriji, John N. "Igboland, Slavery, and the Drums of War and Heroism." In *Fighting the Slave Trade: West African Strategies*, edited by Sylviane A. Diouf, 121–31. Oxford: James Currey, 2003.

Osakwe, C. C. C., and A. Lipede, "The Nigerian Child in War and Peace, 1960 to 1910." *African Journal of History and Culture* 9, no. 8 (August 2017): 64–71.

Patterson, Orlando. *Slavery and Social Death.* Cambridge, MA: Harvard University Press, 1982.

Pedersen, Susan. *Eleanor Rathbone and the Politics of Conscience.* New Haven, CT: Yale University Press, 2004.

———. *The Guardians: The League of Nations and the Crisis of Empire.* Oxford: Oxford University Press, 2015.

Perham, Margery Freda. *Native Administration in Nigeria.* London: Oxford University Press, 1962.

Pinchbeck, Ivy, and Margaret Hewitt. *Children in English Society.* Vol 2, *From the Eighteenth Century to the Children Act 1948.* London: Routledge and Kegan Paul, 1973.

Pitman, Frank Wesley. "The Treatment of the British West Indian Slaves in Law and Custom." *Journal of Negro History* 11, no. 4 (October 1, 1926): 610–28.

Presley, Cora Ann. *Kikuyu Women, the Mau Mau Rebellion, and Social Change in Kenya.* Boulder, CO: Westview Press, 1992.

Rattray, R. S. *Ashanti Law and Constitution*. Oxford: Clarendon Press, 1969.

Razy, Elodie, and Marie Rodet, eds. *Children on the Move in Africa: Past and Present Experiences of Migration*. Suffolk: James Currey, 2016.

Rich, Jeremy. "Searching for Success: Boys, Family Aspirations, and Opportunities in Gabon, ca. 1900–1940." *Journal of Family History* 35, no. 1 (January 2010): 7–24.

Robertson, Claire C., and Martin A. Klein. *Women and Slavery in Africa*. Madison: University of Wisconsin Press, 1983.

Roberts, Richard. "French Colonialism, Imported Technology, and the Handicraft Textile Industry in the Western Sudan, 1898–1918." In "The Tasks of Economic History." Special issue, *Journal of Economic History* 47, no. 2 (June 1987): 461–72.

———. *Litigants and Households: African Disputes and Colonial Courts in the French Sudan, 1895–1912*. Portsmouth, NH: Heinemann, 2005.

Rodet, Marie. "Under the Guise of Guardianship and Marriage: Mobilizing Juvenile and Female Labor in the Aftermath of Slavery in Kayes, French Soudan, 1900–1939." In *Trafficking in Slavery's Wake: Law and the Experience of Women and Children in Africa*, edited by Benjamin N. Lawrance and Richard L. Roberts, 86–100. Athens: Ohio University Press, 2012.

Roe, Jill. "Collisson, Marjorie Chave (1887–1982)." In *Australian Dictionary of Biography*, vol. 17. Canberra: National Centre of Biography, Australian National University. http://adb.anu.edu.au/biography /collison-marjorie-chave-12338.

Ryan, Patrick J. "How New Is the 'New' Social Study of Childhood? The Myth of a Paradigm Shift." *Journal of Interdisciplinary History* 38, no. 4 (April 2008): 553–76.

Samson, K. T. "ILO [International Labor Organization]," *Human Rights* 9, no. 2 (October 1, 1980): 23–43.

Schwelb, Egon. "Marriage and Human Rights." *American Journal of Comparative Law* 12, no. 3 (July 1, 1963): 337–83.

Seddon, David. "Popular Protest and Class Struggle in Africa: An Historical Overview." In *Class Struggle and Resistance in Africa*, edited by Leo Zeilig, 57–86. Chicago: Haymarket Books, 2009.

Sharp, Evelyn. *The African Child: An Account of the International Conference on African Children, Geneva.* Westport, CT: Negro University Press, 1931.

Shell, Sandra Rowoldt. *Children of Hope: The Odyssey of the Oromo Slaves from Ethiopia to South Africa.* Athens: Ohio University Press, 2018.

Slack, Jeremy, Daniel E. Martínez, and Scott Whiteford, eds. *The Shadow of the Wall: Violence and Migration on the U.S.-Mexico Border.* Tucson: University of Arizona Press, 2018.

Slater, Stefan. "Lady Astor and the Ladies of the Night: The Home Office, the Metropolitan Police and the Politics of the Street Offences Committee, 1927–28." *Law and History Review* 30, no. 2 (May 1, 2012): 533–73.

Snow, William F. "The Program of the League of Nations Advisory Committee on the Traffic in Women and the Protection and Welfare of Children and Young People." *Proceedings of the Academy of Political Science in the City of New York* 12, no. 1 (July 1, 1926): 411–17.

Stearns, Peter N. *Growing Up: The History of Childhood in a Global Context.* Charles Edmondson Historical Lectures, Book 28. Waco, TX: Baylor University Press, 2005.

Stilwell, Sean. *Slavery and Slaving in African History.* New York: Cambridge University Press, 2014.

Sundiata, Ibrahim K. *From Slaving to Neoslavery: The Night of Biafra and Fernando Po in the Era of Abolition, 1827–1930.* Madison: University of Wisconsin Press, 1996.

Taylor, Mildred Europa. "How Africa's Largest Tax Rebellion by Igbo Market Women Disrupted Colonisation in 1929." October 9, 2018. https://face2faceafrica.com/article/how-africas-largest-tax-rebellion-by-igbo-market-women-disrupted-colonisation-in-1929.

Traffic in Persons, Chapter 7. "International Agreement for the Suppression of the 'White Slave Traffic,'" May 18, 1904. United Nations Treaty Collection. https://treaties.un.org/Pages/ViewDetails.aspx?src=TREATY&mtdsg_no=VII-8&chapter=7&clang=_en.

Uche, Chibuike Ugochukwu. "Foreign Banks, Africans, and Credit in Colonial Nigeria, c. 1890–1912." *Economic History Review, n.s.,* 52, no. 4 (November 1, 1999): 669–91.

Uchendu, Victor. *The Igbo of Southeast Nigeria*. New York: Van Nostrand Reinhold, 1965.

United Nations. *United Nations Convention against Transnational Organized Crime and the Protocols Thereto*. United Nations Office on Drugs and Crime, 2004. http://www.unodc.org/documents/treaties/UNTOC/Publications /TOC%20Convention/TOCebook-e.pdf.

United Nations Children's Fund, Innocenti Research Center. *Child Trafficking in West Africa: Policy Responses*. Florence, Italy: Tipografia Giuntina, April 2002. https://www.unicef-irc.org/publications/pdf/insight7.pdf.

United States Department of State. "Local Solutions to a Global Problem: Supporting Communities in the Fight against Human Trafficking." https://www.state.gov/reports/2018-trafficking-in-persons-report /#report-toc__section-4.

———. *Trafficking in Persons Report 2017: Nigeria*. https://www.state.gov/j/tip/rls /tiprpt/2017/index.htm.

———. *Trafficking in Persons Report 2018: Nigeria*. https://www.state.gov/j/tip/rls /tiprpt/2018/index.htm.

Universal Declaration of Human Rights, December 10, 1948, Paris. https://www .un.org/en/universal-declaration-human-rights/.

Usoro, Eno J. *The Nigerian Oil Palm Industry*. Ibadan, Nigeria: Ibadan University Press, 1974.

Van Allen, Judith. "'Sitting on a Man': Colonialism and the Lost Political Institutions of Igbo Women." In "The Roles of African Women: Past, Present and Future." Special issue, *Canadian Journal of African Studies/ Revue Canadienne des Études Africaines* 6, no. 2 (January 1, 1972): 165–81.

Van den Bersselaar, Dmitri. "Establishing Facts: P. A. Talbot and the 1921 Census of Nigeria." *History in Africa* 31 (2004): 69–102.

———. "In Search of Igbo Identity: Language, Culture and Politics in Nigeria, 1900–1966." PhD diss., Leiden University, 1998.

———. "Missionary Knowledge and the State in Colonial Nigeria: On How G. T. Basden Became an Expert." *History in Africa* 33 (January 1, 2006): 433–50.

Vaughan, Olufemi. *Nigerian Chiefs: Traditional Power in Modern Politics, 1890s–1990s*. Rochester, NY: University of Rochester Press, 2006.

Weindling, Paul. *International Health Organisations and Movements, 1918–1939.* Cambridge: Cambridge University Press, 1995.

White, Luise. *The Comforts of Home: Prostitution in Colonial Nairobi.* Chicago: University of Chicago Press, 1990.

Whyte, Christine. "'Freedom but Nothing Else': The Legacies of Slavery and Abolition in Post-Slavery Sierra Leone, 1928–1956." In "Exploring Post-Slavery in Contemporary Africa." Special issue, *International Journal of African Historical Studies* 48, no. 2 (2015): 231–50.

Primary Sources

Aba Commission of Inquiry. *Notes of Evidence Taken by the Commission of Inquiry Appointed to Inquire into the Disturbance in the Calabar and Owerri Provinces,* December 1929. London: Waterlow, 1930. Microfilm. Rutgers University Libraries, New Brunswick, NJ.

A Chief. "Concerning the House Rule Ordinance: A Cry from the Central Province of Old Southern Nigeria." *Nigerian Chronicle,* September 25, 1914.

"African Riot Toll Now 1 Man, 43 Women: British Under-Secretary for Colonies Tells Common Cause Is Still Unascertained." *New York Times,* December 24, 1929.

Agbo, Chief Daniel E. N., J. P. Interview conducted by Anayo Enechukwu on behalf of author, Amechi Awkunanaw, Enugu State, Nigeria, August 8, 2012.

Agu, Kinsley. Interview conducted by Ifeoma Obijiaku on behalf of author, Calabar, Cross River State, Nigeria, August 21, 2012.

Agubaram, Chief Anthony Chibueze. Interview conducted by Ifeoma Obijiaku on behalf of author, Calabar, Cross River State, Nigeria, August 22, 2012.

Anderson, Curt. "Human Trafficking Increase Expected during Super Bowl." *PBS New Hour,* January 9, 2020. https://www.pbs.org/newshour/nation /human-trafficking-increase-expected-during-super-bowl/.

"Announcements." *Nigerian Eastern Mail,* January 26, 1946, 24. National Archives of Nigeria, Ibadan.

"The Anti-Slavery and Aborigines Protection Society Formation of the Lagos Auxiliary." *Nigerian Times,* September 6, 1910.

Asawalam, Thomas U. Interview conducted by Cynthia E. Uche on behalf of author, Umuaro, Umunumo, Ehime Mbano, Imo State, August 29, 2012.

Ashley, J. "Pawning of Children: Report by Captain J. Ashley, Assistant District Officer in Charge of Bonny District," March 5, 1923. In I. Tribal Customs and Superstitions of the Southern Province of Nigeria; II. Practice of Pawning Children as Security for Debts of Parents, 89. CSO 26/1/06827, National Archives of Nigeria, Ibadan.

Assistant Inspector-General of Police. Letter from the Assistant Inspector-General of Police, Southern Provinces, Enugu, to the Commissioner of Police, M. F. Powell, Owerri Province, Port Harcourt, October 16, 1933. C136 Child Stealing, Rivprof 2/1/24, 13, National Archives of Nigeria, Enugu.

Azuka, Nze Azubuike. Interview conducted by Ifeoma Obijiaku on behalf of author, Calabar, Cross River State, Nigeria, August 20, 2012.

Bell, C. R. *Slave Dealing and Child Stealing: Monthly Reports, September–November 1934,* Reports on Bende and Owerri, December 4, 1934, 67–88, 93, 100. C136 Child Stealing, Rivprof 2/1/24, 125 pages, National Archives of Nigeria, Enugu.

Beringer, J., Sr. Sanitation Officer. *The Influenza Epidemic of 1918 in the Southern Provinces of Nigeria*, September 5, 1919. CO 583/77, National Archives, Richmond, U.K.

Calabar Province Slave Dealing, 1907–1911. Calabar, Nigeria, 1912, National Archives of Nigeria, Calabar.

Chief Ezeonyodu v. Okanu, January 21, 1925. CSO 26/1/16100, 43, National Archives of Nigeria, Ibadan.

Chief Inspector. Letter to the Commissioner of Police at Port Harcourt, February 3, 1927. In Slave Dealing, OkiDist 4/9/42, National Archive of Nigeria, Enugu.

Christy, Cuthbert, Charles Spurgeon Johnson, and Arthur Barclay. "The 1930 Enquiry Commission to Liberia." *Journal of Royal African Society* 30, no. 120 (July 1931): 277–90.

Clifford, Hugh. Letter from Governor Hugh Clifford to Colonel L. S. Amery, Secretary of State for the Colonies, December 31, 1924. In I. Tribal Customs and Superstitions of the Southern Province of Nigeria; II. Practice of

Pawning Children as Security for Debts of Parents. CSO 26/1/06827, 123, National Archives of Nigeria, Ibadan.

Colonial Currency. African Colonies and Protectorates. West Africa. Vol. 3, *Colony of Southern Nigeria and the Protectorates of Southern and Northern Nigeria.* London: Printed for His Majesty's Stationary Office, 1911, 8. Colonial Office Nigeria, T1/11374, National Archives, Richmond, U.K.

Cooper, J. Letter from J. Cooper, Bank of British West Africa Limited, to the Under Secretary of State, Colonial Office. Treasury Papers, Southern Nigeria. Proposal to Establish a Government Currency Note Issue, April 18, 1908. TI/11226/695, National Archives, Richmond, U.K.

Council for the Representation of Women in the League of Nations: Annual Report, 1929–30. League of Nations, 1930. CO 323/1071/8 Slavery: Slavery of Women, National Archives, Richmond, U.K.

"The Covenant of the League of Nations." *American Journal of International Law* 15, no. 1 (January 1, 1921): 4–13.

Crewe-Milnes, Robert Offley Ashburton. Insert from a letter from Lord Crewe to Sir Walter Egerton. Treasury Papers, Southern Nigeria. Proposal to establish a government currency note Issue, August 7, 1908. TI/11226/695, National Archives, Richmond, U.K.

"Dame Maria Ogilvie Gordon: Geologist and Prominent Worker for Women's Causes." *Glasgow Herald*, June 26, 1939.

Dennett, R. E. "Development of Native Governments in Southern Nigeria." *Nigerian Chronicle*, September 29, 1911.

Devonshire, Mr. Letter from Mr. Devonshire to Sir Hugh Clifford, Governor, December 12, 1922. CSO 26/1/06827, vol. 1, Pawning, 1920s, National Archives of Nigeria, Ibadan.

Dew, H. T. B. Letter from the District Officer of Enugu, H. T. B. Dew, to the Senior Resident of Onitsha, February 12, 1923. In I. Tribal Customs and Superstitions of the Southern Province of Nigeria; II. Practice of Pawning Children as Security for Debts of Parents, 37–39.

Dickins, A. R. A. Letter from A. R. A. Dickins for Secretary, Southern Provinces, to the Resident at Calabar Province, October 24, 1936, 26. Itudist 2/1/28: Slave Dealing, 1933–1938, National Archives of Nigeria, Enugu.

Dickinson, E. Letter from E. Dickinson, Acting District Officer of Owerri, to Major J. W. Garden, D.S.O., November 28, 1933. C136 Child Stealing, Rivprof 2/1/24, National Archives of Nigeria, Enugu.

District Officer at Bende. Letter to the District Officer at Okigwe: Alleged Slave Dealing at Obowo," February 28, 1929. OkiDist 4/11/31. National Archives of Nigeria, Enugu.

District Officer in Awka. Letter to the Senior Resident of Onitsha Province (February 15, 1923). In I. Enactment of Slavery Ordinance, 1916; II. The Slavery (Amendment) Ordinance, 1916. CSO 26/1/03063, National Archives of Nigeria, Ibadan.

District Officer in Okigwi. Letter to Major J. W. Garden, Assistant Commissioner of Police, Owerri Province, Port Harcourt, December 4, 1933. C136 Child Stealing, Rivprof 2/1/24, National Archives of Nigeria, Enugu.

District Officer of Bende. Letter to the District Officer at Okigwe, April 29, 1927. OkiDist 4/9/72 Rex vs Idi, 11, National Archives of Nigeria, Enugu.

District Officer of Okigwi. Letter to the District Officer of Awka, June 1, 1929. OkiDist 4/11/31: Alleged Slave-Dealing, 1929, 10 pages, National Archives of Nigeria, Enugu.

———. Memorandum to the District Officer of Bende, "Alleged Slave Dealing at Obowo," February 28, 1929. OkiDist 4/11/31: Alleged Slave-Dealing, 1929, National Archives of Nigeria, Enugu.

Doro. Letter from Doro, Head Chief and Political Agent, Warri, Nigeria, to Unknown Colonial Representative, April 27, 1914. CSE 8/7/39, Slave Dealing: Extension of Jurisdiction of D.C.'s to Hear and Determine Cases Sitting with Native Court or with Selected Assessors-Requests, 1912–1914, National Archives of Nigeria, Enugu.

Ebubedike, Chief Ohaegbulam. Interview conducted by Cynthia E. Uche on behalf of author, Aba, Abia State, Nigeria, August 31, 2012.

Echewa, Obinkaram T. Interview by author. Philadelphia, PA, May 16, 2009.

Egerton, Walter. Letter from Governor Sir Walter Egerton of Southern Nigeria to the Earl of Elgin, Secretary to the Colonies." Treasury Papers, Southern Nigeria. Proposal to Establish a Government Currency Note Issue, November 30, 1907. TI/11226/695, National Archives, Richmond, U.K.

Eheakandu, Okpala. Statement Given by Okpala Eheakandu of Umuahia Township, March 18, 1934. OkiDist 11/1/214, Child Stealing and Slave Dealing, 1932–1934, 141, 127. National Archives of Nigeria, Enugu.

Ekpeyong, Archibong. Interview conducted by Ifeoma Obijiaku on behalf of author, Calabar, Cross River State, Nigeria, August 20, 2012.

Elgin, Earl of. Letter from the Earl of Elgin, Colonial Secretary, to Sir Walter Egerton. Treasury Papers, Southern Nigeria. Proposal to Establish a Government Currency Note Issue, March 26, 1908. PRO TI/11226/695, National Archives, Richmond, U.K.

I. Enactment of Slavery Ordinance, 1916; II. The Slavery (Amendment) Ordinance, 1916. CSO 26/1/03063, National Archives of Nigeria, Ibadan.

"Europe Is Turning from Child Labor: Greece Passes Law Prohibiting Employment of Children under 12, American Minister Reports. New Agitation in England Yorkshire Education Board Rescinds Measure Permitting Children between 12 and 14 to Be Employed." *New York Times (1857–1922)*, May 19, 1912. https://search-proquest-com.authenticate.library .duq.edu/docview/97304272?accountid=10610.

Ezeji, Nelson Anyanele. Interview conducted by Ezeji Grace on behalf of author, Owerri, Imo State, Nigeria, August 21, 2012.

Ezinna, Cornelius Echeruo. Interview conducted by Cynthia E. Uche on behalf of author, Umuaro, Umunumo, Imo State, Nigeria, August 29, 2012.

———. Follow-up interview conducted by Augustine Onyemauchechukwu Onye on behalf of author, Umuaro, Umunumo, Imo State, Nigeria, September 2012.

Falk, E. "Cases of Slave Dealing," letter from E. Falk, District Officer at Aba, to J. Ashley, Assistant District Officer at Bende, November 7, 1920. OkiDist 4/2/1, 107, National Archives of Nigeria, Enugu.

Ferguson, F. Report: Pawning of Children. In I. Tribal Customs and Superstitions of the Southern Province of Nigeria; II. Practice of Pawning Children as Security for Debts of Parents, March 1, 1923, 1–2. CSO 26/1/06827, National Archives of Nigeria, Ibadan.

Firth, O. W. "Owerri Province Annual Report, 1932." In *Slave Dealing and Child Stealing Investigation*, February 25, 1933. CSO 21/4/28994, National Archives of Nigeria, Ibadan.

Flood, J. E. W. Notes on the position of women in West Africa, League of Nations. Meeting Held in the Secretary of State's Room at 11 a.m. on Tuesday, the 8th of April, 1930, April 8, 1930. CO 323/1071/8 Slavery: Slavery of Women, 3, National Archives, Richmond, U.K.

Garden, J. W. *Slave Dealing: Report for December, 1933: The Assistant Inspector General of Police, Southern Provinces, through the Commissioner of Police, Owerri Province, Port Harcourt*, January 5, 1934, 41. C136 Child Stealing, Rivprof 2/1/24, National Archives of Nigeria, Enugu.

———. *Slave Dealing: Report for January, 1934. From the Acting Commissioner of Police, J. W. Garden to the Assistant Inspector General of Police, Owerri Province, Port Harcourt*, February 10, 1934, 49, 54. C136 Child Stealing, Rivprof 2/1/24, National Archives of Nigeria, Enugu.

———. *Slave Dealing: Monthly Report, February 1934*, Enugu, Nigeria, March 10, 1934, 55–57. C136 Child Stealing, Rivprof 2/1/24, National Archives of Nigeria, Enugu.

———. *Slave Dealing Report: Report for March 1934*, Owerri Province, April 5, 1934, 60. C136 Child Stealing, Rivprof 2/1/24, National Archives of Nigeria, Enugu.

"Geneva Declaration of the Rights of the Child." League of Nations, September 26, 1924. http://www.un-documents.net/gdrc1924.htm.

George, S. P. *Slave Dealing and Child Stealing: Final Report up to 15th July, 1935.* C136 Child Stealing, Rivprof 2/1/24, National Archives of Nigeria, Enugu.

———. *Slave Dealing and Child Stealing Investigation*, Bende, Owerri, February 4, 1935. C136 Child Stealing, Rivprof 2/1/24. Nigeria National Archive, Enugu.

———. *Slave Dealing and Child Stealing Investigation: Monthly Report, March 1935*, Port Harcourt, Owerri Province, April 1, 1935. C136 Child Stealing, Rivprof 2/1/24, 131, National Archives of Nigeria, Enugu.

Glover, John Hawley. Letter from Glover to Administrator in Chief, Sierra Leone, February 11, 1870. National Archives of Nigeria, Ibadan.

———. Letter from Glover to Newcastle, October 9, 1863. CSO 1/1/1, 87, National Archives of Nigeria, Ibadan.

Harlan, Chico, and Stefano Pitrelli. "A Foreign Mafia Has Come to Italy and Further Polarized the Migration Debate." *Washington Post*, June 25,

2019. https://www.washingtonpost.com/world/europe/a-foreign
-mafia-has-come-to-italy-and-further-polarized-the-migration
-debate/2019/06/25/377cf978-8235-11e9-b585-e36b16a531aa_story.html.

Harris, J. H. "The Native House Rule Ordinance." *Nigerian Chronicle*, August 11, 1911.

Haydock-Wilson, H. *Slave Dealing and Child Stealing Campaign: Final Report–up to 9th May, 1936*, Owerri Province, May 11, 1936, 212. C136 Child Stealing, Rivprof 2/1/24, National Archives of Nigeria, Enugu.

"Health and Social Questions Section, 1919–1946." Catalogue, United Nations Archives, Geneva. http://biblio-archive.unog.ch/detail.aspx?ID=405.

Heap, Simon. "'Jaguda Boys': Pickpocketing in Ibadan, 1930–1960." *Urban History* 24, no. 3 (December 1997): 324–43.

Heathcote, G. N. "Cases of Slave Dealing." Memorandum from Assistant District Officer G. N. Heathcote of Bende to the District Officer of Okigwi, July 29, 1920. OkiDist 4/2/1, 153, National Archives of Nigeria, Enugu.

Hives, Frank. Report on the Pawning of Children in the Southern Provinces, Nigeria, as Called for by His Honour Lieutenant-Governor, Southern Provinces, Vice Secretary Southern Provinces' Confidential Memo No. C.2/23, January 17, 1923. CSO 26/1/06827, 1:54, Pawning, 1920s, National Archives of Nigeria, Ibadan.

Ibeawuchi, Anthonia Nkechinyere. Interview conducted by Augustine Onyemauchechukwu Onye on behalf of author, Iho, Ikeduru, Imo State, Nigeria, August 25, 2012.

Ibgocheonwu, Callista Okemmadu. Interview conducted by Cynthia E. Uche on behalf of author, Umuaro, Umunumo, Ehime Mbano, Imo State, Nigeria, August 22, 2012.

Isichei, Elizabeth. *Igbo Worlds: An Anthology of Oral Histories and Historical Descriptions*. London: Macmillan, 1977.

James, F. S. Letter to acting colonial secretary Gerald Bell, Slave Dealing: Extension of Jurisdiction of District Commissioners to Hear and Determine Cases Sitting with the Native Court, 1912–1914, June 13, 1912. CSE 8/7/39, National Archives of Nigeria, Enugu.

Johnson, F. E. G. "Letter from District Commissioner F. E. G. Johnson to the High Provincial Commissioner," November 13, 1911. CSE 8/7/39: Slave

Dealing: Extension of Jurisdiction of D.C.'s to Hear and Determine Cases Sitting with Native Court or with Selected Assessors-Requests, 1912–1914, National Archives of Nigeria, Enugu.

Kaplan, Temma. *Democracy: A World History.* New York: Oxford University Press, 2014.

Kelly, E. J. G. Letter from E. J. G. Kelly, Secretary of the Southern Provinces, to the Chief Secretary to the Government at Lagos, April 20, 1936. C136 Child Stealing, Rivprof 2/1/24, 202–4, National Archives of Nigeria, Enugu.

King, C. D. B., President of Liberia. A Proclamation: Labour for Fernando Poo 1930. FO/458/106, 36, Stanford University Libraries, Stanford, CA.

"Labor Shortage Forcing Children of School Age to Work." *New York Times (1857–1922)*, October 13, 1918.

Laird, MacGregor, and R. A. K. Oldfield. *Narrative of an Expedition into the Interior of Africa, by the Niger River, in the Steam-Vessels Quorra and Alburkah in 1832, 1833, and 1834.* London: Richard Bentley, 1837.

Layton, R. C. Letter from the District Commissioner R. C. Layton at Aba to the Provincial Commissioner at Calabar, September 11, 1911, 1–2. CSE 8/7/39, National Archives of Nigeria, Enugu.

League of Nations. "Slavery Convention: Signed at Geneva on 25 September 1926. Entry into Force: 9 March 1927, in Accordance with Article 12." Office of the High Commissioner for Human Rights, September 25, 1926. https://www.ohchr.org/EN/ProfessionalInterest/Pages/SlaveryConvention.aspx.

Livingstone, David. "Treatment of Native Races. The Heritage and Duty of the British People. Address Delivered by Mr. E. D. Morel at Birkhead." *Nigerian Chronicle,* June 13, 1913. MF 749 CAMP.

Lucas, C. P. Letter from C. P. Lucas, the Under Secretary of State, Colonial Office (London), to the Secretary to the Treasury. Treasury Papers, December 31, 1909. PRO TI/11226/26021, Public Records Office, London.

Lugard, F. D. *Lugard and the Amalgamation of Nigeria: A Documentary Record, Being a Reprint of the Report by Sir F. D. Lugard on the Amalgamation of Northern and Southern Nigeria and Administration, 1912–1919.* London: Frank Cass, 1968.

———. "Memorandum from Lord Lugard High Commissioner: Memo No. 6-Slavery Questions," September 1906. http://www.tubmaninstitute.ca/sites/default/files/file/memo6.pdf (no longer available).

Lugard, Frederick D. *The Diaries of Lord Lugard*. Vol. 4, *Nigeria, 1894–5 and 1898*. Edited by Margery Perham and Mary Bull. London: Faber, 1963.

———. Letter to L. G. S. [Charles Strachey], including copy of minutes by H. E., April 26, 1916. Calprof 13/6/103, 2–3, National Archives of Nigeria, Enugu.

Marcellenus, Ahanotu. Interview conducted by Augustine Onyemauchechukwu Onye on behalf of author, Awo Mbieri, Mbaitoli, Imo State, Nigeria, August 23, 2012.

McKenzie, Rev. T. "A Few Words of Interest Relating to Missionary Life in Southern Nigeria, West Africa, 1919–1921," June 1922. MMS 1204, SOAS University of London.

"The Moneylender's Bill." *Nigerian Chronicle*, June 21, 1912.

Murphy, G. E. "Pawning of Children: Report by Mr. G. E. Murphy, District Officer in Charge of Ahoada District (February 15th, 1923)." In I. Tribal Customs and Superstitions of the Southern Province of Nigeria; II. Practice of Pawning Children as Security for Debts of Parents. Vol. 1, CSO 26/1/06827, 88, National Archives of Nigeria, Ibadan.

"The Native House Rule Amendment Ordinance Discussed." *Nigerian Chronicle*, February 16, 1912.

"The Native House Rule Ordinance in Southern Nigeria." *Nigerian Chronicle*, October 13, 2011.

Native Unrest in Nigeria (letter from Mr. Bottomley to Sir. S. Wilson), December 1929. CO 583/168/14, National Archives, Richmond, U.K.

"News of the Week." *Nigerian Chronicle*, June 28, 1912.

"Nigeria 'Baby Factory' Raided in Imo State," May 10, 2013. https://www.bbc.com /news/world-africa-22484318.

Nigerian Correspondent. "The Disturbances in S.E. Nigeria: The Special Commission's Report Reviewed," October 11, 1930. CO 583/176/10, 1450, National Archives, Richmond, U.K.

Numa, Chief Dore. Letter to the Governor General Frederick Lugard. Slave Dealing: Extension of Jurisdiction of District Commissioners to Hear and Determine Cases Sitting with the Native Court, April 27, 1914. CSO 8/7/39, National Archives of Nigeria, Enugu.

Nwadinko, Anthony. Interview conducted by Ezeji Grace on behalf of author, Owerri, Imo State, Nigeria, August 21, 2012.

Obuta, Lolo Alias. "Statement of Lolo Alias Obuta," March 1932. OkiDist 11/1/214 Child Stealing and Slave Dealing, 1932–1934, 6, National Archives of Nigeria, Enugu.

Oduomyenma. "Statement Given by Oduomyenma of Okigwe," March 31, 1934. OkiDist 11/1/214 Child Stealing and Slave Dealing, 1932–1934, 129, Nigeria National Archive, Enugu.

Okanu of Ochida. Letter to the Resident of the Southern Province, Lagos, July 2, 1925. CSO 26/1/16100, National Archives of Nigeria, Ibadan.

Okofo, Mgboli. "Statement of a Girl Named Mgboli Okofo," June 24, 1932. OkiDist 11/1/214 Child Stealing and Slave Dealing, 1932–1934, 28, National Archives of Nigeria, Enugu.

Okolo, Abraham, Elder. Interview conducted by Anayo Enechukwu on behalf of author, Amorji-Nike, Enugu State, Nigeria, August 2, 2012.

Okolo, HRH Igwe Dr. Titus. Interview conducted by Anayo Enechukwu on behalf of author, Igwe Palace, Amorji-Nike, Enugu State, Nigeria, August 2, 2012.

Ormsby-Gore, William. Letter from Mr. Ormsby-Gore, Assistant to the Secretary of State, to Governor Hugh Clifford, March 31, 1925. CSO 26/1/06827, National Archives of Nigeria, Ibadan.

Owerri Province Annual Report for 1921, 1921. CSO 26/03928, 1–63, National Archives of Nigeria, Ibadan.

Owerri Province Annual Report for 1922, n.d. CSO 26/03928. National Archives of Nigeria, Ibadan.

Owolabi, Tife, and Libby George. "Nigerian Police Free Children, Pregnant Teens from 'Baby Factory,'" Reuters, February 27, 2020. https://www.reuters.com /article/us-nigeria-captives-babies/nigerian-police-free-children-pregnant -teens-from-baby-factory-idUSKCN20L2MI.

"The Pawnbrokers Bill." *Nigerian Chronicle*, June 7, 1912.

"Pawnbrokers Order in Council." *Nigerian Chronicle*, February 21, 1913, 1.

Provincial Commissioner at Calabar. Letter to the Colonial Secretary at Lagos, October 22, 1915. Calprof 13/6/103, 2, National Archives of Nigeria, Enugu.

Punch, Cyril. Slave Dealing: Extension of Jurisdiction of District Commissioners to Hear and Determine Cases Sitting with the Native Court-Precis of Views by Officers in Regard to Difficulties Experienced Containing Conviction before the Supreme Court, November 15, 1911. CSE 8/7/39, Slave Dealing: Extension of Jurisdiction of D.C.'s to Hear and Determine Cases Sitting with Native Court or with Selected Assessors-Requests, 1912–1914, National Archives of Nigeria, Enugu.

Pusey, Allen. "June 3, 1918: Child Labor Law Declared Unconstitutional." *ABA Journal*, June 1, 2015. http://www.abajournal.com/magazine/article /june_3_1918_child_labor_law_declared_unconstitutional.

"Republic of Liberia: 'Slavery Does Exist: International Commission's Findings.'" *African World*, November 1, 1930, Labour for Fernando Poo 1930. FO/458/106, 10, Stanford University Libraries, Stanford, CA.

Resident of Owerri Province. Letter to the Secretary of the Southern Provinces at Lagos (March 23, 1923)." In I. Tribal Customs and Superstitions of the Southern Province of Nigeria; II. Practice of Pawning Children as Security for Debts of Parents. CSO 26/1/06827, National Archives of Nigeria, Ibadan.

Resident of Owerri Province. Letter to the Secretary, Southern Provinces at Enugu, April 15, 1936. C136 Child Stealing, Rivprof 2/1/24, 202, National Archives of Nigeria, Enugu.

Reuben, Chief Ugwuefi. Interview conducted by Anayo Enechukwu on behalf of author, Nike, Enugu State, Nigeria, August 5, 2012.

Rex v. Mbakwe of Avutu and three others, Child Stealing, November 1929. OkiDist 4/11/46, National Archives of Nigeria, Enugu.

Rex v. Mbakwe of Avutu and three others, Child Stealing, November 1929. OkiDist 4/11/58, National Archives of Nigeria, Enugu.

Rex v. Wilson Edom of Umuariam Obowo, April 13, 1925. OkiDist 11/1/267, Child Stealing, 1935, 3, National Archives of Nigeria, Enugu.

Ross, W. A. Letter from W. A. Ross, Senior Resident, Oyo Province, to Secretary of Southern Provinces," March 14, 1923. CSO 26/1/06827, vol. 1, Pawning, 26–27, National Archives of Nigeria, Ibadan.

Sessional Papers: Annual Report on the Police Department of the Southern Provinces of Nigeria for the Year 1915, Sessional Papers, December 7, 1916. PRO 657/3, National Archives, Richmond, U.K.

Simkin, John. "Margery Corbett Ashby." *Spartacus Educational*, September 1997 (updated January 2020). http://www.spartacus-educational.com/Washby.htm.

Slave Dealing: Extension of Jurisdiction of District Commissioners to Hear and Determine Cases Sitting with the Native Court, 1912–1914. CSE 8/7/39, National Archives of Nigeria, Enugu.

Slave Dealing: Precis of Views by Officers in Regard to Difficulties Experienced in Containing Conviction before the Supreme Court and Suggestions Submitted for Remedying Detection and Conviction More Effective, May 13, 1912. CSE 8/7/39, National Archives of Nigeria, Enugu.

"Slavery: Slavery of Women," 1930. CO 323/1071/8, National Archives, Richmond, U.K.

Smith, David. "Nigerian 'Baby Farm' Raided—32 Pregnant Girls Rescued." *Guardian*, June 2, 2011. https://www.theguardian.com/law/2011/jun/02/nigeria-baby-farm-raided-human-trafficking.

Southern Provinces, Nigeria. *Annual Report on the Prison Department of the Southern Provinces of Nigeria for the Year*, 1915–1937. Lagos: Government Printer, 1916–38. http://dds.crl.edu/CRLdelivery.asp?tid=20048.

Statement by chiefs to the commissioner of Warri, May, 26, 1914. Slave Dealing, CSE 8/7/39, National Archives of Nigeria, Enugu.

Stead, W. T. "The Maiden Tribute of Modern Babylon: The Report of Our Secret Commission." *Pall Mall Gazette*, July 6, 1985. https://www.attackingthedevil.co.uk/pmg/tribute/mt1.php#3.

Stevenson, Major. Letter from District Officer at Owerri, Major Stevenson, to the Senior Resident, Owerri Province," June 17, 1933. C136 Child Stealing, Rivprof 2/1/24, National Archives of Nigeria, Enugu.

"Supplement." *London Gazette*, January 1, 1955.

Thomas, James Henry. Letter from J. H. Thomas, Chief Secretary to the Government, to the Resident of the Onitsha Province, W. Buchanan Smith, November 23, 1933. CSO 21/4/28994, Nigeria National Archives, Ibadan.

Treasury Papers, Southern Nigeria. Proposal to Establish a Government Currency Note Issue, March 26, 1908. TI/11226/695, National Archives, Richmond, U.K. Tribal Customs and Superstitions of Southern Nigeria (Pawning), 1920s. Files of the Egba Judicial Council. CSO 26/1/06827, Pawning of Children, National Archives of Nigeria, Ibadan.

BIBLIOGRAPHY

I. Tribal Customs and Superstitions of the Southern Province of Nigeria; II. Practice of Pawning Children as Security for Debts of Parents. CSO 26/1/06827, National Archives of Nigeria, Ibadan.

Ugwu, Obiageli Nwakaego. Interview conducted by Anayo Enechukwu on behalf of author, Obollo Eke, Enugu State, Nigeria, August 8, 2012.

Ugwu, Ugwu Nwangwu, Elder Chief. Interview conducted by Anayo Enechukwu on behalf of author, Ibeagwa Nike, Enugu State, Nigeria, August 5, 2012.

Uncle Mike. "Beware of Human Wolves." *Lagos (Nigeria) Daily Times,* August 11, 1956, National Archives of Nigeria, Ibadan.

Uzor-Eghelu, Sammy. Letter from Sammy Uzor-Eghelu of Ichida to chief secretary of the colony, May 26, 1925. CSO 26/1/16100, National Archives of Nigeria, Ibadan.

————. Letter from Sammy Uzor-Eghelu of Ichida to chief secretary of the colony, May 29, 1925. CSO 26/1/16100, National Archives of Nigeria, Ibadan.

"Welfare of the Young." *Nigerian Eastern Mail*, August 17, 1946, 6, National Archives of Nigeria, Ibadan.

Women's Consortium of Nigeria. "Trafficking in Nigeria," n.d. https://www .womenconsortiumofnigeria.org/?q=content/nigeria.

Wozniak, Mark. "Inmates Rights Groups Protest Use of Prison labor for state's new hand sanitizer." March 11, 2020. https://news.wbfo.org/post /inmate-rights-groups-protest-use-prison-labor-states-new-hand-sanitizer.

Young, Jess. "Time to Raise the Bar: The Bittersweet Truth about Cocoa." *London Economic*, March 11, 2020. https://www.thelondoneconomic.com/opinion /time-to-raise-the-bar-the-bittersweet-truth-about-cocoa/11/03/.

INDEX

Page numbers in *italics* refer to figures